Half Sisters of History

DATE			

Half Sisters of History

SOUTHERN

WOMEN

AND THE

AMERICAN

PAST

Catherine Clinton

Editor

DUKE UNIVERSITY PRESS

Durham and London

1994

for

Carol Bleser

and

Jean Baker

Nolite te bastardes carborundorum

Designed by Cherie Holma Westmoreland

Typeset in Adobe Caslon by Keystone Typesetting, Inc.

Library of Congress Cataloging-in-Publication Data appear on the last printed page of this book.

Credits: Chapter by Jones from Hoffman and Albert, *Women in the Age of the American Revolution* (Capitol Historical Society, University of Virginia Press, 1989); Perdue from Walter J. Fraser et al., eds., *The Web of Southern Social Relations* (University of Georgia Press 1985) (copyright by author); White from *Journal of Family History* (vol. 8, Fall 1983, JAI Press); Scott from *Journal of American History* (vol. 6, June 1974); Painter from *Georgia Historical Quarterly* (Summer 1992); Lebsock from *Journal of Southern History* (May 1977); Clinton from Georgia Historical Quarterly (Summer 1992) (copyright by author); Fox-Genovese from *American Quarterly* (vol. 33, Fall 1981, Johns Hopkins University Press); Hall from *Journal of American History* (vol. 73, 1986) (copyright by author); Evans from *Personal Politics* (Alfred A. Knopf, 1979).

ACR 99160

Contents

Preface

The title of this book is especially poignant for me not only because I have spent most of my academic career as a historian of southern women, but because I have also been a half sister. I think the family metaphor is apt for dealing with a subject as internecine and incestuous as historical fields. I am perhaps more attuned to this imagery having started out as a student of slavery—a scholarly battlefield strewn with fratricidal shoot-outs and blood feuds.

The metaphor in my title will not become some belabored thematic device—identifying a "Big Daddy" or "wicked stepmother" is not the purpose of this volume. Rather, I examine the historical roots of southern women's history before outlining some of the significant scholarship by pioneering historians which constitutes the now flourishing field of southern women's history.

Serious consideration of southern women has been handicapped by the sexism of American history in general and southern history in particular, combined with the regional chauvinism of women's history. These parochial elements have been retarding. Many assumed that women's historical experience would be the exclusive domain of female historians and those working in women's history. Most scholars in women's history rarely mention, much less examine southern women, perhaps fearful that "*half sisters*" might unravel the neatly woven canvas of their re-created pasts.

This double marginalization has created some interesting and pioneering results. Historians of southern women may have been the first scholars of women's history to realize the indelible impact of race on assessing gender relations. Also, they must contend with the looming significance of class in a region where economic and social nuances are extreme and rigid. Finally, many researchers have learned that toiling in the fields may not bring overnight results, but patience and steady effort will reap a bounteous harvest.

When academic efforts are measured too often in terms of who can cross the finish line first, many historians of southern women have been consigned to the status of also-rans. But contemporary scholars of southern women are rapidly recovering their edge. Not unlike the tortoise racing the hare, those pursuing southern women's history may finish ahead of authors of northern (*a.k.a. American*) women's history. Historians working on southern women might not just catch up but surpass others if they can avoid the mishaps of their predecessors. At the same time, I prefer to think that historians of southern women might be able to convince their more fast-lane colleagues that it's not the destination but the journey which should be of primary interest to us as scholars—not simply the glittering prizes, but the glimmers of recognition we can wrench from readers and listeners.

Like all pioneers of new fields, practitioners in southern women's history face controversial questions. If we are only given access within a segregated domain or in the spirit of symbolic tokenism, can we claim progress? If the representation of southern women is merely southern *qua* southern and never *qua* American, have we created a community for nurture or carved out turf for isolation? If we build a southern women's history power base, what criteria are employed for membership and allegiance, and after putative empowerment, who decides how to parcel out resources? How will we deal with the inevitable splinter groups whose distinctive voices reveal the emergence of key subcultures? How do Appalachian women, Cajun women, and other groups fit under the umbrella? Will our ghettoizations be so different from what we are attacking?

Trying to recapture the frustration of working under such conditions, colleagues have encouraged me to share some of the patronizing remarks passed on by journals which indicated the reader feared I might be sending out a manuscript from an institution other than a university: Why was I focusing *exclusively* on southern women? Why didn't I give more thought to comparisons with northern women? How does this relate more generally to *American* women (as if southern women weren't American women)? At the Ivy League school where I was finishing my dissertation, the subject of my thesis—the role of the plantation mistress in antebellum slave society—was ridiculed, nicknamed "Whips and Chains in the Old South." The sting from these criticisms has transformed itself into a twisted sort of nostalgia—for all the character building these critics imposed upon me.

I also learned from my forays in the South that scholars and archivists could be as warm and welcoming as I might ever hope to find. At the same time, I know I will always first be asked: "Where are you from?" Because I have never settled in the South, my response fails to satisfy the initial inquiry, which is then followed by: "But where were you born? Why are you interested in southern history?" I always wonder why audiences invariably treat any non-southerner interested in the southern past with curiosity if not downright suspicion.

Again and again, since I did not teach in the South, nor boast a southern accent and three names, it was assumed that I would claim southern ancestry and talk about my family. I always prefer to sidestep this issue, because although I remain proud of my Missouri heritage, I resent this line of questioning—a southern pedigree may add cachet but does not confer authenticity.

When I was younger I would offer a lengthy, complex intellectual response and watch the questioner's eyes glaze over. I have never resorted to genealogical gambits. When pressed now ("What got you interested in the South?") I smile and respond: "I guess I was just born naturally bright." I know I am cheating my audience of an important point, but I want them to appreciate my work as well as to hear my ideas. I suppose my years of travel and research throughout the South do count for something—I learned about honey from some of the finest beekeepers in the world.

Conflicted memories of my adventures in southern women's history fade considerably when I contrast them with the crystal-clear vision of shared challenge and cheerful camaraderie which prevailed for those of us on the research trail in the seventies and eighties. And in the buoyant present, the long stride and mighty tide of southern women's history erodes resentment. My only regret is that so many who came before will not be here to celebrate with us as we approach the twenty-first century. For them, let us pay tribute to our legacy of struggle, our battle for our full and rightful place, with continuing good works.

There are so many people to thank for making this book possible, but I am especially grateful to the nine scholars whose work I have included in this volume. I am equally indebted to all the contributors to the wonderful work in southern women's history that continue to make working in the field a comfort and joy, especially to archivists and librarians throughout the South who give so generously.

Further, I am extremely glad that the Jackies, Hall and Jones, have been such cooperative and steadfast cheerleaders of my work on this project. As you well know, I have no trouble telling you apart, but you have been indistinguishably dear and generous colleagues, for which I remain in your debt.

Ellen Fitzpatrick has been a strong and invaluable force for good in my academic career the past decade. With humor and cheer and mounting phone bills, we remain close. She and I will live to tell handmaids' tales and more. For her infinite wisdom and rollicking wit, I am eternally grateful. Further, Ellen introduced me to my editor for this project, Rachel Toor, who has been a vibrant and visionary whirlwind herself.

Rachel rescued this project from the limbo to which all too many of my ambitions are consigned. She transforms loose talk at a convention into a cause for publication. She pushed and prodded and spun me onward, and I am grateful to her for her enthusiasm and talent.

And although a bounty of women are acknowledged and thanked and celebrated throughout this text (and the book is dedicated to two of the finest), I must close by thanking a trio of absolutely stellar fellows: Daniel, Drew, and Ned Colbert. Not all feminists get such arduous training—daily life outnumbered in an unarmed camp. And few women enjoy the luxury I have of a household full of supportive, spectacular males. Each and every book I write takes its toll on my family, and for that I am regretful. In closing, I remain grateful for your patience and understanding. You guys are the greatest.

Catherine Clinton

Riverside Connecticut

Introduction

Southern women truly are half sisters of history. But it is my contention that half sisters may have an advantage over their comfortably ensconced siblings; as both family and outsiders, they possess doubled perspectives. With these multiple lenses on the past, scholars in southern women's history are not condemned to the tunnel vision which has so hampered the fields within which they labor. They recognize that context does not merely add to our understanding but literally defines what we study. The shifting of definitions and contents dramatically reconfigures our perceptions of the past, with each new generation and over time.

Women's history in the nineteenth century consisted primarily of biographical sketches of notable women who had made patriotic contributions to the nation. Many of these collective biographies are wonderful sources, but they rarely offer insight into historical periodization, gender constructions, and other issues critical to women's history today. When feminists tackled women's history in the closing decades of the last century, all too many writers confined their sights to women's traditional roles: women in education, women in religion, and women's contributions to what was increasingly designated "the domestic sphere." When production moved from the household into a separate workplace, scholars argue, roles and responsibilities became more gendered throughout American society. Women's activities were increasingly confined to sex-segregated areas, and home and family were labeled "woman's sphere."

There were always dissenters from this conventional view, but it wasn't until near the end of the last century that a distinguished body of women historians began to challenge this masculine hegemony. Most exemplary is Annie Nathan Meyer's *Woman's Work in America* (1891), which presented pioneering material on female professionals. Nearly a half century later, still only a handful of pathbreaking books could be cited, such as Mary Sumner Benson's *Women in Eighteenth Century America* (1935) and Julia Cherry Spruill's *Women's Life and Work in the Southern Colonies* (1938). But by the late thirties a hardy band of scholars were interested in redefining both women's experience and women's place in American history. Dynamic scholars such as Arthur Schlesinger, Sr., Mary Beard, Eleanor Flexner, and others scoured archives, published prolifically, and steered an entire generation of scholars into the nascent field of women's history.

By the 1960s the seeds from this earlier generation were blossoming in riotous profusion. The modern movement for women's liberation and other social protests forced redefinition of the past, as well as the present and future. Feminist scholars not only invaded the archives but began to break down barriers. Tenured appointments and newly created positions in "women's history" began to stimulate campuses across the country. Undergraduates and doctoral candidates alike sought increasing awareness of women's past and the possibilities for women's history. Janet James, a student of Arthur Schlesinger, Sr., coedited *Notable American Women* (1971), a three-volume reference text. This project and many bibliographic and collaborative efforts which followed demonstrated the clout and permanence this movement intended.

Gerda Lerner and Anne Firor Scott, pioneers in these efforts, both went on to serve as president of the Organization of American Historians during the 1980s. Although Scott and Lerner both had done work on southern women, and indeed Scott was primarily associated with her work in southern women's history, the flood of scholars that followed immediately was overwhelmingly involved in northern women's history, which was referred to simply as American women's history. Southern women rarely made it into the footnotes of the work of those most influential books and articles of the seventies, the "required reading" by Barbara Welter,

Mary Ryan, Ellen DuBois, Nancy Cott, Kathryn Kish Sklar, Linda Kerber, Carroll Smith-Rosenberg, Linda Gordon, and Mary Jo Buhle, to name some prominent and influential scholars. Even Mary Beth Norton's token inclusion of southern women in her work was a rare exception to the rule of neglect.

Feminist scholars targeted and explored rich areas for ongoing historical research: the cult of domesticity, the impact of urbanization and industrialization, the organization of labor, the growth of reform movements, club and voluntary organizations, "female culture," education, religion, family and kinship, sexuality and homosocial relations, courtship and marriage patterns, fertility and birth control, and even women's involvement in traditionally male spheres such as war and electoral politics. Yet in this provocative body of work, southern women were barely visible.

This shadow status fostered conceptual frameworks that were deeply flawed. The rise of the factory system in the North fostered industrialization and consequent trends, for example the rise in never-married women, declining birth rates, and so on. However, in the South, the invention of the cotton gin spurred another kind of growth—the expansion of the plantation system, both geographically and in size. Many southern women increased their family size during this boom era and the proportion of single women consequently dwindled. White southern women did not merely manifest patterns which lagged behind northern sisters: during this critical era their paths diverged radically.

Attention to racial dynamics has profoundly shaped southern women's history during the past decade. The new visibility of another group significant to the southern past, slaves, has dramatically altered our notions of historical agency in the American past. After the founding of the nation, the majority of slaves were southern and the majority of that majority were women. Given the marginalization of color, region, and gender considerations in mainstream history and popular culture, black southern women are a strong starting point to rescue half sisters from benign neglect.

Some of these uphill battles on the not-so-level playing field have rendered historians of southern women scrappy fighters. By necessity, many of us have become embroiled in heated historical controversies, besieged on many fronts. Several of the articles included in this volume are the work of champion debaters. Our field has been blessed and cursed by debate since its inception. Clashes over race and sex have erupted both within the American past and within contemporary academic and intellectual politics. Historians of southern women have contributed vital new perspectives on these areas of scholarly inquiry.

Certainly the role of elite white women in antebellum culture has been a matter of considerable dispute. Were these women closet abolitionists? Were they so circumscribed by responsibilities as plantation mistresses that they came to resent their husband's property? Did elite women living in urban areas differ in their views from their rural sisters? Did they exert more autonomy, chafe more against the bonds of economic and political constraints? Did slaveowners' wives seek and secure power through their own crucial function within the plantation economy? What of the vast majority of women in the South, the white farm women and working-class poor whose interests were far removed from slavery? How has modernity been incorporated or ignored by increasingly complex work on twentieth-century southern women? How have whites used gender and race to divide and conquer in the southern public arena? What roles do class relations play within these complex gender dynamics?

How closely does the image of the southern lady reflect reality? Why has she symbolized southern women when the image of slave women stands so vividly alongside? How have women of color been marginalized? How have their contributions been overlooked? Slave women's labor was a bedrock for the political economy of their own people as well as plantation culture. How have the mammy and the lady been defining forces for gender behavior within plantation culture? Are they interlocking? Interdependent? What role have men played in shaping these gendered definitions? These questions offer a hint of the controversies tackled by scholars in what follows.

Southern women's history is always at the crossroads, but even more so during contemporary debates over fragmentation, multiculturalism, and inclusion. How can we accomplish anything by depicting unintegrated parallel lives? Are we building identity or increasing intellectual isolationism? Jacquelyn Dowd Hall has suggested that "we need a historical practice that turns on partiality, that is self-conscious about perspective, that releases multiple voices rather than competing orthodoxies, and that, above all nurtures an 'internally differing but united political community.'"[1] In this spirit, we can look forward to ongoing negotiations as we struggle to build a diverse yet unified community.

Community has been and continues to be an important element in understanding all pasts, but particularly the southern experience. Many of the scholars featured within this collection have worked hard to call attention to new sources and research in the field.[2] In many ways southern women's history has been the product of an extraordinary extended family of scholars, archivists, teachers, and organizers trying to preserve and celebrate competing communities within the southern past.

However, the goal of this collection is not to feature exclusively those issues which have divided early practitioners of southern women's history, although such issues are certainly present in many of the essays. Rather, I have tried to bring together powerful and provocative pieces which symbolize some of the best work of the past quarter century. I have tried to select those voices within southern women's history that have been speaking to us loud and clear and will, I hope, continue well into the next century.

Half Sisters of History follows nearly a century of intense interest but a much shorter period marking the coming of age of southern women's history. In the late nineteenth century and on into the twentieth, women of letters appear alongside the grand old men of southern literature. A small but surprisingly influential group churned out recollections after the turn of the century: Belle Kearney's *A Slaveholder's Daughter* (1900), Rebecca Latimer Felton's *Country Life in the Days of My Youth* (1919), and Susan Bradford Eppes's *Through Some Eventful Years* (1926). Many of these "memoirs" are what I call "remembrance of things imagined," some more propagandistic than others, but confabulations of days gone by, tinted rosy for effect.

The "memoirization" of southern belles and ladies continued unabated through the Depression and into the post–World War II era. Edmund Wilson, in his definitive *Patriotic Gore: Studies in the Literature of the American Civil War* (1962), praised diarists Kate Stone, Sarah Morgan, and the increasingly popular Mary Chesnut. But if we search Wilson's index the only Mitchell we find is

"Silas Weir," although the most famous name associated with Civil War fiction remains Margaret Mitchell.

Gone With The Wind (1936) was a runaway international best-seller. It was reviewed by historians, imitated by novelists, and heralded by the motion picture industry, which adapted it to the silver screen for a 1939 release. Margaret Mitchell's portrait of the Civil War past has dominated American popular culture and considerably hampered our attempts to demystify this era. Clearly, when the book became a bestseller again in 1991 (propelled back onto the top ten list by its sequel, *Scarlett,* also a record-breaking success), Americans revealed their infatuation with a fictionalized past.

Movements in the 1960s geared to raising consciousness concerning race and gender had a considerable impact on the historical profession. The conspicuous absence of historical publishing on southern women characterized most of the 1940s and 1950s. Yet there were exceptions: A. Elizabeth Taylor's efforts to chart victories and defeats of the southern suffrage movement began with an article on Georgia in a 1944 issue of the *Georgia Historical Quarterly.* Taylor, like many scholars who followed, found heroic efforts underappreciated.

But the sisterhood of historical scholarship trickled southward, increasing odds that even half sisters inherited space on library shelves, in bibliographies, and eventually in the classroom. Certainly, Gerda Lerner's *The Grimké Sisters from South Carolina: Rebels Against Slavery* (1967) and Anne Scott's *The Southern Lady: From Pedestal to Politics* (1970) provided a new generation of students with formidable foremothers—scholars whose research, service, and activism would energize the next generation of dissertation writers.

Inspiration was found both within and outside the walls of academe. Indeed, one of the most powerful pieces challenged the silence within groves of academe when it appeared in 1971: Angela Davis's "Reflections on the Black Woman's Role in the Community of Slaves." This essay, produced by Davis during her incarceration in a California jail, was a tour de force that in effect repudiated researchers' pleas concerning limited resources. Davis presented a defiant and eloquent case against scholarly indifference to race, sex, and class. Her provocative essay challenged comfortable assumptions about historical perspective and raised

issues embraced seriously by a new generation of southern scholars struggling to hear the "multiple voices" Hall encouraged us to
heed.

In too many ways southern women's history was an orphan
during the storm of work which exploded into anthology form
during the 1970s and 1980s. And here we see the disadvantages of
half sisters. There are a growing number of essays which are critical for students trying to grasp the dynamics of southern women's
history. Too many remain available only in journal form or tucked
away in a scattered array of specialist volumes. Equally distressing,
many anthologies of American women's history neglect southern
experience and rarely mention sectionalism or regional variants.
Some focus exclusively on slave women in an unusual, although
understandable, reversal of fortune between black and white
southern women.

There are very real obstacles for those of us committed to
teaching southern women's history. What follows is meant to ease
our burden. Ten essays cannot pretend to be comprehensive, yet
this cohesive collection designed for classroom use touches on
critical questions central to our field today. These two handfuls
illustrate the increasing clout of southern women's history in the
broader field of American history. Several authors have garnered
major prizes, many hold chairs at distinguished universities, and
all have influence and impact within the field of southern wom-
en's history.

It would have been tempting to publish the essays in the chronological order of publication, beginning with Anne Firor Scott's
from 1974 closing with Nell Painter's from 1992. Instead, each
piece appears in the volume in the chronological order of the topic
addressed, again with an eye to the classroom.

Selections reveal the work of those who have profoundly
shaped *my* thinking in southern women's history and, again and
again, have engaged my students. Countless citations and references to these scholars in secondary literature confirm my faith.
Classroom discussions about these pieces will, I hope, stir up
more interest and arguments and stimulate revisions in the decades to come.

There is no question that Jacqueline Jones's work on African
American women has profoundly reshaped our perception of

southern women's experience, and indeed her work has had a wider impact on the way we view American women's history. From her early work on teachers of freedpeople in Georgia and her widely acclaimed study of black women from slavery to the present, on to her most recent research on migrant labor, Jones insists that race and class are dynamics *essential* to our appreciation of any historical era. In the piece adapted for inclusion in this volume, "Race, Sex, and Self-Evident Truths: The Status of Slave Women during the Era of the American Revolution" (1989), Jones confronts the rhetorical heyday of freedom and independence. Her razor-sharp rereading of this period provides a critical examination of black women's stake during this era of emerging nationalism. She focuses on that most emblematic of founding fathers, slaveowner George Washington. Her vivid and impassioned reconstruction of the world of work and African-American responses to rigid socioeconomic structures skewers considerably our perception of "life, liberty and the pursuit of happiness." Her radical perspective reworks facile understandings of identity and opportunity at the end of the eighteenth century. Traditional treatments of the era clearly leave black women as actors *out* while counting them in as a permanent poor to be trampled at the bottom rung of the ladder. Slave women, anchored on plantations, may have been absent from the debates surrounding the formation of the state, but Jones reconfigures dynamics to delineate the critical role of race, class, and gender within the emerging political hierarchy. The labor of black women and their political disempowerment symbolized the bedrock upon which elites could comfortably build a white man's democracy.

Theda Perdue's impressive body of work in American Indian history is represented here by her creative and pathbreaking "Southern Indians and the Cult of True Womanhood" (1985). Perdue allows us to view the intricate cultural clashes between native and white peoples in the antebellum South by exploring especially Cherokee women's transformation through exposure to the doctrines of "true womanhood" and its zealous advocates. As white missionaries and southern planters subscribed to notions of "separate gender spheres" and "woman's proper place," many American Indians accommodated these prescriptives. The process of assimilation, Perdue gracefully illuminates, had a decisive

impact on women's role within tribal power structures. She specu-
lates on how and why Cherokee adaptiveness spelled dramatic
transformations and the precipitous shift, if not decline, in female
status as a result.

Deborah Gray White's pioneering studies on slave women on
antebellum plantations stirred considerable debate as she challenged conventional views on role, status, and personality within
the slave community. As traditional views bemoaned the "emas-
culation of the slave," her introduction of gender considerably
undermined single-sex assessments. White makes a persuasive
case in her "Female Slaves: Sex Roles and Status in the Antebellum Plantation South" (1983) that plantation life reflected gendered values among the slave community, as well as among slaveowners. White combines a feminist sensibility with a keen eye to
class and race factors, which within her framework are not viewed
as "categories" so much as "influences." She does not make static
claims, but through her use of anthropological and sociological
frameworks chooses to enhance our crude interpretations to render slave life simultaneously more raw and more refined. Her
perceptive analysis shows us how we can tackle questions of authority and control, choice and cultural coercion, family and individual identity without the availability of abundant traditional
source material. Her emphasis on a female slave network within
the plantation community has had considerable impact.

Anne Firor Scott's germinal work really brought southern
women's history into the limelight with her pathbreaking study of
the southern lady from 1830 to 1930. She has continued her research on southern women in voluntary societies, suffrage movements, and many other aspects of women's experiences from the
colonial period onward. Her significant and prolific contributions
to journals and anthologies make it difficult to select just one
piece for this collection, but "Women's Perspective on the Patriarchy in the 1850s" (1974) perhaps stimulated more younger scholars in the field than any other essay she has published before or
since, and the essay's final phrase, "but it is worth a good deal
of study," was practically a call to arms. Scott outlines many critical issues revolving around intellectual ferment and sectional crises. She presents gripping evidence of discontent within plantation society, highlighting private and public considerations set

against the larger storms gathering on the horizon. Scott deftly sketches the larger political questions while preserving the voices of women in this compact, engaging essay.

Nell Irvin Painter's contribution, "Of *Lily,* Linda Brent, and Freud: A Non-Exceptionalist Approach to Race, Class, and Gender in the Slave South" (1992), captures the heady spirit which infuses most new work in the field. Painter represents those who have been drawn into the growing community of scholars in southern women's history by the sheer depth and expanse this intriguing field promises. Although Painter's early work on African-American migrants, her portrait of the Communist Hosea Hudson, and, most recently, her study of the Progressive era might not seem to lead directly into the tangle of ideas with which she wrestles in this essay, Painter emphatically stakes a claim with this piece. She has produced a provocative introductory essay for the journal of Ella Gertrude Clanton Thomas and ongoing investigations of sexuality and race. Her essay provides the most historiographical, as well as one of the most original contributions to this volume. Her critique of previous studies is not mere commentary but her agenda for future work—her own as well as others. Painter sends forth a call for scholars to embrace questions of class, race, region, and *sexuality,* not just gender. Painter boldly proclaims, "What my approach means for southern history is a renunciation of a 'the South' way of thinking. . . . I insist on going beyond lazy characterizations in the singular."

Suzanne Lebsock's creative and much admired work on women in Petersburg, Virginia, demonstrated the ways in which public documents might give voice to a previously silenced urban majority: women in southern towns and cities. Her book on women in Virginia history (which accompanied a traveling museum exhibit) demonstrated the ways in which private lives can be recovered and reintegrated into public history through ambitious programs. Further, her current and ongoing research on women involved in suffrage politics in the South serves to remind us of our responsibility to work against divides which artificially segregate "women's history" and "political history." It is only fitting that her creative and consciousness-raising piece, "Radical Reconstruction and the Property Rights of Southern Women" (1977), be included. Lebsock, considerably updating the work of

Julia Cherry Spruill, provides us with a dazzling array of evidence culled from court records and legislative debates. She further demonstrates one of the great ironies of southern history, that women have all too often made feminist gains for reasons having nothing to do with feminism, as she warns, "The legal status of southern women hinged on the decisions of lawmakers for whom the status of women per se was rarely the paramount concern." Lebsock amply documents the nuances behind these statutory reforms and creates a model for explorations in southern women's legal and social history.

My own view of southern women's history has been shaped by early work on plantation sources, a survey text in nineteenth-century women's history, and the editing of a collection of essays on American women's history through individual lives where my two contributions (Maria Chapman and Ella Baker) were separated by a century but united in their commitment to challenging the status quo concerning American race relations. My most recent work on the Civil War, an anthology on gender relations, and my new book on realities and images of African American and white women in the wartime South, is reflected in my own essay "Bloody Terrain: Freedwomen, Sexuality, and Violence during Reconstruction" (1992). I have struggled to integrate questions involving images of women (iconography and popular culture) and topics involving sexuality throughout most of my work on southern women. The recovery of both black and white southern women's experiences, reintegrating their voices, remains a primary concern within my scholarly writing.

Elizabeth Fox-Genovese's career in southern women's history has followed a very different path from previous contributors. Perhaps because of, not in spite of, her training in European intellectual history, she brings a very distinctive sensibility to her interpretations of southern women, but a distinctiveness which is showcased in her study of plantation mistresses and slaves. Fox-Genovese has produced, as well, a staggering outpouring of articles covering topics from slave women's autobiographies to white women's fictions, falling inside as well as far afield from the plantation household. Her commitment to interdisciplinary perspective and her insistence upon what she calls "feminism without illusions" have garnered her widespread attention. For this collection an essay which combines her keen cultural instincts and dense theoretical insights has been chosen: "Scarlett O'Hara: The Southern Lady as New Woman" (1981). This sharply focused deconstruction of Margaret Mitchell and her heroine is one of the best of a growing body of article literature which focuses on southern women as cultural icons. Much work has been done during the past decade to bridge the gap between cultural criticism and historical writing in the field of southern women. Fox-Genovese has been a leading proponent of this movement, and her creative rerendering of *Gone With The Wind*'s layered meanings sheds new and important light on Scarlett O'Hara and her emblematic role within southern cultural representation.

The work of Jacquelyn Dowd Hall provides us with an embarrassment of riches. Her own early study of Jessie Daniel Ames and the anti-lynching movement, as well as her study giving voice to textile workers in the modern South, remain widely cited. These prize-winning volumes have influenced several academic generations of southern scholars. Hall has always advocated that close attention be paid to questions of gender and sexuality and was an early crusader in this regard. Further, she has struggled to integrate class, gender, race, and ethnicity in her ongoing research, most recently on workers in Atlanta after the turn of the twentieth century. Hall's individual achievement and her collaborative efforts have provided models for research. She has extensively employed oral history in her work and literally and figuratively embellishes her scholarship with women's voices. Her "Disorderly Women: Gender and Labor Militancy in the Appalachian South" (1986) is representative of the scholar's dilemma when approaching southern women's history, confronting females who, "because they contradicted conventional wisdom, were easily dismissed." Hall does not dismiss her rowdy and complex subjects. Instead, she relishes the uncharted territory—tracing women's entry "into public space and political struggles previously monopolized by men." This allows her to see these women without the lenses of "class and cultural 'otherness.'"

Sara Evans's piece, the final essay in this volume, is a fitting conclusion in many ways. Evans has written extensively about activism and social justice, from her first book on the roots of the women's liberation movement in the student movement and civil rights crusade of the 1960s to her most recent publications on wage justice and democratic movements. "Black Power: Catalyst for Feminism" (1979) charts intersections of feminism and civil rights activism, vividly bringing to life the lives of the men and women involved in these struggles. Evans, herself once active in the movements she explores, prepared this essay as a scholar, an activist, and a witness to her times. Although several distinguished bestsellers have emerged on the Civil Rights era and a dozen or more studies of male leaders have been published, African American women seem condemned to the footnotes and dedication pages of scholarly literature rather than given the featured roles in the texts that they deserve. Women, black and white, are prominent in Evans's pioneering work, as she forces us to contend with the ways in which women's marginalization triggered the social movement for female equality. Women's secondhand status within political reform crusades not only transformed women activists, but had a tremendous impact within organizations and grassroots movements.

Feminism's stormy origins, Evans suggests, developed within a very highly charged political climate, spontaneously combusting within civil rights activism during its student protest heyday. Evans expertly tracks the fissures that divided, the contexts that propelled women with identical responses into opposing camps, and the layers of complexity surrounded these questions of sex, race, and class. As a result, we more fully appreciate southern women as activists—as catalysts for change and as pioneering social activists.

It has been my good fortune over the past two decades to read and benefit from the work of the scholars selected for this volume. It also has been my great pleasure to meet some of the students of these energetic scholars. It is no surprise that these mentors have nurtured and trained well over a score of master's and doctoral candidates in southern women's history during the past decade, with more in the pipeline.

The authors I have brought between two covers for *Half Sisters of History* may on occasion hold diametrically opposed points of view and speak only to intellectual issues, rather than to one another. Despite disputes and differences, we are bound together by our commitment to southern women's history, and it is in this spirit of camaraderie that I have undertaken this volume. I hope that this collection will nurture a new generation of scholars who may want to reinvent the field and, if all succeeds, doubtless will.

With the raised consciousness of scholars and the increased interest of bookbuyers and publishers, we now have a flourishing enterprise. Indeed, so burgeoning is this field that we have reached an important second stage. Anne Scott's recent volume *Unheard Voices: The First Historians of Southern Women* (1993), selections from the work of five pioneering scholars, sheds light on the disjointed, unheralded achievements of the first wave. Scott sketched how lonely and stoic these women were, the pain and perseverance such publications cost. *Half Sisters of History* includes articles demonstrating a range and intensity that would bedazzle historical foremothers. Also, the Southern Association of Women Historians (SAWH) now honors the best book written in southern women's history with the Julia Cherry Spruill Prize.

I remember in the early eighties attending a Southern Historical Association meeting and being begged to put together on the spot a program for the following year. I was warned that if I didn't there wouldn't be any panel dealing with southern women during the entire meeting. Those days are certainly over. Besides a respectable representation of southern women's history at the Southern Historical Association Meeting, at the American Studies Association annual meeting, and on the program of the Organization of American Historians convention, the SAWH holds meetings every three years (Spartanburg in 1988, Chapel Hill in 1991, and Houston in 1994) demonstrating the collective identity and spirit of feminism southern women's history has fostered.

Publication of primary sources has exploded in the past decade. The *Schomburg Library of Nineteenth-Century Black Women Writers* (40 volumes), edited by Henry Louis Gates, Jr., features a wide array of texts, including the writings of Ida Wells-Barnett and Anna Julia Cooper.[3] Gerda Lerner, Dorothy Sterling and Darlene Clark Hine have edited impressive collections on black women that contain rich material on southern women.[4] Carol Bleser is the editor of an equally impressive series, "Southern Voices From the Past: Women's Letters, Diaries and Writings," which provides a significant resource.[5]

Southern women's history has prospered because of the published findings of a growing body of talented scholars—Jean

Friedman on religion, Anne Goodwyn Jones on southern women writers, Sally McMillen on motherhood, Barbara Bellows and Julia Blackwelder on urban women, Martha Swain on women in government, Jane deHart on feminism and antifeminism, Susan Tucker in oral history, Steven Stowe on courtship, Ann Malone on family, Jan Lewis and Jane Turner Censer on marriage, Joan Cashin on migration, Dolores Janiewski on labor, Nancy Hewitt on work and ethnicity, George Rable, Donna Krug, and Drew Faust on the Civil War, Kathleen Berkeley on Memphis, Nina Silber on gender and sectionalism, Christine Farnham on education, Sara Evans on the civil rights movement, Linda Reed on the Southern Conference Movement, Jacqueline Rouse and Cynthia Neverdon-Morton on reform, Bertram Wyatt-Brown on the Percy women, Darden Pyron on Margaret Mitchell, Ann Loveland on Lillian Smith—as well as scholarship exploring relatively uncharted territory: Martha Hodes on sex across the color line, Adele Logan Alexander on free women of color, and Melton McLaurin on rape and its consequences for one slave woman.

Additionally the work of a dynamic group of emerging scholars will surely challenge and expand our definitions of southern women and gender studies. Recent studies by Victoria Bynum on "disorderly women," by Marjorie Spruill Wheeler on the southern suffrage movement, by Stephanie McCurry on gender dynamics and the yeoman class, by Lee Ann Whites on the Civil War as a crisis in gender, by Elsa Barkley Brown on community and race in Richmond, by Brenda Stevenson on family and slavery in antebellum Virginia, by Glenda Gilmore on gender and Jim Crow, by Nancy MacLean on women and the Klan—all are expanding our visions of southern women's past.

Forthcoming studies on law and family by Peter Bardaglio, on Indian women by Nancy Shoemaker, an enthnohistorical approach to Creek women by Kathryn E. Holland Braund, on Cherokee women and material culture by Sarah Hill, on a free woman of color by Kent Leslie, on planter women in South Carolina by Marli Wiener, on gender and Mardi Gras by Karen Leatham, on memory and the civil rights movement by Kathryn Nasstrom, on girlhood in the post–Civil War South by Cita Cook, on reconstruction by Leslie Schwalm, by Laura Edwards, by Carol Montgomery, and by Nancy Bercaw, on household workers by Tera Hunter, on servants by Stephanie Cole, on antebellum Mississippi by Dale Edwyna Smith, on working-class women in Atlanta by Gretchen Maclachlan, on the Jewish community by Leah Hagedorn, on Creole culture in the Gulf South by Virginia Gould, on sex and race in colonial Virginia by Kathleen Brown, on Appalachian women by Kathleen Blee and by Nyoka Hawkins, on women in antebellum Virginia by Elizabeth Varon, on Kentucky suffragists by Claudia Knott, on women's reform in North Carolina by Sarah Wilkerson-Freeman, on women's organizations in North Carolina by Anastasia Sims, on antisuffrage by Elna Green, on Mississippi reformers by Joanne Hawks, on Galveston by Elizabeth Turner, on women reformers in Texas by Judith MacArthur, on Pattie Ruffner Jacobs by Wayne Flynt and Marlene Rikard, and on Maria Bryan by Carol Bleser—these scholars and many others will contribute to the exponential growth within the field. This list is just a sampling of the new crop of southern women's history being cultivated as our harvest becomes more bounteous with each passing year.

We are all engaged in a great enterprise to make southern women's history a lively and compelling challenge. We come together as readers and writers, researchers and preservationists, to awaken something within. Some seek out audiences in libraries and classrooms, others at conferences and scholarly forums, still others at rallies and protests. We build together, bound by stories and footnotes, confabulations and deadlines, spreading the gospel. We may bicker and brag and occasionally stub our egos, but most often we work together, if not like a family, then as a community, to fight for a better past. Despite ideological conflicts and sharply differentiated perspectives, we must learn to bury the hatchet—but not in one another's backs. Sharing memories, retelling stories, collecting the evidence, reaching out to a wider family of scholars makes us better historians. We are born as children—what we make of our lives is in the past as well as the future. What we can make of our history, as half sisters and scholars, remains to be done.

Notes

1. Jacquelyn Dowd Hall, "Partial Truths: Writing Southern Women's History," *Signs* 14, no. 4 (Summer 1989): 911.

2. See for example Deborah G. White, "Mining the Forgotten: Manuscript Sources for Black Women's History," *Journal of American History* 74 (1987): 2; Jacquelyn Dowd Hall and Anne Firor Scott, "Women of the South," in John B. Boles and Evelyn T. Nolen, eds., *Interpreting Southern History* (Baton Rouge, 1987).

3. New York (Oxford University Press).

4. Lerner, *Black Women in White America* (New York, 1972); Sterling, *We Are Your Sisters: Black Women in the Nineteenth Century* (New York, 1985); Hine, *Black Women in United States History* (New York, 1990).

5. Athens (University of Georgia Press).

Race, Sex, and Self-Evident Truths

THE STATUS OF SLAVE WOMEN DURING THE

ERA OF THE AMERICAN REVOLUTION

JACQUELINE JONES

Jacqueline Jones is Harry S. Truman Professor of American Civili-
zation at Brandeis University. Her first book, Soldiers of Light and
Love: Northern Teachers and Georgia Blacks, 1865–1873 *(1980),*
revealed her central interest in sex, race, and region in the American
past. Her second book, Labor of Love, Labor of Sorrow: Black
Women, Work and Family from Slavery to the Present *(1985) won*
the Bancroft Prize, the Letitia Brown Prize, the Julia Cherry Spruill
Prize, the Philip Taft Prize, and was a finalist for the Pulitzer Prize.
Her most recent study, The Dispossessed: America's Underclasses
from the Civil War to the Present *(1992), explores the interlocking*
systems of class, race, and gender oppression in the American past.
The article that follows is an abridgement of an essay prepared for a
symposium in Washington, D.C. that examined women at the end of
the eighteenth century. The papers from the conference, sponsored by
the Capitol Historical Society, were published under the title Women
in the Age of the American Revolution *(University of Virginia*
Press, 1989).

Amid the political turmoil that accompanied the founding of
the new nation in the 1780s, George Washington managed to retreat periodically to his beloved Mount Vernon. Of all his public
roles—including military commander, lawmaker, statesman, and
chief executive—Washington embraced that of Virginia planter
with a special passion.[1] According to Washington's diaries, the
slaves who collected manure from the barnyard, and later spread it

around the fallow fields, were almost always females: the observation "woman heaping dung" appeared regularly in reference to all seasons of the year and on all different quarters.[2]

The image of the proud *pater patriae* astride his horse surveying the menial toil of his female slaves has compelling symbolic value. Nevertheless, such a static portrait reveals little about the political system that sustained this superficially placid scene, or the human emotions that threatened to undermine it. As delegates to the Constitutional Convention of 1787, Washington and his compatriots acted decisively to protect the rights of slaveholders; the American Revolution solidified the legal institution of bondage even as it guaranteed certain rights and privileges to all white men. Edmund Morgan has shown that the simultaneous legitimization of black slavery and the expansion of white freedom was more than coincidental; Virginia aristocrats like Washington "could more safely preach equality in a slave society than in a free one."[3] On a daily basis, apparently, the conjunction of slaveholding and revolutionary-republican responsibilities rested lightly on George Washington's shoulders.

For the historian, race, as a socially defined category of human relationships, should constitute a central consideration in exploring the self-evident truths of this country's past.[4] More specifically, during the era of the American Revolution, the status of all black women differed in fundamental ways from the status of all white women. Together, slave women and men endured the agony of bondage, and together blacks, both enslaved and free, struggled to form families that eventually served as the foundation of a distinctive Afro-American culture. The military conflict between loyalists and rebels intensified physical hardship among blacks, while the ensuing social and economic turmoil afforded some of their race the opportunities for a basic kind of freedom that white women and men—for all their rhetoric about the evils of tyranny—already enjoyed. Therefore, any discussion of the war's impact on American women must first highlight racial factors before dealing with issues related to class, regional, ethnic, and religious diversity in the late eighteenth-century population.

Yet within the confines of the slave system, and within the boundaries of their own households and communities, black women shouldered burdens that set them apart from their menfolk. In the period from 1750 to 1800, the nature and extent of these burdens varied according to whether a woman was African or American born; whether she lived in the North or South, in a town or rural area; whether she toiled in the swampy South Carolina lowcountry or on a Virginia wheat farm. This is not to suggest that black women suffered more than black men under the oppressive weight of the racial caste system, only that gender considerations played a significant role in shaping the task assignments parceled out to blacks by slaveholders and in shaping the way blacks structured relationships among themselves. By 1800 transformations wrought by the Revolutionary War had intensified racial divisions in American society, as large-scale cotton cultivation introduced a new and brutal chapter in the history of slavery. At the same time, sexual divisions within the Afro-American community became more obvious, as an explicit sexual division of labor emerged within the private and public lives of free blacks.

To assess the status of black women in late eighteenth-century America, we must confront the central paradox in their collective experience: that a stable family life was the source of both their personal strength and their vulnerability. While kin ties provided all slaves with love and affection, a world of their own within a nation controlled by whites, those ties remained painfully fragile. Therefore it is necessary to consider whether various regions and local economies inhibited or encouraged the growth of the black family and add this factor to general findings related to legal status and work obligations. Although their position remained distinct from that of white women, black women experienced racial prejudice in different ways, depending upon the demographic, economic, social, and political characteristics of the area in which they lived.

The ordeal of black women as wives, mothers, and workers encapsulates all the ironies and tensions that marked the history of slavery during the era of the American Revolution. In their efforts to create and preserve a viable family life, these women sought to balance caution and daring, fear and hope, as they reacted to the peculiar matrix of individual circumstances. Regardless of their work and family status in Boston, on a small farm in Pennsylvania, on George Washington's plantation, or in the

South Carolina lowcountry, they saw freedom through the prism of family life. Consequently they perceived this revolutionary idea in ways fundamentally different from the white men who tried to claim the War for Independence as their own, and from the white women who remained so awkwardly suspended between their racial prerogatives on the one hand and gender and class liabilities on the other. Caught in the crossfire of sexual and racial oppression, black women contributed to the definition of liberation in these turbulent times. Indeed, through their modest everyday struggles, these wives and mothers offered a vision of freedom that was, by virtue of its consistency and fairness, more enduring than the one articulated so eloquently by the founding fathers.

One way to combine historiographical perspectives on the gender and racial caste systems is to focus on the theme of black women's roles in the family. Responsible for child rearing and other tasks in their own households, these women affirmed affective family values in defiance of the slaveholder's crass materialism. As Angela Davis has suggested, tending the home fires under such adverse circumstances amounted to a political act of resistance against white hegemony.[5] At the same time, the black family, with its rather explicit sexual division of labor and its developing kin networks, served as the cornerstone of Afro-American culture, the key building block of black nationalism. Thus, an exploration of black women's history is crucial to a full understanding of the priorities of black and white women and men and their respective responses to the personal and political conflicts that engulfed them all during the revolutionary era. An analysis of black women's work as slaves and as family members affords an overview of their general position in the new American nation. Recent scholarship reveals the necessity of paying special attention to the regional variations in the slave system, from the large, isolated rice plantations of the South Carolina and Georgia lowcountry to the smaller, more diversified estates of the upper South and the small farms and commercial centers of New England and the Middle Colonies.[6] It is helpful here to consider several factors that determined the well-being of slave women: their material standard of living (defined by the adequacy of their food, clothing, and shelter); their ability to form kin relationships and then to preserve them; the amount of control they exercised over their own productive energies; and the arduousness of, or physical danger associated with, their labor.

Within eighteenth-century slave economies, the sexual division of labor included the kinds of work slave women were forced to do by whites and the types of services they provided for their own households, kin, and communities. From the slaveholder's perspective, black women's labor presented problems in terms of plantation management. Theoretically, these women were, of course, able to perform almost any task as field laborers, house servants, or artisans. But as black females' reproductive capacity gradually assumed greater significance in the course of the eighteenth century, most southern planters came to reject the policies followed by their West Indian counterparts—white men who found it more convenient to work to death successive groups of imported Africans than to purchase large numbers of women and encourage them to have children. In addition, the mainland colonists' set ideas about the nature of women's domestic work (ideas that transcended racial boundaries) revealed that cultural bias, as well as economic imperatives, shaped the task assignments meted out to slave women.

The history of black women's work roles is intimately connected to the history of the black family. Here it is worthwhile to consider a major irony in the history of the slave family—the fact that no matter how subversive the institution to slaveholders' claims on black people's time and energies, and no matter how comforting kin ties to a folk constantly under siege, the natural reproduction of the bound labor force greatly enriched whites in the long run, and by the late eighteenth century contributed directly to the expansion of the staple crop economy. The revolutionary period marks the convergence of these two mutually supportive developments—on the one hand, the emergence of a relatively stable slave family combined with a vital Afro-American culture, and, on the other hand, white men's tacit recognition that some form of tolerance for, if not positive encouragement of, family relations would promote plantation harmony and yield greater returns on investment. The issue turned on maintaining a balanced sex ratio within individual farm units and on providing slaves with a certain measure of freedom to form marital ties. As one aspiring planter noted on the eve of the Revolution:

"[Husband-wife relations] will greatly tend to keep them [men] at home and to make them Regular and tho the Women will not work all together so well as ye Men, Yet Amends will be sufficiently made in a very few years by the Great Encrease of Children who may easily [be] traind up and become faithfully attached to the Glebe and to their Master."[7]

A limited amount of evidence indicates that at least a few southern slaveholders in the seventeenth and early eighteenth centuries took deliberate steps to force slave women to bear children. A North Carolinian reported in 1737 that after two or three years of marriage, childless wives were compelled "to take a second, third, fourth, fifth or more husbands or bedfellows—a fruitful woman amongst them very much valued by the planters and a numerous issue esteemed the greatest riches in this country." Yet the proclivities of individual owners did not translate into a policy universally accepted among planters during this period, nor did it guarantee any sort of viable family life for the slaves involved.[8] In fact, the dynamics of the African slave trade conspired against a natural increase of the black population until the second quarter of the eighteenth century in the South, and probably later in the North. Individual planters had some control over this process; nevertheless, certain demographic and economic variables remained impervious to the deepest desires of either whites or blacks.

Whether or not a slave woman was expected to bear children for her master's use, she remained vulnerable to his sexual advances, and the constant threat of rape injected raw-edged tensions into black family life. Any offspring that resulted from rape or concubinage served to enhance the wealth of labor-hungry planters, who thus had positive inducements to wreak havoc on the integrity of slave husband-wife relations. In crowded northern cities the economic benefits of such behavior were less apparent; nonetheless, many domestic servants found themselves at the mercy of lascivious masters and their teenaged sons. Some owners indulged in ritualistic sex games with their bondswomen, while others boasted proudly of their conquests in the slave quarters. The degree of public acceptance of these unions varied throughout the colonies—from tacit disapproval in the North to open acceptance in aristocratic South Carolina, where, according to

Josiah Quincy, Jr., in 1773, "the enjoyment of a negro mulatto woman is spoken of as quite a common thing; no reluctance, delicacy or shame is made about the matter." But the ensuing harm to black family life was universal. In no way could a master more dramatically demonstrate his racial and sexual prerogatives to his own wife as well as to his slaves. For southern planters, especially, this combination of self-indulgence and economic self-interest proved irresistible; it also served to terrorize their female slaves and to humiliate all black men.[9]

At this point it is useful to contrast the work assigned to slave women with that performed by white women of various social classes. Obviously, wives of the wealthiest masters found themselves freed from much of the most arduous and tedious household labor, although they frequently bemoaned the supervisory responsibilities incumbent upon them as slave mistresses. Young women of the elite planter class might learn to knit or do fancy needlework, but they rarely engaged in cloth production themselves. According to Julia Cherry Spruill, "Unlike northern and frontier housewives, the southern mistress in the settled counties did not generally spin and weave the clothing of her family"; she relied instead on either "Negresses . . . trained as spinners" or foreign imports of cloth. With the onset of the Revolution, "flax was planted. Negresses were taught to spin, and wheels were set in motion on every plantation."[10]

Poorer white women in all areas of the colonies performed essentially the same kinds of domestic tasks as female slaves. However, we may assume that the quality of their work experience was considerably enhanced (at least in a relative sense), for white housewives retained some control over the pace of their labor and derived a measure of satisfaction from it when it directly benefited their own families. Though they might have followed the same techniques in preparing meals, the black cook in the "big house" and the white woman of modest means had divergent perceptions of the value of their own labor.[11]

The issue of women's field work is more problematic, for white women in frontier households probably did their share of stump clearing, plowing, and harvesting. Still, a few generalizations seem warranted: first, white women of the elite and middling classes confined themselves to the house and its immediate environs during the workday; this sexual division of labor between white partners was a matter of pride for husbands, a matter of self-respect for wives. Second, white female indentured servants, North or South, might be sent to the fields, according to the demands of the crop, but they were "not ordinarily so employed." Contrasting the status of female slaves and indentured servants in Virginia in 1722, Robert Beverley wrote: "A white woman is rarely or never put to work in the ground, if she be good for anything else; and to discourage all planters from using any women so, their law makes female servants working in the ground tithables, while it suffers all other white women to be absolutely exempted; whereas, on the other hand, it is a common thing to work a woman slave out of doors, nor does the law make any distinction in her taxes, whether her work be abroad or at home." Slave women were a regular part of the South's agricultural labor force, while white women (regardless of class status) were not.[12]

Significantly, the primitive techniques associated with staple-crop cultivation in the colonial era (chiefly indigo, rice, and tobacco) made this an exceedingly difficult, disagreeable, and even dangerous kind of intensive labor. Of the rice grown in Georgia swamps, one observer noted, "The labor required for the cultivation is fit only for slaves, and I think the hardest work I have seen them engaged in."[13] Another source suggested in the 1770s that even toil in large bodies of stagnant water was "not so fatal as the excessive hard labor of beating the rice in mortars [that is, slave women's work]. . . . This (where there is a severe overseer) generally carries of[f] great numbers every winter."[14] Thus both the physical and political contexts of black women's labor merit consideration. White female indentured servants were routinely exploited (both economically and sexually) for the benefit of their masters, but they were exempt from the grueling pace of forced labor in the fields, they served for a set number of years, and they bore free children.

The cultural dimension of black women's experience sheds additional light on their work patterns. Ira Berlin has pointed out the close connection between the location and nature of slaves' labor and the degree of their assimilation into the larger white society. Masters favored Afro-Americans (that is, "country-born Negroes" as opposed to native Africans) for skilled jobs. These more privileged male slaves and their families were concentrated in urban areas, where they lived in close proximity to whites and where their African heritage became more diffuse as time passed. On the other hand, Africans isolated on large lowcountry rice plantations (South Carolina) or remote upcountry tobacco quarters (Virginia) learned English only gradually (if at all) and preserved many elements of common West African cultural forms related to religion and crop production. According to Berlin, "By the eve of the Revolution, deep cultural differences separated those blacks who sought to improve their lives through incorporation into the white world and those who determined to disregard the white man's ways."[15]

These differences manifested themselves in the types of work that black women performed on behalf of their own families. The task system associated with rice cultivation permitted women a certain amount of freedom in following traditional African gardening, cooking, and bartering practices. On at least some early eighteenth-century southern plantations, black wives and mothers prepared meals communally along the lines of West African tribes that practiced polygyny.[16] In contrast, workers organized in gangs, and domestic servants in towns and cities, were more closely supervised by whites, and the time available for chores in the quarters correspondingly limited. Of all black women, those in northern and southern cities probably became most rapidly adept at household skills traditionally assigned to women of English or West European backgrounds.

Men held most formal positions of authority in the slave community (preachers and skilled craftsmen are prime examples), but elderly women often gained informal influence by virtue of their knowledge of herbal medicine, poisons, conjuring, and midwifery. When they delivered a baby or prescribed a root tea for some physical or spiritual malady, grandmothers commanded the respect of their kin and neighbors. When they offered their services to abort a pregnancy, concoct a deadly potion for the master's food, or foretell the consequences of a contemplated slave uprising, they posed a direct threat to the institution of bondage itself. Records of the eighteenth-century North Carolina slave courts contain numerous instances of slave women charged with such offenses (like Hannah, convicted of giving "powder" to her mistress), proof that the alleged crimes were serious enough to warrant action on the part of public officials rather than be left to the discretion of the individual master.[17]

Clearly, the significance of the slave family—defined in terms of both the nuclear unit and the convergence of kin networks that created and sustained Afro-American life—transcended the affective realm that bound parent to child and cousin to cousin. Free blacks often used their hard-earned cash not for purposes of individual self-aggrandizement but rather to liberate loved ones from bondage, and slaves who petitioned for freedom frequently cited not only the abrogation of their own rights as individuals but also their inability as spouses and parents to enjoy a stable family life: "Thus we are deprived of every thing that hath a tendency to make life even tolerable, the endearing ties of husband and wife than our masters or mistresses thinkes proper marred or onmarred. Our children are also taken from us by force."[18]

If the ideology of democratic republicanism reduced to successful practice represented the genius and creativity of eighteenth-century white men in America, then attempts by slaves to preserve the integrity of family life represented an analogous spirit (that is, an impulse similarly revealing of a group's cultural priorities) among slave women and men. The patriots' public attempts to secure the rights of property owners found their private counterpart in the initiative and daring required of black family members either to preserve or recover ties to loved ones that were threatened by whites.

Short of poisoning her master, torching his house, barn, or crop, or plotting an armed revolt against him, an eighteenth-century slave woman could most directly challenge the system of bondage by seizing control over her own person and depriving whites of her labor. Though less spectacular than the shedding of blood or destruction of property, this act too required (in most cases) advance planning, subterfuge, and a great deal of raw courage. Family considerations played a major role in determining when, why, and how slave women ran away from their owners, just as duties to their kin could (more often than not) discourage such behavior.[19] Young and childless women at times took advantage of their lack of child-rearing responsibilities to strike out on their own and rejoin other family members. Out of sheer desperation, Charleston's Robert Pringle finally decided to sell young Esther in 1740, though he lamented losing such a good worker permanently. He advised potential buyers that she could "doe any House Work, such as Makeing Beds, Cleaning Rooms, Washing, Attending at Table &c & talks good English being this Province Born, & is not given to any Vice"—except, apparently, the unfortunate habit of trying to flee to her parents on one of Pringle's other plantations outside the city.[20] Presumably Esther's new master would find her more tractable once he removed her from the vicinity of Charleston.

But other black women, like the Virginia slave Mary, had to assume the added risk of absconding with children, who enriched their newfound (if temporary) sense of freedom but at the same time slowed their flight and made them more obvious to white authorities; this twenty-six-year-old mother ran away "with a boy sucking at the breast named Billy . . . [and] a girl named Lidia, about 9 years old, of a yellow complexion like the mother." In South Carolina, Kate attempted a daring escape when, in the eighth unwieldy and obvious month of pregnancy, she took her stuttering son and deserted her master, who was (according to the white man) "extremely ill in bed, her mistress in another, and two of [his] children not able to help each other." The white man damned Kate, the "inhuman creature," for leaving his family in dire straits, and suggested she "must be conscious of some crime" to disappear at such an inopportune moment. About the same time, Darque took her "child about 8 or 9 months old" with her when she left her Georgia owner, prompting historian Betty Wood to note that, in this case, as well as others involving slave women fugitives, "the fear of being separated from their offspring or actual separation from the child's father had prompted them to run away." Indeed, for women especially, the decision to leave was often a family affair. The New York mother who ran off "in an advanced state of pregnancy" together with her husband must have been overjoyed at the possibility of offering her baby a life of (relative) freedom.[21]

In their attempts to rid themselves of chronic runaways through sale or to retrieve offenders through public notices, eighteenth-century slaveholders acknowledged the intelligence, resourcefulness, and boldness of their bondswomen. Descriptions of these slaves belie the conventional stereotypes that became popular during the early nineteenth century—the notion that both black people and females were by nature obedient, passive, and lacking in imagination or strength. Revolutionary-era runaways included Milly, "a sly subtle Wench, and a great Lyar"; Cicely, "very wicked and full of flattery"; and Hannah, "very insinuating and a notorious thief."[22] Women condemned as guileful, cunning, proud, and artful often assumed the demeanor of free blacks, a feat accomplished most often in cities and with the help of relatives, both slave and free. These examples must of course be juxtaposed to the experiences of most slave women, who made the calculated decision to remain in their master's household and thereby provide for loved ones in less dramatic, though often equally surreptitious, ways. In sum, the complex relationships between the work and family life of slave women make it exceedingly difficult to generalize about their status in the eighteenth century, even allowing for regional variations in demography and economy.

The Revolutionary War years did little to change the basic work and family obligations that assumed a kaleidoscope of patterns in the lives of different groups of black women. Nevertheless, the conflict made much clearer the cleavage in status (if not consciousness) between free blacks and slaves, for while almost all of them faced unprecedented hardships, some emerged from the crucible of war free (or at least freer) to labor on behalf of their own families and communities, while others entered a new and brutal slave regime in the Cotton South.

Benjamin Quarles has estimated that five thousand black men served in the patriot armed forces, including the Continental army and navy, and state militias. This figure includes slaves who deserted their loyalist owners to fight with the rebels and free blacks (almost all in the North) who volunteered for duty. But a far larger number of blacks perceived their best interests to lie with the British, a conviction no doubt encouraged early on by Virginia's royal governor, Lord Dunmore, who in 1775 promised to liberate all the slaves of patriots who joined his army. As a slaveholder, Dunmore promoted policies that reflected the opportunistic attitude of the British toward blacks in general: they were considered worthy of decent treatment only insofar as they furthered the king's cause as soldiers, manual laborers, or insurgents who deprived the colonists of much needed labor. According to Sylvia Frey, British authorities showed little inclination to offer refuge to the slaves of loyalists. Dunmore himself refused sanctuary to runaways whom he could not readily use in his current military campaigns.[23]

As might be expected, few slave women found a haven behind British lines. Army camps along the coast of Virginia were crowded and disease ridden, with black people of both sexes and all ages suffering from exposure, hunger, and smallpox. The grisly image of a child seeking nourishment from the breast of its dead mother on Gwynne Island in 1776 conveys the bitter reality of black life—and death—in refugee camps.[24] The image itself is also a reminder of the unique forms of oppression that impelled slave women to flee their owners' plantations and the lack of concern for their plight among officials on either side of the conflict. Few white women had cause to risk so much during the war.

In occupied cities and towns, the British exploited black female labor whenever it suited their purposes. Military commanders supervised black workers who had been acquired (through whatever means) to perform unskilled labor. In Philadelphia fifteen women toiled as part of a "Company of Black Pioneers" forced to "assist in Cleaning the Streets and Removing All Newsiances being thrown into the Streets." Some army units bought slaves outright: "late in 1782 the artillery department at Charleston owned forty-four Negro women and their children, and the 'Horse Department' owned six women and their children."[25] These slaves probably cooked and washed for the soldiers and did the most disagreeable chores related to the routine maintenance of horses and equipment. Whatever their political differences, the white male combatants seemed to share similar notions about "black women's work."

The black people evacuated with British troops after the war faced an uncertain future indeed. At least fifteen thousand black women and men left the country aboard British ships that sailed from Savannah, Charleston, and New York; some were self-defined loyalists, others served loyalist masters, and still others hoped to benefit from British efforts to deprive their conquerors of personal property. The wide range of experiences that awaited individual women—a lifetime of slavery in the West Indies; a struggle to survive in the fledgling British colony of Sierra Leone; or a new beginning of health, safety, and freedom in Nova Scotia—mirrored the crosscurrents of hardship and liberation that characterized the status of slave women during the Revolutionary War.[26]

In the 1780s and 1790s, free and slave women together actively participated in the creation of an "institutional core" for Afro-American life—the formation of churches, schools, and benevolent societies separate and distinct from those of whites, blending an African heritage with American political realities.[27] Although several historians have described in detail the emergence of black organized religion after the war, the role of women in that story remains untold. Positions of public influence were dominated by male preachers, like Philadelphia clergyman Richard Allen, who formalized black worship traditions, and southern itinerants, who expanded their ministry among white and black, slave and free congregants in accordance with the racially egalitarian impulses of the Great Awakening.[28]

However, black women exerted considerable religious influence within their own communities in compelling but less formal ways. Some, like the visionary Elizabeth (and later Jarena Lee) had large followings, though as women they could not qualify for ordination within any Protestant denomination.[29] Other women continued along the time-honored path of their African foremothers and offered a combination of folk-medicine remedies and spiritual counseling to persons of both sexes. And, finally, large numbers of working wives and mothers sustained local churchwork through their meager wages; the high proportion of gainfully employed free black women (compared to whites) indicated that their voluntary contributions were integral to the religious vitality of the postwar black community.

During these years the exhilaration of freedom experienced by some black women contrasted mightily with the plight of many more who remained condemned to slavery. The late eighteenth-century southern economy echoed colonial themes and at the same time presaged dominant antebellum trends. Upper South whites became less reliant on large-scale plantation slavery and hired out bondsmen and women to smaller farms and craft establishments. But here again the old pattern of tradeoffs applied to the status of slave women. Individual black men acquired skills and relative freedom of movement when they could earn ready cash for their masters. Children worked as apprentices and menial laborers. But women, who were more difficult to hire out, bore the brunt of, in Sarah S. Hughes's words, the consequent "discontinuities in household composition"; this mode of slavery sacrificed black family stability to the flexibility of the new nonplantation economy.[30]

Later, the cotton boom years of the antebellum period would recapitulate and intensify the most callous features of the early eighteenth-century rice plantation system. Masters fully appreciated a self-replenishing labor force, but their efforts each year to grow as much cotton as humanly possible worked to the detriment of childbearing females. Most white men did not fully comprehend the connection between overwork and high miscarriage and infant mortality rates; the result was untold pain and grief for slave mothers.[31] As the institution of bondage renewed itself, so too did the drive for hegemony among ambitious men on the make as well as among the sons of revolutionary-era slaveholders—a drive that held sacred the tenet of private property (no matter what its form) and eventually provoked a war far bloodier than the rebellion of 1776. While their free sisters kept alive the spirit of Afro-American community autonomy, black mothers and wives in the Cotton South would continue to eat the bitter fruit borne of a white man's political and economic revolution.

Notes

1. Donald Jackson and Dorothy Twohig, eds., *The Diaries of George Washington*, 6 vols. (Charlottesville, 1976–79), vol. 5:170, 510, 215.

2. Ulrich Bonnell Phillips, *American Negro Slavery* (New York, 1918), 83–84; Jackson and Twohig, eds., *Diaries of Washington*, vol. 5:261, 105, 302, 305; Lois Green Carr and Lorena S. Walsh, "The Transformation of Production on the Farm and in the Household in the Chesapeake, 1658–1820" (Paper presented at the Washington Area Seminar on Early American History, March 1985), 59.

3. Edmund S. Morgan, *American Slavery, American Freedom: The Ordeal of Colonial Virginia* (New York, 1975), 380.

4. Barbara J. Fields, "Ideology and Race in American History," in J. Morgan Kousser and James M. McPherson, eds., *Region, Race, and Reconstruction: Essays in Honor of C. Vann Woodward* (New York, 1982), 143–78; George M. Fredrickson, "Self-Made Hero," *New York Review of Books*, June 27, 1985.

5. Angela Davis, "Reflections on the Black Woman's Role in the Community of Slaves," *Black Scholar* 3 (1971):2–15.

6. Ira Berlin, "Time, Space, and the Evolution of Afro-American Society in British Mainland North America," *American Historical Review* 85 (1980):44–78.

7. Planter (1769) quoted in Daniel C. Littlefield, *Rice and Slaves: Ethnicity and the Slave Trade in Colonial South Carolina* (Baton Rouge, 1981), 65.

8. North Carolinian quoted in John Spencer Bassett, *Slavery and Servitude in the Colony of North Carolina* (Baltimore, 1896), 57; Wesley Frank Craven, *White, Red, and Black: The Seventeenth-Century Virginian* (New York, 1971), 100–101.

9. Edgar J. McManus, *A History of Negro Slavery in New York* (Syracuse, 1966), 66; Gerald W. Mullin, *Flight and Rebellion: Slave Resistance in Eighteenth-Century Virginia* (New York, 1972), 65; Quincy quoted in Littlefield, *Rice and Slaves,* 170.

10. Catherine Clinton, *The Plantation Mistress: Women's World in the Old South* (New York, 1982); Spruill, *Women's Life and Work in the Southern Colonies* (1938; reprint, New York, 1972), 74–75. See also Alice Morse Earle, *Home Life in Colonial Days* (1898; reprint, Stockbridge, Mass., 1974).

11. Julia Cherry Spruill, *Women's Work.* These themes are explored more fully in Jacqueline Jones, *Labor of Love, Labor of Sorrow: Black Women, Work, and the Family from Slavery to the Present* (New York, 1985).

12. Spruill, *Women's Work,* 83; James Curtis Ballagh, *A History of Slavery in Virginia* (Baltimore, 1902), 107; "Robert Beverly Distinguishes between Servants and Slaves," in William Lee Rose, ed., *A Documentary History of Slavery in North America* (New York, 1976), 26.

13. For descriptions of the cultivation techniques for each crop during this period, see Phillips, *American Negro Slavery:* Georgia observer quoted in Ralph Betts Flanders, *Plantation Slavery in Georgia* (Cos Cob, Conn., 1967), 42. According to Flanders, "The exclusive use of the hoe in the cultivation, the primitive methods of threshing and reaping, and the constant exposure exacted the greatest amount of physical exertion from

the laborer," 42. See also David O. Whitten, "American Rice Cultivation, 1680–1980: A Tercentenary Critique," *Southern Studies* 21 (1982):5–15.

14. "Benjamin West Sympathizes with Slaves in South Carolina," in Rose, ed., *Documentary History*, 55–56.

15. Berlin, "Time, Space, and Afro-American Society," 67.

16. Allan Kulikoff, "The Beginnings of the Afro-American Family in Maryland," in Aubrey C. Land, Lois Green Carr, and Edward C. Papenfuse, eds., *Law, Society, and Politics in Early Maryland* (Baltimore, 1977), 117–80. See also Betty Wood, *Slavery in Colonial Georgia, 1730–1775* (Athens, 1984), 147; William R. Bascom, "Acculturation among the Gullah Negroes," *American Anthropologist* 43 (1941):43–50; Philip D. Morgan, "Work and Culture: The Task System and the World of Lowcountry Blacks, 1700–1880," *William and Mary Quarterly*, 3d ser. 39 (1982):563–99.

17. On the political significance of slave women's labor in the quarters, see Davis, "Reflections on the Black Woman's Role," 3–15. Alan D. Watson, "North Carolina Slave Courts, 1715–1785," *North Carolina Historical Review* 60 (1983):28.

18. Petition (1773) in Herbert Aptheker, ed., *A Documentary History of the Negro People*, vol. 1, *From Colonial Times through the Civil War* (Secaucus, N.J., 1951), 9. See also Ruth Bogin, ed., "'Liberty Further Extended': A 1776 Anti-Slavery Manuscript by Lemuel Haynes," *William and Mary Quarterly* 3d ser. 40 (1983):85–105.

19. See for example Mullin, *Flight and Rebellion*, 104; Daniel E. Meadors, "South Carolina Fugitives as Viewed through Local Colonial Newspapers with Emphasis on Runaway Notices, 1732–1801," *Journal of Negro History* 60 (1975); Edgar J. McManus, *Black Bondage in the North* (Syracuse, 1973), 114–15; Lorenzo Johnston Greene, "The New England Negro as Seen in Advertisements for Runaway Slaves," Journal of Negro History 29 (1944):125–46; Wood, *Slavery in Colonial Georgia*, 157, 172, 187.

20. Pringle quoted in Peter H. Wood, *Black Majority: Negroes in Colonial South Carolina through the Stono Rebellion* (New York, 1974), 249.

21. Virginia advertisement quoted in Mullin, *Flight and Rebellion*, 104, 105; South Carolina advertisement quoted in Meadors, "South Carolina Fugitives," 311; Wood, *Slavery in Colonial Georgia*, 172; McManus, *Black Bondage in the North*, 114–15.

22. Advertisements quoted in Mullin, *Flight and Rebellion*, 104. See also "Masters Describe Their Runaway Slaves," in Rose, ed., *Documentary History*, 57; Littlefield, *Rice and Slaves*, 133, 167; Jeffrey J. Crow, *The Black Experience in Revolutionary North Carolina* (Raleigh, 1977), 41;

Kenneth Wiggins Porter, "Negroes on the Southern Frontier, 1670–1763," *Journal of Negro History* 33 (1948):78.

23. Benjamin Quarles, *The Negro in the American Revolution* (1961; reprint, New York, 1973), ix; Sylvia P. Frey, "Between Slavery and Freedom: Virginia Blacks in the American Revolution," *Journal of Southern History* 49 (1983):383–84.

24. Frey, "Slavery and Freedom," 391.

25. Quarles, *Negro in the American Revolution*, 135, 157.

26. Mary Beth Norton, "'What An Alarming Crisis Is This': Southern Women and the American Revolution," in Jeffrey J. Crow and Larry E. Tise, eds., *The Southern Experience in the American Revolution* (Chapel Hill, 1978), 214–15; Mary Beth Norton, "The Fate of Some Black Loyalists of the American Revolution," *Journal of Negro History* 58 (1973):402–6.

27. Ira Berlin, "The Revolution in Black Life," in Alfred F. Young, ed., *The American Revolution: Explorations in the History of American Radicalism* (De Kalb, Ill., 1976), 376.

28. See for example Carol V. R. George, *Segregated Sabbaths: Richard Allen and the Emergence of Independent Black Churches, 1760–1840* (New York, 1973); Albert J. Raboteau, "The Slave Church in the Era of the American Revolution," in Berlin and Hoffman, eds., *Slavery and Freedom*, 193–213; Marcus W. Jernegan, "Slavery and Conversion in the American Colonies," *American Historical Review* 21 (1916):504–27; Crow, *Black Experience*, 48–50, 95; Luther P. Jackson, "Religious Development of the Negro in Virginia from 1760 to 1860," *Journal of Negro History* 16 (1931):168–239.

29. Marilyn Richardson, *Black Women and Religion: A Bibliography* (Boston, 1980), 18; Bert Loewenberg and Ruth I. Bogin, eds., *Black Women in Nineteenth-Century American Life: Their Words, Their Thoughts, Their Feelings* (University Park, Pa., 1976), 127–41. See also Jean M. Humez, "'My Spirit Eye': Some Functions of Spiritual and Visionary Experience in the Lives of Five Black Women Preachers, 1810–1880," in Barbara J. Harris and JoAnn K. McNamara, eds., *Women and the Structure of Society* (Durham, N.C., 1984).

30. Sarah S. Hughes, "Slaves for Hire: The Allocation of Black Labor in Elizabeth City County, Virginia, 1782 to 1810," *William and Mary Quarterly*, 3d ser. 35 (1978):263.

31. See for example Michael P. Johnson, "Smothered Slave Infants: Were Slave Mothers at Fault?" *Journal of Southern History* 47 (1981):493–520.

Southern Indians and
the Cult of True Womanhood

THEDA PERDUE

*Theda Perdue is Professor of History at the University of Kentucky.
Her first book,* Slavery and the Evolution of Cherokee Society,
1540–1865 *(1979) demonstrated her compelling talent for placing Indians within southern history. Her most recent books,* Native Carolinians *(1985) and* The Cherokee *(1988) demonstrate her continuing
interest in combining southern history and the history of American
Indians. She is the editor of* Cherokee Editor: The Writings of
Elias Budinot *(1983) and* An Oral History of the Five Civilized
Tribes, *first published in 1980, with a revised edition in 1993.*

*Perdue's essay was prepared for a symposium held at Georgia
Southern College in 1984. Her piece, which first appeared in a volume
of papers from this conference—entitled* The Web of Family Relations: Women, Family and Education in the South *(University of
Georgia Press, 1985), represents her ongoing work on American Indian women.*

Southern Indians stand apart culturally and historically from
other native Americans.[1] Building of temple mounds, an elaborate ceremonial life, a complex belief system, riverine agriculture,
and matrilineal descent characterized their aboriginal culture.
Southern Indians embraced European culture with such enthusiasm and success that they came to be known as the "five civilized
tribes." They acquired this sobriquet in the half century after the
ratification of the United States Constitution, a time when many
southern Indians came to believe that their physical survival de-

pended on adopting an Anglo-American lifestyle and value system. These Indians gradually abandoned hunting and subsistence agriculture, the practice of blood vengeance, their traditional religious beliefs and practices, and other aspects of their aboriginal way of life. Some individual Indians succeeded so well that they became culturally indistinguishable from their white neighbors. They owned large plantations, operated successful businesses, attended Christian churches, promoted formal legal and judicial systems, and wrote and conversed in the English language.[2]

An integral part of this cultural transformation was a redefinition of gender roles. Just as men could no longer follow their aboriginal pursuits of hunting and warfare, women could no longer behave in what was perceived to be a "savage" or "degraded" way.[3] Instead, they had to attempt to conform to an Anglo-American ideal characterized by purity, piety, domesticity, and submissiveness.[4] By the second quarter of the nineteenth century, the glorification of this ideal had become so pervasive in American society that the historian Barbara Welter has called it the "cult of true womanhood." A true woman was essentially spiritual rather than physical. She occupied a separate sphere apart from the ambition, selfishness, and materialism that permeated the man's world of business and politics. Her proper place was the home, and because of her spiritual nature, she imbued her home with piety, morality, and love. The home was a haven from the outside world, and in its operation a true woman should excel. Openly submissive to men, a true woman influenced them subtly through her purity and piety.

Traditionally southern Indians had a very different view of womanhood. Indian women occupied a separate sphere from that of men, but they had considerable economic, political, and social importance. While men hunted and went to war, women collected firewood, made pottery and baskets, sewed clothes, cared for children, and cooked the family's food. These tasks certainly fell within the nineteenth-century definition of domesticity, but the sphere of Indian women extended beyond home and hearth to encompass economic activities that seemed far less appropriate to their sex. In particular, women farmed in a society that depended primarily on agriculture for subsistence, and women performed most of the manual labor with men assisting only in clearing fields and planting corn. This inequitable division of labor elicited comments from most Euro-American observers. In 1775, Bernard Romans described the women he encountered on a journey through east and west Florida: "Their strength is great, and they labor hard, carrying very heavy burdens great distance." On his 1797 tour of the Cherokee country, Louis-Philippe, who later would become king of France, observed: "The Indians have all the work done by women. They are assigned not only household tasks; even the corn, peas, beans, and potatoes are planted, tended, and preserved by the women." In the economy of southern Indians, therefore, women did what Euro-Americans considered to be work—they farmed—while men did what was considered sport—they hunted.[5]

This arrangement was amazing in that women did not seem to object to doing most of the work. In the early nineteenth century, a missionary commented on the willingness with which the women toiled: "Though custom attached the heaviest part of the labor of the women, yet they were cheerful and voluntary in performing it. What others have discovered among the Indians I cannot tell, but though I have been about nineteen years among the Cherokees, I have perceived nothing of that slavish, servile fear, on the part of women, so often spoke of." One reason women may have worked so gladly was that they received formal recognition for their economic contribution, and they controlled the fruit of their labor. In the Green Corn Ceremony, the southern Indians' most important religious event, women ritually presented the new crop, which was sacrificed to the fire, and when Europeans occasionally purchased corn from the Indians in the eighteenth century, they bought it from women.[6] Women may also have labored without complaint because farming was one of the determinants of gender. Southern Indians distinguished between the sexes on other than merely biological grounds. Women were women not only because they could bear children but also because they farmed, and men who farmed came to be regarded sexually as women. Men hunted, therefore, because hunting was intrinsically linked to male sexuality; women farmed because farming was one of the characteristics that made them women.[7]

The matrilocal residence pattern of southern Indians probably contributed to the association of women and agriculture. A man lived in the household of his wife's lineage, and buildings, garden plots, and sections of the village's common field belonged to her lineage. A man had no proprietary interest in the homestead where he lived with his wife or in the land his wife farmed. Nor was a husband necessarily a permanent resident in the household of his wife's lineage. Polygamy was common, and he might divide his time between the lineages of his wives. Furthermore, southeastern Indians frequently terminated their marriages, and in the event of divorce, a man simply left his wife's household and returned to his mother's house and his own lineage. Because southeastern Indians were also matrilineal, that is, they traced kinship only through the female line, children belonged to the mother's lineage and clan rather than to the father's, and when divorce occurred, they invariably remained with their mothers. Men, therefore, had no claim on the houses they lived in or the children they fathered.[8]

John Lawson tried to explain matrilineal lineage, which he considered an odd way of reckoning kin, by attributing it to "fear of Imposters; the Savages knowing well, how much Frailty possesses *Indian* women, betwixt the Garters and the Girdle."[9] Women in southern Indian tribes did enjoy considerable sexual freedom. Except for restraints regarding incest and menstrual taboos, Indian women were relatively free in choosing sexual partners, engaging in intercourse, and dissolving relationships. All southern Indians condoned premarital sex and divorce, which were equally female or male prerogatives, but attitudes toward adultery varied from one tribe to another.

Indian women usually displayed a sense of humor and a lack of modesty regarding sexual matters. One member of Lawson's expedition took an Indian "wife" for a night. The couple consummated their marriage in a room occupied by other members of the company and guests at the wedding feast. In the morning the groom discovered that both his bride and his shoes were gone.[10] So brazen and skilled were most Cherokee women that Louis-Philippe concluded that "no Frenchwomen could teach them a thing." When his guide made sexual advances to several Cherokee women in a house they visited, he recorded in his journal that "they were so little embarrassed that one of them who was lying on a bed put her hand on his trousers before my very eyes and said scornfully, *Ah, sick.*"[11]

Compared to the other southern Indians, Louis-Philippe de-

cided, the Cherokees were "exceedingly casual" about sex. Although all southern Indians had certain common characteristics—they were matrilineal and matrilocal, women farmed, and
both sexes enjoyed some sexual freedom—Cherokee women had
the highest degree of power and personal autonomy. The trader
James Adair maintained that the Cherokees "have been a considerable while under a petticoat-government." In Cherokee society,
women spoke in council and determined the fate of war captives.
Some even went on the warpath and earned a special title, "War
Woman."[12] In fact, Cherokee women were probably as far from
the "true women" of the early nineteenth-century ideal as any
women Anglo-Americans encountered on the continent. When
the United States government and Protestant missionaries under-
took the "civilization" of native Americans in the late eighteenth
century, however, the Cherokees proved to be the most adept at
transforming their society.[13] Because the Cherokees provide the
greatest contrast between the aboriginal role of women and the
role that emerged in the early nineteenth century as a consequence of civilization, I will examine the impact of the cult of true
womanhood on the status of Cherokee women.

Until the late eighteenth century, Europeans had few relations
with Cherokee women other than sexual ones. Europeans were
primarily interested in Indian men as warriors and hunters and
considered women to be of little economic or political significance. After the American Revolution, native alliances and the
deerskin trade diminished in importance. All the Indians still had
that Europeans valued was land. George Washington and his
advisers devised a plan which they believed would help the Indians recover economically from the depletion of their hunting
grounds and the destruction experienced during the Revolution
while making large tracts of Indian land available for white settlement. They hoped to convert the Indians into farmers living on
isolated homesteads much like white frontiersmen. With hunting
no longer part of Indian economy, the excess land could be ceded
to the United States and opened to whites.

The Cherokees traditionally had lived in large towns located
along rivers. These towns were composed of many matrilineal
households containing several generations. A woman was rarely
alone: her mother, sisters, and daughters, with their husbands,

lived under the same roof, and other households were nearby. Beyond the houses lay large fields which the women worked communally. Originally, these towns had served a defensive purpose, but in the warfare of the eighteenth century, they became targets of attack. In the French and Indian War and the American Revolution, soldiers invaded the Cherokee country and destroyed towns and fields. As a result, Cherokees began abandoning their towns even before the United States government inaugurated the civilization program. When a government agent toured the Cherokee Nation in 1796, he passed a number of deserted towns; at one site he found a "hut, some peach trees and the posts of a town house," and at another there was only a "small field of corn, some peach, plumb and locust trees."[14]

Agents appointed to implement the civilization program encouraged this trend. They advised the Cherokee to "scatter from their towns and make individual improvements also of cultivating more land for grain, cotton &c. than they could while crowded up in towns." The Cherokees complied: "They dispersed from their large towns,—built convenient houses,—cleared and fenced farms, and soon possessed numerous flocks and herds." By 1818 missionaries complained that "there is no place near us where a large audience can be collected as the people do not live in villages, but scattered over the country from 2 to 10 miles apart." The breaking up of Cherokee towns resulted in a very isolated existence for women because new households often consisted of only one nuclear family. This isolation occurred just at the time when the work load of women was increasing.[15]

In a letter of 1796, George Washington advised the Cherokees to raise cattle, hogs, and sheep. He pointed out that they could increase the amount of corn they produced by using plows and that they could also cultivate wheat and other grains. Apparently addressing the letter to the men, Washington continued: "To these you will easily add flax and cotton which you may dispose of to the White people, or have it made up by your own women into clothing for yourselves. Your wives and daughters can soon learn to spin and weave."[16] Washington apparently knew nothing about traditional gender roles, and the agents he sent usually had little sympathy for the Indian division of labor. They provided plows to the men and instructed them in clearing fields, tilling soil, and building fences. Women received cotton cards, spinning wheels, and looms.

The women, politically ignored in the eighteenth century and bypassed in the earlier hunting economy, welcomed the opportunity to profit from contact with whites. In 1796, agent Benjamin Hawkins met with a group of Cherokee women and explained the government's plan. He reported to Washington that "they rejoiced much at what they had heard and hoped it would prove true, that they had made some cotton, and would make more and follow the instruction of the agent and the advice of the President." According to a Cherokee account, the women proved far more receptive to the civilization program than the men: "When Mr. Dinsmore, the Agent of the United States, spoke to us on the subject of raising livestock and cotton, about fifteen years ago, many of us thought it was only some refined scheme calculated to gain an influence over us, rather than to ameliorate our situation and slighted his advice and proposals; he then addressed our women, and presented them with cotton seeds for planting; and afterwards with cards, wheels and looms to work it. They acquired the use of them with great facility, and now most of the clothes we wear are of their manufacture." Two censuses conducted in the early nineteenth century reveal the extent to which women accepted their new tasks. In 1810 there were 1,600 spinning wheels and 467 looms in the Cherokee Nation; by 1826 there were 2,488 wheels and 762 looms.[17]

In 1810, one Cherokee man observed that the women had made more progress toward civilization than the men: "The females have however made much greater advances in industry than the males; they now manufacture a great quantity of cloth; but the latter have not made proportionate progress in agriculture; however, they raise great herds of cattle, which can be done with little exertion." At the same time, women continued to do most of the farming, and many even raised livestock for market. This extension of woman's work concerned government agents because many men were not acquiring the work habits considered essential to "civilized" existence.[18] They had not been able to accomplish a shift in gender roles merely by introducing the tools and techniques of Western culture. Gender roles as well as many other aspects of Cherokee culture proved extremely difficult to change.

Cultural change came more easily, however, among Cherokees who already had adopted the acquisitive, materialistic value system of white Americans. Turning from an economy based on hunting, they took advantage of the government's program and invested in privately owned agricultural improvements and commercial enterprises. They quickly became an economic elite separated from the majority of Cherokees by their wealth and by their desire to emulate whites. In the early nineteenth century, members of this economic elite rose to positions of leadership in the Cherokee Nation because of the ease and effectiveness with which they dealt with United States officials. Gradually they transformed Cherokee political institutions into replicas of those of the United States.[19] This elite expected Cherokee women to conform to the ideals of the cult of true womanhood, that is, to be sexually pure, submissive to fathers and husbands, concerned primarily with spiritual and domestic matters, and excluded from politics and economic activities outside the home. In 1818, Charles Hicks, who later would become principal chief, described the most prominent men in the nation as "those who have kept their women & children at home & in comfortable circumstances."[20] Submissive, domestic wives were a mark of prominence.

Cherokees learned to be true women primarily through the work of Protestant missionaries whom tribal leaders welcomed to the nation. In 1800 the Moravians arrived to open a school, and in the second decade of the nineteenth century Congregationalists supported by the interdenominational American Board of Commissioners for Foreign Missions, Baptists, and Methodists joined them. Except for the Methodists, missionaries preferred to teach children in boarding schools, where they had "the influence of example as well as precept." In 1819 President James Monroe visited the American Board's Brainerd mission and approved "of the plan of instruction; particularly as the children were taken into the family, taught to work, &c." This was, the president believed, "the best, & perhaps the only way to civilize and Christianize the Indians."[21] For female students, civilization meant becoming true women.

Mission schools provided an elementary education for girls as well as boys. Either single women or the wives of male missionaries usually taught the girls, but all students studied the same academic subjects, which included reading, writing, spelling, arithmetic, geography, and history. Examinations took place annually and were attended by parents. The teachers questioned students in their academic subjects as well as Bible history, catechism, and hymns, and "the girls showed specimens of knitting, spinning, mending, and fine needlework."[22]

Mastery of the domestic arts was an essential part of the girls' education because, according to one missionary, "all the females need is a proper education to be qualified to fill any of the relations or stations of domestic life." The children at the mission schools performed a variety of tasks, and the division of labor approximated that in a typical Anglo-American farming family. The boys chopped wood and plowed fields, and the girls milked, set tables, cooked meals, washed dishes, sewed clothing, knitted, quilted, did laundry, and cleaned the houses.[23] Because their fathers were wealthy, many students were not accustomed to such menial labor. Missionaries endeavored to convince them that "the charge of the kitchen and the mission table" was not degrading but was instead a "most important station," which taught them "industry and economy."[24]

The great advantage of teaching Cherokee girls "industry and economy" was the influence they might exert in their own homes. One girl wrote: "We have the opportunity of learning to work and to make garments which will be useful to us in life." Another girl expressed gratitude that missionaries had taught the students "how to take care of families that when we go home we can take care of our mothers house." A missionary assessed the impact of their work: "We cannot expect that the influence of these girls will have any great immediate effect on their acquaintance—but I believe in each case it is calculated to elevate the families in some degree, with which they are connected." Although missionaries and students expected the domestic arts learned in the mission schools to improve the parental home, they believed that the primary benefit would be to the homes the girls themselves established. Missionary Sophia Sawyer specifically hoped to "raise the female character in the Nation" so that "Cherokee gentlemen" could find young women "sufficiently educated for companions." In 1832 missionaries could report with satisfaction that the girls who had married "make good housewives and useful members of society."[25]

The marriages missionaries had in mind were not the Cherokees' traditional polygamous or serial marriages. Louis-Philippe had believed that such a marriage "renders women contemptible in men's eyes and deprives them of all influence." A monogamous marriage was supposedly liberating to women because these "serve exclusively to heighten the affections of a man."[26] Although the Cherokee elite accepted most tenets of Western civilization, some balked at abandoning the practice of polygamy. The chief justice was one who had more than one wife, but these marriages differed from traditional ones in which a man lived with his wives in their houses. Polygamous members of the elite headed more than one patriarchal household. They recognized the desirability of monogamous unions, however, encouraged others to enter into them, and sent their children to mission schools, where they were taught that polygamy was immoral.

In practice, religious denominations confronted the problem of polygamy in different ways. Moravians apparently allowed converts to keep more than one wife. The American Board required a man "to separate himself from all but the first." Perhaps because some of their chief supporters were polygamists, the governing body in Boston advised missionaries in the field to be "prudent and kind" when dealing with this "tender subject" and to instruct polygamous converts "in the nature and design of marriage, the original institution, and the law of Christ, that they may act with an enlightened conviction of duty." American Board ministers sometimes remarried in a Christian service couples who had lived for years in "a family capacity." Missionaries also rejoiced when they united in matrimony young couples of "industrious habits & reputable behavior" who were "very decent and respectable in their moral deportment."[27]

Achieving "moral deportment" at the mission schools was no simple matter, but missionaries considered the teaching of New England sexual mores to be one of their chief responsibilities. According to some reports, they enjoyed success. In 1822, American Board missionaries reported: "Mr. Hall thinks the moral influence of the school has been considerable. . . . The intercourse between the young of both sexes was shamefully loose. Boys & girls in their teens would strip & go into bathe, or play ball together naked. They would also use the most disgustingly indecent language, without the least sense of shame. But, when better instructed, they became reserved and modest." To maintain decorum, the missionaries tried to make certain that girls and boys were never alone together: "When the girls walk out any distance from the house they will be accompanied by instructors." Male and female students normally attended separate classes. When Sophia Sawyer became ill in 1827 she reluctantly sent the small girls to the boys' school but taught the larger girls in her sickroom. Miss Sawyer so feared for the virtue of the older girls that she asked the governing board "could not the boys at Brainerd be at some other school." The Moravians did resort to separate schools. The American Board, however, simply put locks on the bedroom doors.[28]

Even with these precautions, difficulties arose. In 1813 the Moravians recorded in their journal: "After prayer we directed our talk toward Nancy, indirectly admonishing her to abstain from the lust which had gripped her. She seemed not to have taken it to heart, for instead of mending her ways she continues to heap sin upon sin." Nancy Watie later moved to an American Board mission along with her cousin Sally Ridge. Their fathers were prominent in the Cherokee Nation, and they had left strict instructions that their daughters be supervised constantly and their purity preserved. A problem occurred when teenage boys in the neighborhood began calling on the girls at the mission. At first, the young people decorously sat in front of the fire under the watchful eyes of the missionaries, but soon the conversation shifted from English to Cherokee, which none of the chaperons understood. Suspecting the worst, the missionaries ordered the suitors to "spend their evenings in some other place." A year later, however, the missionaries reported that despite their care, the girls "had given themselves up to the common vices."[29]

The missionaries did not, of course, intend to cloister the young women to the extent that they did not meet suitable young men. Sophia Sawyer observed: "Like all females they desire the admiration of men. They can easily be shown that the attention, or good opinion of men without education, taste, or judgement is not worth seeking, & to gain the affection or good opinion of the opposite character, their minds must be improved, their manner polished, their persons attended to, in a word they must be qualified for usefulness." Attracting the right young men was permissible and even desirable.[30]

The girls' appearance was another concern of the missionaries. Ann Paine related an attempt to correct the daughter of a particularly prominent Cherokee: "Altho' her parents supplied her with good clothes, she was careless and indifferent about her appearance.—I often urged her attention to these things and offered as a motive her obligation to set a good example to her nation as the daughter of their chief. Told her how the young ladies of the North were taught to govern their manners and tempers and of their attention to personal appearance. She never appeared more mortified than in hearing of her superiority of birth, and of the attention she ought to pay to her personal appearance." Paine soon had "the satisfaction of witnessing her rapid improvement." Four years later, Sophia Sawyer complained about the female students in general: "I have had to punish several times to break bad habits respecting cleanliness in their clothes, books, & person—I found them in a deplorable situation in this respect. The largest girls I had in school were not capable of dressing themselves properly or of folding their clothes when taken off." Sometimes concern for the students' appearance went beyond clothing. One girl wrote a correspondent: "Mr. Ellsworth told me I had better alter my voice. He said I spoke like a man."[31]

In addition to a neat, feminine appearance, respectable men presumably also admired piety in young women and probably expected them to be more pious than they themselves were. The missionaries clearly believed that the female students in mission schools were more serious about religion than the male students, and they encouraged this emotion. Nancy Reece wrote her northern correspondent that "after work at night the girls joined for singing a special hymn Mr. Walker wrote for them & then go to worship services." Many of the girls wrote about their spiritual lives. A ten-year-old confided in a letter that "some of the girls have been serious about there wicked hearts and have retired to their Chambers to pray to God. . . . I feel as though I am a great sinner and very wicked sinner."[32]

The piety of the girls at the mission station was manifest in other ways. They organized a society to raise money to send missionaries into heathen lands. The American Board agreed to pay them for clothing they made, and they in turn donated the money to mission work. They also sold their handiwork to local Cherokee women. The piety of the girls extended beyond the school and into the community. Once a month, neighboring women would gather at the mission for a prayer meeting "that missionary labors may be blessed." One missionary reported with satisfaction that "the females have a praying society which is well attended, and they begin to do something by way of benevolence."[33]

Of the several hundred Cherokee girls who attended mission schools, the best example of "true womanhood" was Catharine Brown. She was sixteen or seventeen years old when she arrived at the Brainerd mission. She had some European ancestry, and although she had grown up in a fairly traditional Cherokee household, she spoke and read a little English. The missionaries reported that, despite the absence of a Christian influence in her childhood, "her moral character was ever good." Her biographer added: "This is remarkable, considering the looseness of manners then prevalent among the females of her nation, and the temptations to which she was exposed, when during the war with the Creek Indians, the army of the United States was stationed near her father's residence. . . . Once she even fled from her home into the wild forest to preserve her character unsullied." When she applied for admission to Brainerd, the missionaries hesitated because they feared that she would object to the domestic duties required of female students. They later recalled that she was "vain, and excessively fond of dress, wearing a profusion of ornaments in her ears." Catharine "had no objection" to work, however, and shortly after her admission, her jewelry disappeared "till only a single drop remains in each ear." After she became a part of the mission family, Catharine became extremely pious: "She spent much time in reading the Scriptures, singing, and prayer." She attended weekly prayer meetings and helped instruct the younger girls in the Lord's Prayer, hymns, and catechism. In 1819, Catharine received baptism. Her intellectual achievements were also remarkable, and soon the missionaries sent her to open a female school at the Creek Path Mission station. There she fulfilled not only her spiritual and educational responsibilities but also her domestic ones. Visitors reported: "We arrived after the family had dined, and she received us, and spread a table for our refreshment with the unaffected kindness of a sister." When her father proposed to take the family to Indian territory, Catharine was appropriately submissive. Although she did not want to go, she acquiesced to his wishes and prepared to leave for the West. Catharine's health, however, was fragile. She became ill, and "as she approached nearer to eternity her faith evidently grew stronger." In July 1823, "this lovely convert from heathenism died."[34]

Few women in the Cherokee Nation could equal Catharine Brown, and perhaps the majority of Cherokee women had little desire to be "true women." The historical record contains little information about the Cherokee masses, but from the evidence that does exist, we can infer that many Cherokees maintained a relatively traditional way of life. Continuing to exist at the subsistence level, they rejected Christianity and mission schools and relied on local councils rather than the central government dominated by the elite. Borrowing selectively from the dominant white society, a large number of women also maintained a semblance of their aboriginal role. As late as 1817, a council of women petitioned the Cherokee National Council to refrain from further land cessions, and in 1835 at least one-third of the heads of households listed on the removal roll were women.[35] Some probably were like Oo-dah-less, who, according to her obituary, accumulated a sizable estate through agriculture and commerce. She was "the support of a large family" and bequeathed her property "to an only daughter and three grand children."[36] Other women no doubt lived far more traditionally, farming, supervising an extended household, caring for children and kinsmen, and perhaps even exercising some power in local councils.

Although the feminine ideal of purity, piety, submissiveness, and domesticity did not immediately filter down to the mass of Cherokees, the nation's leaders came to expect these qualities in women. Therefore, the influence of the cult of true womanhood probably far exceeded the modest number of women trained in mission schools. The Cherokee leaders helped create a new sphere for women by passing legislation that undermined matrilineal kinship and excluded women from the political process. In the first recorded Cherokee law of 1808, the national council, which apparently included no women, established a police force "to give their protection to children as heirs to their father's property, and to the widow's share." Subsequent legislation gave further recognition to patrilineal descent and to the patriarchal family structure common among men of wealth. In 1825 the council extended citizenship to the children of white women who had married Cherokee men, another act that formally reordered descent. Legislation further isolated women by prohibiting polygamy and denied women the right to limit the size of their families by outlawing the traditional practice of infanticide. In 1826 the council decided to call a constitutional convention to draw up a governing document for the tribe. According to legislation that provided for the election of delegates to the convention, "No person but a free male citizen who is full grown shall be entitled to vote." Not surprisingly, when the convention met and drafted a constitution patterned after that of the United States, women could neither vote nor hold office. The only provisions in the Cherokee legal code reminiscent of the power and prestige enjoyed by aboriginal women were laws that protected the property rights of married women and prohibited their husbands from disposing of their property without consent.[37]

The elite who governed the Cherokee Nation under the Constitution of 1827 regarded traditionalists with considerable disdain. Having profited from the government's civilization program, most truly believed in the superiority of Anglo-American culture. Some leaders and, to an even greater extent, United States officials tended to question the ability of traditionalists to make well-informed, rational decisions. This lack of faith provided a justification for those highly acculturated Cherokees who in 1835, without tribal authorization, ceded Cherokee land in the Southeast contrary to the wishes of the vast majority of Indians.[38] The failure of many Indian women to conform to the ideals of womanhood may well have contributed to the treaty party's self-vindication. Perhaps they believed that the land could have little meaning for the Cherokees if women controlled it, that the Indians must still depend primarily on hunting if women farmed, and that the Indians had no notion of ownership if men had no proprietary interest in their wives.

Of all the southern tribes, the Cherokees provide the sharpest contrast between the traditional role of women and the role they were expected to assume in the early nineteenth century. In this period, the Cherokees excluded women, who originally had participated in tribal governance, from the political arena. Women in other tribes had been less active politically; consequently, their status did not change as dramatically. All southern nations, however, did move toward legally replacing matrilineal with patrilineal descent and restricting the autonomy of women. In 1824, for example, the Creeks passed one law prohibiting infanticide and another specifying that upon a man's death, his children "shall have the property and his other relations shall not take the property to the injury of His children."[39]

Men of wealth and power among the Creeks, Choctaws, and Chickasaws as well as the Cherokees readily accepted the technical assistance offered through the government's civilization program and gradually adopted the ideology it encompassed. Although these changes occurred at different rates among southern Indians, women began to fade from economic and political life in the early nineteenth century. Just as the traditional female occupation, farming, became commercially viable, men took over and women became only secondarily involved in subsistence. Women, of course, still had their homes and families, but their families soon became their husbands' families, and domesticity brought influence, not power. Similarly, purity and piety seemed almost anachronistic in a culture and age that tended to value the material above the spiritual. Perhaps all that remained for women was what historian Nancy Cott has called "bonds of womanhood," but Indian women did not even develop closer ties to other women.[40] Living a far more isolated existence than ever before, they no longer shared labor and leisure with mothers, daughters, and sisters. Instead they spent most of their time on remote homesteads with only their husbands and children.

This separate sphere in which Indian women increasingly lived in the nineteenth century could hardly give rise to a women's rights movement, as some historians have suggested it did among white women, because true womanhood came to be associated with civilization and progress.[41] Any challenge to the precepts of the cult of true womanhood could be interpreted as a reversion to savagery. Ironically, by the end of the century, some white Americans had come to view the traditional status of Indian women in a far more favorable light. In 1892 the author of an article in the

Albany Law Review applauded the revision of property laws in the United States to protect the rights of married women and noted that such a progressive practice had long existed among the Choctaw and other southern Indians.[42] This practice, however, was only a remnant of a female role that had been economically productive, politically powerful, and socially significant but had been sacrificed to the cult of true womanhood.

Notes

1. For studies of the aboriginal Southeast, see John R. Swanton, *The Indians of the Southeastern United States* (Washington, D.C., 1946), and Charles Hudson, *The Southeastern Indians* (Knoxville, Tenn., 1976).

2. Works on the "five civilized tribes" include Henry T. Malone, *Cherokees of the Old South: A People in Transition* (Athens, Ga., 1956); Theda Perdue, *Slavery and the Evolution of Cherokee Society, 1540–1866* (Knoxville, 1979); Arrell M. Gibson, *The Chickasaws* (Norman, Okla., 1971); Angie Debo, *The Rise and Fall of the Choctaw Republic* (Norman, Okla., 1934); Angie Debo, *The Road to Disappearance* (Norman, Okla., 1941); Michael D. Green, *The Politics of Indian Removal: Creek Government and Society in Crisis* (Lincoln, Neb., 1982); Daniel F. Littlefield, Jr., *Africans and Creeks: From the Colonial Period to the Civil War* (Westport, Conn., 1979); Edwin C. McReynolds, *The Seminoles* (Norman, Okla., 1957). Acculturation was limited among the Seminoles.

3. Mary E. Young, "Women, Civilization, and the Indian Question," in Mabel E. Deutrich and Virginia C. Purdy, eds., *Clio Was a Woman: Studies in the History of American Women* (Washington, D.C., 1980).

4. Barbara Welter, "The Cult of True Womanhood, 1820–1860," *American Quarterly* 18 (1966): 151–74. Although Welter begins her discussion in 1820, the "cult" had been emerging since the mid-eighteenth century.

5. Bernard Romans, *A Concise Natural History of East and West Florida* (facsimile repr. of 1775 edition, Gainesville, Fla., 1962), 62; Louis-Philippe, *Diary of My Travels in America,* trans. Stephen Becker (New York, 1977), 73. For details of women's work, see James Adair, *Adair's History of the American Indian,* ed. Samuel Cole Williams (Johnson City, Tenn., 1927), 434–41, 447, 453–56; William Bartram, "Observations on the Creek and Cherokee Indians, 1789," *Transactions of the American*

Ethnological Society 3, pt. 1 (1853): 31, 82; Samuel Cole Williams, ed., *Early Travels in the Tennessee County, 1540–1800* (Johnson City, Tenn., 1928), 100–101, 257–58, 478; John Lawson, *Lawson's History of North Carolina,* ed. Francis Lathan Harris (Richmond, 1937), 199, 220.

6. The comment about the attitude of women toward work was made by Daniel Butrick of the American Board of Commissioners for Foreign Missions, John Howard Payne Papers, 4:27, Newberry Library, Chicago. For a description of the Green Corn Ceremony, see Adair, *History,* 105–17.

7. I base this assertion on Cherokee mythology, the role assigned to women in the Green Corn Ceremony, the reaction of southeastern Indians to men who did not hunt or go to war, and the presence of transvestites among the Choctaws and Chickasaws (and perhaps other groups as well). See James Mooney, *Myths of the Cherokee* (Washington, D.C., 1900), 242–48; Adair, *History,* 109, 163; Romans, *Concise Natural History,* 70, 83.

8. Bartram, "Observations," 40, 66; Lawson, *History,* 184, 195–96; Louis-Philippe, *Diary,* 77; Williams, ed., *Early Travels,* 261; Adair, *History,* 462. Also see John R. Swanton, *Social Organization and Social Usages of the Indians of the Creek Confederacy* (Washington, D.C., 1928); John Phillip Reid, *A Law of Blood: Primitive Law of the Cherokee Nation* (New York, 1970); and Alexander Spoehr, *Changing Kinship Systems: A Study in the Acculturation of the Creeks, Cherokee, and Choctaw* (Chicago, 1947).

9. Lawson, *History,* 37–38, 197–98.

10. *Ibid.,* 37–38.

11. Louis-Philippe, *Diary,* 84–85.

12. Adair, *History,* 152–53; Pat Alderman, *Nancy Ward: Cherokee Chieftainess* (Johnson City, Tenn., 1978).

13. The major study of United States policy in this period is Francis Paul Prucha, *American Indian Policy in the Formative Years: The Indian Trade and Intercourse Acts, 1790–1834* (Cambridge, Mass., 1962). For mission work, see Robert F. Berkhofer, Jr., *Salvation and the Savage: An Analysis of Protestant Missions and American Indian Response* (Lexington, Ky., 1965), and William G. McLoughlin, *Cherokees and Missionaries, 1789–1839* (New Haven, Conn., 1984).

14. Payne Papers, 4:34; William L. McDowell, *Documents Relating to Indian Affairs, May 21, 1750–Aug. 7, 1754* (Columbia, S.C., 1958), 246–47, 149; Benjamin Hawkins, *Letters of Benjamin Hawkins, 1796–1806* (Savannah, 1916), 16–18.

15. Payne Papers, 9:53; Brainerd Journal, December 29, 1818, American Board of Commissioners for Foreign Missions Papers (hereinafter cited as American Board Papers), Houghton Library, Harvard University, Cambridge, Mass.

16. The *Cherokee Phoenix* printed the letter March 20, 1828.

17. Hawkins, *Letters,* 20; John Norton, *The Journal of Major John Norton, 1816,* ed. Carl F. Klinck and James J. Talman (Toronto, 1970), 36; Elias Boudinot, *An Address to the Whites* (Philadelphia, 1826), 8.

18. Report from Willstown, October 10, 1828, American Board Papers; Hawkins, *Letters,* 20–21.

19. William G. McLoughlin and Walter H. Conser, Jr., "The Cherokees in Transition: A Statistical Analysis of the Federal Census of 1835," *Journal of American History* 64 (1977): 678–702; Malone, *Cherokees of the Old South.*

20. Ard Hoyt, Moody Hall, William Chamberlain, and D. S. Butrick to Samuel Worcester, July 25, 1818, American Board Papers.

21. Cyrus Kingsbury to Samuel Worcester, November 28, 1816, Brainerd Journal, May 27, October 29, 1819, American Board Papers.

22. Payne Papers, 8:10–12; William Potter to Jeremiah Evarts, August 16, 1826, American Board Papers.

23. Sophia Sawyer to Jeremiah Evarts, August 21, 1824, Appendix to Memoranda of the Cherokee Mission, May 16, 1822, Brainerd Journal, December 14, 1822, June 11, 1823, American Board Papers; Payne Papers, 8:6, 9, 11, 18, 39.

24. Brainerd Journal, June 19, 1818, August 2, 1821; Memoranda of the Cherokee Mission No. 2, May 1822; Ann Paine to Jeremiah Evarts, November 8, 1821, American Board Papers; Payne Papers, 8:51.

25. Sophia Sawyer to Jeremiah Evarts, August 21, 1824, Elizur Butler to Evarts, August 3, 1829, Lucy A. Butler to Daniel Green, September 29, 1832, American Board Papers; Payne Papers, 8:34, 49.

26. Louis-Philippe, *Diary,* 72.

27. Samuel Worcester to Ard Hoyt, November 11, 1818, Moody Hall's Journal, April 21, 1824, Brainerd Journal, February 9, 1820, September 18, 1823, American Board Papers; McLoughlin, *Cherokees and Missionaries,* 204–5.

28. Memoranda Relative to the Cherokee Mission No. 1, April and May 1822, D. S. Butrick to Jeremiah Evarts, October 17, 1824, Sophia Sawyer to Evarts, August 11, 1825, October 19, 1827, American Board Papers; "Diary of the Moravian Mission at Spring Place," trans. Carl C.

Mauleshagen, typescript, Georgia Historical Commission, Department of Natural Resources, Atlanta.

29. Moravian Mission Diary, April 11, 1813; Frederick Ellsworth to Jeremiah Evarts, May 25, August 12, 1825, American Board Papers.

30. Sophia Sawyer to Jeremiah Evarts, August 21, 1824.

31. Ann Paine, Notebook 2, December 20, 1820, Sophia Sawyer to Jeremiah Evarts, June 25, 1824; Payne Papers, 8:39.

32. Brainerd Journal, August 9, 1818, American Board Papers; Payne Papers, 8:1, 20, 41.

33. Payne Papers, 8:9, 16; William Chamberlain to Jeremiah Evarts, January 8, 1829, American Board Papers.

34. Rufus Anderson, *Memoir of Catharine Brown, a Christian Indian of the Cherokee Nation* (Boston and New York, 1825).

35. Kingsbury Journal, February 13, 1817, American Board Papers; Census of 1835, Indian Affairs, Record Group 75, National Archives, Washington, D.C. Cherokee speaker Robert Bushyhead kindly provided the gender for names on the census.

36. *Cherokee Phoenix*, July 2, 1828.

37. *Laws of the Cherokee Nation: Adopted by the Council at Various Times, Reprinted for the Benefit of the Nation*, vol. 5 of *The Constitutions and Laws of the American Indian Tribes* (Wilmington, Del., 1973), 3, 4, 5, 10, 53, 57, 73, 79, 120–21, 142–43.

38. In "Letters and Other Papers Relating to Cherokee Affairs," treaty signer Elias Boudinot wrote: "We can see strong reasons to justify the action of a minority of fifty persons—to do what the majority *would do* if they understood their condition" (Theda Perdue, ed., *Cherokee Editor: The Writings of Elias Boudinot* [Knoxville, Tenn., 1983], 162).

39. Antonio J. Waring, ed., *Laws of the Creek Nation*, University of Georgia Miscellaneous Publications, no. 1 (Athens, Ga., 1969), pp. 19, 24.

40. Nancy F. Cott, *The Bonds of Womanhood: "Woman's Sphere" in New England, 1780–1835* (New Haven, Conn., 1977).

41. *Ibid.*, 197–206; Aileen S. Kraditor, *Up from the Pedestal* (Chicago, 1968).

42. "Current Topic," *Albany Law Journal* 45 (1982): 199.

Female Slaves

SEX ROLES AND STATUS IN THE

ANTEBELLUM PLANTATION SOUTH

DEBORAH GRAY WHITE

Deborah Gray White is Professor of History and Africana Studies at Rutgers University. Her first book, Ar'n't I a Woman: Female Slaves in the Antebellum South *won the Letitia Brown Prize. The article that follows outlines some of the arguments in this award-winning book.*

White is extensively published in journals of American history and feminist theory and her articles have been widely reprinted. The piece that follows is taken from the Journal of Family History, *where it was first published in 1983.*

In his study of the black family in America, sociologist F. Franklin Frazier theorized that in slave family and marriage relations, women played the dominant role. Specifically, Frazier wrote that "the Negro woman as wife or mother was the mistress of her cabin, and, save for the interference of master and overseer, her wishes in regard to mating and family matters were paramount." He also insisted that slavery had schooled the black woman in self-reliance and self-sufficiency and that "neither economic necessity nor tradition had instilled in her the spirit of subordination to masculine authority."[1] The Frazier thesis received support from other social scientists, including historians Kenneth Stampp and Stanley Elkins, both of whom held that slave men had been emasculated and stripped of their paternity rights by slave masters who left control of slave households to slave women.[2] In his infamous 1965 national report, Daniel Patrick Moynihan lent further confirmation to the Frazier thesis when he alleged that the fundamental problem with the modern black family was the "often reversed roles of husband and wife," and then traced the origin of the "problem" back to slavery.[3]

Partly in response to the criticism spawned by the Moynihan Report, historians reanalyzed antebellum source material, and the matriarchy thesis was debunked. For better or worse, said historians Robert Fogel and Stanley Engerman, the "dominant" role in slave society was played by men.[4] Men were dominant, they said, because men occupied all managerial and artisan slots, and because masters recognized the male head of the family group. From historian John Blassingame we learned that by building furnishings and providing extra food for their families, men found indirect ways of gaining status. If a garden plot was to be cultivated, the husband "led" his wife in the family undertaking.[5] After a very thoughtful appraisal of male slave activities, historian Eugene Genovese concluded that "slaves from their own experience had come to value a two-parent, male-centered household, no matter how much difficulty they had in realizing the ideal."[6] Further tipping the scales toward patriarchal slave households, historian Herbert Gutman argued that the belief that matrifocal households prevailed among slaves was a misconception. He demonstrated that children were more likely to be named after their fathers than mothers, and that during the Civil War slave men acted like fathers and husbands by fighting for their freedom and by protecting their wives and children when they were threatened by Union troops or angry slaveholders.[7]

With the reinterpretation of male roles came a revision of female roles. Once considered dominant, slave women were now characterized as subordinated and sometimes submissive. Fogel and Engerman found proof of their subordinated status in the fact that they were excluded from working in plow gangs and did all of the household chores.[8] Genovese maintained that slave women's "attitude toward housework, especially cooking, and toward their own femininity" belied the conventional wisdom "according to which women unwittingly helped ruin their men by asserting themselves in the home, protecting their children, and assuming other normally masculine responsibilities."[9] Gutman found one Sea Island slave community where the black church imposed a submissive role upon married slave women.[10]

In current interpretations of the contemporary black family the woman's role has not been "feminized" as much as it has been "deemphasized." The stress in studies like those done by Carol Stack and Theodore Kennedy is not on roles per se but on the black family's ability to survive in flexible kinship networks that are viable bulwarks against discrimination and racism.[11] These interpretations also make the point that black kinship patterns are not based exclusively on consanguineous relationships but are also determined by social contacts that sometimes have their basis in economic support.

Clearly then, the pendulum has swung away from the idea that women ruled slave households, and that their dominance during the slave era formed the foundation of the modern-day matriarchal black family. But how far should that pendulum swing? This paper suggests that we should tread the road that leads to the patriarchal slave household and the contemporary amorphous black family with great caution. It suggests that, at least in relation to the slave family, too much emphasis has been placed on what men could not do rather than on what women could do and did. What follows is not a comprehensive study of female slavery but an attempt to reassess Frazier's claim that slave women were self-reliant and self-sufficient, through an examination of some of their activities, specifically their work, their control of particular resources, their contribution to their households, and their ability to cooperate with each other on a daily basis. Further, this paper will examine some of the implications of these activities and their probable impact on the slave woman's status in slave society and the black family.

At the outset a few points must be made about the subject matter and the source material used to research it. Obviously, a study that concentrates solely on females runs the risk of overstating woman's roles and their importance in society. One must therefore keep in mind that this is only one aspect, although a very critical one, of slave family and community life. In addition, what follows is a synthesis of the probable sex role of the average slave woman on plantations with at least twenty slaves.[12] In the process of constructing this synthesis I have taken into account such variables as plantation size, crop, region of the South, and the personal idiosyncrasies of slave masters. Finally, in drawing conclusions about the sex role and status of slave women, I have detailed their activities and analyzed them in terms of what anthropologists know about women who do similar things in analogous settings. I took this approach for two reasons. First, information about female slaves cannot be garnered from sources left by slave women because they left few narratives, diaries or letters. The dearth of source material makes it impossible to draw conclusions about the slave woman's feelings. Second, even given the ex-slave interviews, a rich source material for this subject, it is almost impossible to draw conclusions about female slave status from an analysis of their individual personalities. Comments such as that made by the slave woman Fannie to her husband Bob, "I don't want no sorry nigger around me," perhaps say something about Fannie, but not about all slave women.[13] Similarly, for every mother who grieved over the sale of her children there was probably a father whose heart was also broken. Here, only the activities of the slave woman will be examined in an effort to discern her status in black society.

Turning first to the work done by slave women, it appears that they did a variety of heavy and dirty labor, work which was also done by men. In 1853, Frederick Olmsted saw South Carolina slaves of both sexes carting manure on their heads to the cotton fields where they spread it with their hands between the ridges in which cotton was planted. In Fayetteville, North Carolina, he noticed that women not only hoed and shoveled but they also cut down trees and drew wood.[14] The use of women as lumberjacks occurred quite frequently, especially in the lower South and Southwest, areas which retained a frontier quality during the antebellum era. Solomon Northrup, a kidnapped slave, knew women who wielded the ax so perfectly that the largest oak or sycamore fell before their well-directed blows. An Arkansas ex-slave remembered that her mother used to carry logs.[15] On southwestern plantations women did all kinds of work. In the region of the Bayou Boeuf women were expected to "plough, drag, drive team, clear wild lands, work on the highway," and do any other type of work required of them.[16] In short, full female hands frequently did the same kind of work as male hands.

It is difficult, however, to say how often they did the same kind of field work, and it would be a mistake to say that there was no differentiation of field labor on southern farms and plantations.

The most common form of differentiation was that women hoed while men plowed. Yet, the exceptions to the rule were so numerous as to make a mockery of it. Many men hoed on a regular basis. Similarly, if a field had to be plowed and there were not enough male hands to do it, then it was not unusual for an overseer to command a strong woman to plow. This could happen on a plantation of twenty slaves or a farm of five.[17]

It is likely, however, that women were more often called to do the heavy labor usually assigned to men after their childbearing years. Pregnant women, and sometimes women breastfeeding infants, were usually given less physically demanding work.[18] If, as recent studies indicate, slave women began childbearing when about twenty years of age and had children at approximately two-and-a-half-year intervals at least until age thirty-five, slave women probably spent a considerable amount of time doing tasks which men did not do.[19] Pregnant and nursing women were classified as half hands or three-quarters hands, and such workers did only some of the work that was also done by full hands. For instance, it was not unusual for them to pick cotton or even hoe, work done on a regular basis by both sexes. But frequently, they were assigned to "light work" like raking stubble or pulling weeds, which was often given to children and the elderly.[20]

Slave women might have preferred to be exempt from such labor, but they might also have gained some intangibles from doing the same work as men. Anthropologists have demonstrated that in societies where men and women are engaged in the production of the same kinds of goods and where widespread private property is not a factor, participation in production gives women freedom and independence.[21] Since neither slave men nor women had access to, or control over, the products of their labor, parity in the field may have encouraged egalitarianism in the slave quarters. In southern Togo, for instance, where women work alongside their husbands in the field because men do not alone produce goods which are highly valued, democracy prevails in relationships between men and women.[22]

But bondswomen did do a lot of traditional "female work" and one has to wonder whether this work, as well as the work done as a "half-hand," tallied on the side of female subordination. In the case of the female slave, domestic work was not always confined to the home, and often "woman's work" required skills that were highly valued and even coveted because of the place they could purchase in the higher social echelons of the slave world. For example, cooking was definitely "female work" but it was also a skilled occupation. Good cooks were highly respected by both blacks and whites, and their occupation was raised in status because the masses of slave women did not cook on a regular basis. Since field work occupied the time of most women, meals were often served communally. Female slaves, therefore, were for the most part relieved of this traditional chore, and the occupation of "cook" became specialized.[23]

Sewing too was often raised above the level of inferior "woman's work." All females at one time or another had to spin and weave. Occasionally each woman was given cloth and told to make her family's clothes, but this was unusual and more likely to happen on small farms than on plantations. During slack seasons women probably did more sewing than during planting and harvesting seasons, and pregnant women were often put to work spinning, weaving, and sewing. Nevertheless, sewing could be raised to the level of a skilled art, especially if a woman sewed well enough to make the white family's clothes. Such women were sometimes hired out and allowed to keep a portion of the profit they brought their master and mistress.[24]

Other occupations which were solidly anchored in the female domain, and which increased a woman's prestige, were midwifery and doctoring. The length of time and extent of training it took to become a midwife is indicated by the testimony of Clara Walker, a former slave interviewed in Arkansas, who remembered that she trained for five years under a doctor who became so lazy after she had mastered the job that he would sit down and let her do all the work. After her "apprenticeship" ended she delivered babies for both slave and free, black and white.[25] Other midwives learned the trade from a female relative, often their mother, and they in turn passed the skill on to another female relative.

A midwife's duty often extended beyond delivering babies, and they sometimes became known as "doctor women." In this capacity they cared for men, women, and children. Old women, some with a history of midwifery and some without, also gained respect as "doctor women." They "knowed a heap about yarbs [herbs]," recalled a Georgia ex-slave.[26] Old women had innumerable cures, especially for children's diseases, and since plantation "nurseries" were usually under their supervision, they had ample opportunity to practice their art. In sum, a good portion of the slaves' medical care, particularly that of women and children, was supervised by slave women.

Of course, not all women were hired-out seamstresses, cooks, or midwives; a good deal of "female work" was laborious and mundane. An important aspect of this work, as well as of the field work done by women, was that it was frequently done in female groups. As previously noted, women often hoed while men plowed. In addition, when women sewed they usually did so with other women. Quilts were made by women at gatherings called, naturally enough, "quiltins." Such gatherings were attended only by women and many former slaves had vivid recollections of them. The "quiltin's and spinnin' frolics dat de women folks had" were the most outstanding remembrances of Hattie Anne Nettles, an Alabama ex-slave.[27] Women also gathered, independent of male slaves, on Saturday afternoons to do washing. Said one ex-slave, "They all had a regular picnic of it as they would work and spread the clothes on the bushes and low branches of the tree to dry. They would get to spend the day together."[28]

In addition, when pregnant women did field work they sometimes did it together. On large plantations the group they worked in was sometimes known as the "trash gang." This gang, made up of pregnant women, women with nursing infants, children, and old slaves, was primarily a female work gang.[29] Since it was the group that young girls worked with when just being initiated into the work world of the plantation, one must assume that it served some kind of socialization function. Most likely, many lessons about life were learned by twelve-year-old girls from this group of women who were either pregnant or breastfeeding or who were grandmothers many times over.

It has been noted that women frequently depended on slave midwives to bring children into the world; their dependence on other slave women did not end with childbirth but continued through the early life of their children. Sometimes women with infants took their children to the fields with them. Some worked with their children wrapped to their backs; others laid them under a tree. Frequently, however, an elderly woman watched slave children during the day while their mothers worked in the field. Sometimes the cook supervised young children at the master's house.[30] Mothers who were absent from their children most of the day, indeed most of the week, depended on these surrogate mothers to assist them in child socialization. Many ex-slaves remember these women affectionately. Said one South Carolinian: "De old lady, she looked after every blessed thing for us all day long en cooked for us right along wid de mindin'."[31]

Looking at the work done by female slaves in the antebellum South, therefore, we find that sex role differentiation in field labor was not absolute but that there was differentiation in other kinds of work. Domestic chores were usually done exclusively by women, and certain "professional" occupations were reserved for females. It would be a mistake to infer from this differentiation that it was the basis of male dominance. A less culturally biased conclusion would be that women's roles were different or complementary. For example, in her overview of African societies, Denise Paulme notes that in almost all African societies, women do most of the domestic chores, yet they lead lives that are quite independent of men. Indeed, according to Paulme, in Africa, "a wife's contribution to the needs of the household is direct and indispensable, and her husband is just as much in need of her as she of him."[32] Other anthropologists have suggested that we should not evaluate women's roles in terms of men's roles because in a given society, women may not perceive the world in the same way that men do.[33] In other words, men and women may share a common culture but on different terms, and when this is the case, questions of dominance and subservience are irrelevant. The degree to which male and female ideologies are different is often suggested by the degree to which men and women are independently able to rank and order themselves and cooperate with members of their sex in the performance of their duties. In societies where women are not isolated from one another and placed under a man's authority, where women cooperate in the performance of household tasks, or where women form groups or associations, women's roles are usually complementary to those of men, and the female world exists independently of the male world. Because women control what goes on in their world, they rank and order themselves vis-à-vis other women, not men, and they are able to influence decisions made by their society because they exert pressure as a group. Ethnographic studies of the Igbo women of Eastern Nigeria, the Ga women of Central Accra in Ghana, and the Patani of Southern Nigeria confirm these generalizations.[34] Elements of female slave society—the chores done in and by groups, the intrasex cooperation and dependency in the areas of child care and medical care, the existence of high-echelon female slave occupations—may be an indication, not that slave women were inferior to slave men, but that the roles were complementary and that the female slave world allowed women the opportunity to rank and order themselves and obtain a sense of self which was quite apart from the men of their race and even the men of the master class.

That bondswomen were able to rank and order themselves is further suggested by evidence indicating that in the community of the slave quarters certain women were looked to for leadership. Leadership was based on either one or a combination of factors, including occupation, association with the master class, age, or number of children. It was manifested in all aspects of female slave life. For instance, Louis Hughes, an escaped slave, noted that each plantation had a "forewoman who . . . had charge of the female slaves and also the boys and girls from twelve to sixteen years of age, and all the old people that were feeble."[35] Bennett H. Barrow repeatedly lamented the fact that Big Lucy, one of his oldest slaves, had more control over his female slaves than he did: "Anica, Center, Cook Jane, the better you treat them the worse they are. Big Lucy, the Leader, corrupts every young negro in her power."[36] When Elizabeth Botume went to the Sea Islands after the Civil War, she had a house servant, a young woman named Amy, who performed her tasks slowly and sullenly until Aunt Mary arrived from Beaufort. In Aunt Mary's presence the obstreperous Amy was "quiet, orderly, helpful and painstaking."[37]

Another important feature of female life bearing on the ability of women to rank and order themselves independently of men was the control women exercised over each other by quarreling. In all kinds of sources there are indications that women were given to fighting and irritating each other. From Jesse Belflowers, the overseer of the Allston rice plantation in South Carolina, Adele Petigru Allston learned that "mostly mongst the Woman," there was "goodeal of quarling and disputing and telling lies."[38] Harriet Ware, a northern missionary writing from the Sea Islands in 1863, blamed the turmoil she found in black community life on the "tongues of the women."[39] The evidence of excessive quarreling among women hints at the existence of a gossip network among female slaves. Anthropologists have found gossip to be a principal strategy used by women to control other women as well as men. Significantly, the female gossip network, the means by which community members are praised, shamed, and coerced, is usually found in societies where women are highly dependent on each other and where women work in groups or form female associations.[40]

In summary, when the activities of female slaves are compared to those of women in other societies a clearer picture of the female slave sex role emerges. It seems that slave women were schooled in self-reliance and self-sufficiency, but the "self" was more likely the female slave collective than the individual slave woman. On the other hand, if the female world was highly stratified and if women cooperated with each other to a great extent, odds are that the same can be said of men, in which case neither sex can be said to have been dominant or subordinate.

There are other aspects of the female slave's life that suggest that her world was independent of the male slave's and that slave women were rather self-reliant. It has long been recognized that slave women did not derive traditional benefits from the marriage relationship, that there was no property to share and essential needs like food, clothing, and shelter were not provided by slave men.[41] Since in almost all societies where men consistently control women, that control is based on male ownership and distribution of property and/or control of certain culturally valued subsistence goods, these realities of slave life had to contribute to female slave self-sufficiency and independence from slave men. The practice of "marrying abroad," having a spouse on a different plantation, could only have reinforced this tendency, for as ethnographers have found, when men live apart from women, they cannot control them.[42] We have yet to learn what kind of obligations brothers, uncles, and male cousins fulfilled for their female kin, but it is improbable that wives were controlled by husbands whom they saw only once or twice a week. Indeed, "abroad marriages" may have intensified female intradependency.

That marriage did not yield traditional benefits for women, and that "abroad marriages" existed, does not mean that women did not depend on slave men for foodstuffs beyond the weekly rations, but since additional food was not guaranteed, it probably meant that women along with men had to take initiatives in supplementing slave diets. So much has been made of the activities of slave men in this sphere that the role of slave women has been overlooked.[43] Female house slaves, in particular, were especially able to supplement their family's diet. Mary Chesnut's maid, Molly, made no secret of the fact that she fed her offspring and other slave children in the Confederate politician's house. "Dey gets a little of all dat's going," she once told Chesnut.[44] Frederick Douglass remembered that his grandmother was not only a good nurse but a "capital hand at catching fish and making the nets she caught them in."[45] Eliza Overton, an ex-slave, remembered how her mother stole, slaughtered, and cooked one of her master's hogs. Another ex-slave was not too bashful to admit that her mother "could hunt good ez any man."[46] Women, as well as men, were sometimes given the opportunity to earn money. Women often sold baskets they had woven, but they also earned money by burning charcoal for blacksmiths and cutting cordwood.[47] Thus, procuring extra provisions for the family was sometimes a male and sometimes a female responsibility, one that probably fostered a self-reliant and independent spirit.

The high degree of female cooperation, the ability of slave women to rank and order themselves, the independence women derived from the absence of property considerations in the conjugal relationship, "abroad marriages," and the female slave's ability to provide supplementary foodstuffs are factors which should not be ignored in considerations of the character of the slave family. In fact, they conform to the criteria most anthropologists list for that most misunderstood concept—matrifocality.[48] Matrifocality is a term used to convey the fact that women *in their role as mothers* are the focus of familial relationships. It does not mean that fathers are absent; indeed two-parent households can be matrifocal. Nor does it stress a power relationship where women rule men. When *mothers* become the focal point of family activity, they are just more central than are fathers to a family's continuity and survival as a unit. While there is no set model for matrifocality, Smith has noted that in societies as diverse as Java, Jamaica, and the Igbo of eastern Nigeria, societies recognized as matrifocal, certain elements are constant.[49] Among these elements are female solidarity, particularly in regard to their cooperation within the domestic sphere. Another factor is the economic activity of women which enables them to support their children independent of fathers *if they desire to do so or are forced to do so.* The most important factor is the supremacy of the mother-child bond over all other relationships.[50]

Female solidarity and the "economic" contribution of bondswomen in the form of medical care, foodstuffs, and money has already been discussed; what can be said of the mother-child bond? We know from previous works on slavery that certain slaveholder practices encouraged the primacy of the mother-child relationship.[51] These included the tendency to sell mothers and small children as family units, and to accord special treatment to pregnant and nursing women and women who were exceptionally prolific. We also know that a husband and wife secured themselves somewhat from sale and separation when they had children.[52] Perhaps what has not been emphasized enough is the fact that it was the wife's childbearing and her ability to keep a child alive that were the crucial factors in the security achieved in this way. As such, the insurance against sale which husbands and wives received once women had borne and nurtured children heads the list of female contributions to slave households.

In addition to slaveowner encouragement of close mother-child bonds there are indications that slave women themselves considered this their most important relationship.[53] Much has been made of the fact that slave women were not ostracized by slave society when they had children out of "wedlock."[54] Historians have usually explained this aspect of slave life in the context of slave sexual norms which allowed a good deal of freedom to young unmarried slave women. However, the slave attitude concerning "illegitimacy" might also reveal the importance that women, and slave society as a whole, placed on the mother role and the mother-child dyad. For instance, in the Alabama community studied by Charles S. Johnson in the 1930s, most black women felt no guilt and suffered no loss of status when they bore children out of wedlock.[55] This was also a community in which, according to Johnson, the role of the mother was "of much greater importance than in the more familiar American family group." Similarly, in his 1956 study of the black family in British Guiana, Smith found the mother-child bond to be the strongest in the whole matrix of social relationships, and it was manifested in a lack of condemnation of women who bore children out of legal marriage.[56] If slave women were not ostracized for having children without husbands, it could mean that the mother-child relationship took precedence over the husband-wife relationships.

The mystique which shrouded conception and childbirth is perhaps another indication of the high value slave women placed on motherhood and childbirth. Many female slaves claimed that they were kept ignorant of the details of conception and childbirth. For instance, a female slave interviewed in Nashville noted that at age twelve or thirteen, she and an older girl went around to parsley beds and hollow logs looking for newborn babies. "They didn't tell you a thing," she said.[57] Another ex-slave testified that her mother told her that doctors brought babies, and another Virginia ex-slave remembered that "people was very particular in them days. They wouldn't let children know anything."[58] This alleged naiveté can perhaps be understood if examined in the context of motherhood as a *rite de passage*. Sociologist Joyce Ladner found that many black girls growing up in a ghetto area of St. Louis in the late 1960s were equally ignorant of the facts concerning conception and childbirth. Their mothers had related only "old wives' tales" about sex and childbirth even though the community was one where the mother-child bond took precedence over both the husband-wife bond and the father-child bond.[59] In this St. Louis area, having a child was considered the most important turning point in a black girl's life, a more important *rite de passage* than marriage. Once a female had a child all sorts of privileges were bestowed upon her. That conception and childbirth were cloaked in mystery in antebellum slave society is perhaps an indication of the sacredness of motherhood. When considered in tandem with the slave attitude toward "illegitimacy," the mother-child relationship emerges as the most important familial relationship in the slave family.

Finally, any consideration of slaves' attitudes about mother-hood and the expectations which the slave community had of childbearing women must consider the slaves' African heritage. In many West African tribes the mother-child relationship is and has always been the most important of all human relationships.[60] To cite one of many possible examples, while studying the role of women in Ibo society, Sylvia Leith-Ross asked an Ibo woman how many of ten husbands would love their wives and how many of ten sons would love their mothers. The answer she received demonstrated the precedence which the mother-child tie took: "Three husbands would love their wives but seven sons would love their mothers."[61]

When E. Franklin Frazier wrote that slave women were self-reliant and that they were strangers to male slave authority he evoked an image of an overbearing, even brawny woman.[62] In all probability visions of Sapphire danced in our heads as we learned from Frazier that the female slave played the dominant role in courtship, marriage and family relationships, and later from El-kins that male slaves were reduced to childlike dependency on the slave master.[63] Both the Frazier and Elkins theses have been overturned by historians who have found that male slaves were more than just visitors to their wives' cabins, and women some-thing other than unwitting allies in the degradation of their men. Sambo and Sapphire may continue to find refuge in Ameri-can folklore but they will never again be legitimized by social scientists.

However, beyond the image evoked by Frazier is the stark reality that slave women did not play the traditional female role as it was defined in nineteenth-century America, and regardless of how hard we try to cast her in a subordinate or submissive role in relation to slave men, we will have difficulty reconciling that role with the plantation realities. When we consider the work done by women in groups, the existence of upper-echelon female slave jobs, and the intradependence of women in child care and medical care, and if we presume that the quarreling or "fighting and dis-puting" among slave women is evidence of a gossip network and that certain women were elevated by their peers to positions of respect, then what we are confronted with is slave women who are able, within the limits set by slaveowners, to rank and order their female world, women who identified and cooperated more with other slave women than with slave men. There is nothing abnormal about this. It is a feature of many societies around the world, especially where strict sex role differentiation is the rule.

Added to these elements of female interdependence and cooperation were the realities of chattel slavery that decreased the bondsman's leverage over the bondswoman, made female self-reliance a necessity, and encouraged the retention of the African tradition which made the mother-child bond more sacred than the husband-wife bond. To say that this amounted to a matrifocal family is not to say a bad word. It is not to say that it precluded male-female cooperation, or mutual respect, or traditional romance and courtship. It does, however, help to explain how African-American men and women survived chattel slavery.

Notes

1. E. Franklin Frazier, *The Negro Family in the United States* (Chicago, 1939), 125.

2. Kenneth Stampp, *The Peculiar Institution: Slavery in the Ante-Bellum South* (New York, 1956), 344; Stanley M. Elkins, *Slavery: A Problem in American Institutional and Intellectual Life*, 2d ed. (Chicago, 1959), 130

3. Daniel Patrick Moynihan, *The Negro Family: The Case for National Action* (Washington, D.C., 1965), 31.

4. Robert William Fogel and Stanley Engerman, *Time on the Cross: The Economics of American Negro Slavery* (Boston, 1974), 141.

5. John W. Blassingame, *The Slave Community: Plantation Life in the Antebellum South* (New York, 1972), 92.

6. Eugene Genovese, *Roll, Jordan, Roll: The World the Slaves Made* (New York, 1974), 491–92.

7. Herbert Gutman, *The Black Family in Slavery and Freedom, 1750–1925* (New York, 1976), 188–91, 369–86.

8. Fogel and Engerman, *Time on the Cross*, 141–42.

9. Genovese, *Roll, Jordan, Roll*, 500.

10. Gutman, *Black Family*, 72.

11. Carol Stack, *All Our Kin: Strategies for Survival in a Black Community* (New York, 1974); Theodore R. Kennedy, *You Gotta Deal with It: Black Family Relations in a Southern Community* (New York, 1980).

12. The majority of the available source material seems to be from plantations or farms with more than one or two slave families. Relatively few ex-slave interviewees admit to being one of only three or four slaves. If Genovese is right and at least half of the slaves in the South lived on units of twenty slaves or more, this synthesis probably describes the life of a majority of slave women (Genovese, *Roll, Jordan, Roll*, 7).

13. Ophelia S. Egypt, J. Masuoka, and Charles S. Johnson, eds., *Unwritten History of Slavery: Autobiographical Accounts of Negro Ex-Slaves* (Nashville, 1945), 184.

14. Frederick L. Olmsted, *The Cotton Kingdom*, ed. David Freeman Hawke (New York, 1971), 67, 81.

15. Gilbert Osofsky, ed., *Puttin' on Ole Massa* (New York, 1969), 308–9; George Rawick, ed., *The American Slave: A Composite Autobiography* (19 vols., Westport, Conn., 1972), 10, pt. 5: 54.

16. Osofsky, *Puttin' on Ole Massa*, 313.

17. For other examples of work done by female slaves and indications that they did the same work required of men, see Thomas Nairne, *A Letter from South Carolina* (London, 1732), 60; Frances Anne Kemble, *Journal of a Residence on a Georgian Plantation*, ed. John A. Scott (New York, 1961), 65; Olmsted, *Cotton Kingdom*, 67–81; Frederick L. Olmsted, *A Journey in the Back Country* (New York, 1907), 81; Benjamin Drew, *The Refugee: A North Side View of Slavery* (Boston, 1969), 92; Rawick, *American Slave*, 13, pt. 4: 357; 6: 46, 151, 158, 270, 338.

18. See Rawick, *American Slave*, 4, pt. 3: 160; 10, pt. 7: 255; Louis Hughes, *Thirty Years a Slave* (Milwaukee, 1897), 22; Frederick L. Olmsted, *Journey in the Seaboard Slave States* (New York, 1856), 430; *Plantation Instructions* (Southern Historical Collection, University of North Carolina [hereafter SHC] n.d.); Olmsted, *Cotton Kingdom*, 78, 175; Kemble, *Journal of a Residence*, 87, 179; Drew, *Refugee*, 128; Adwon Adams Davis, *Plantation Life in the Florida Parishes of Louisiana 1836–1846 as Reflected in the Diary of Bennet H. Barrow* (New York, 1943), 127.

19. Although Fogel and Engerman cite the slave woman's age at first birth as 22.5, other historians, including Gutman and Dunn, found that age to be substantially lower—Gutman a range from 17 to 19, and Dunn (average age at first birth on Mount Airy, Virginia, plantation) 19.22 years. More recently, economists Trussell and Steckel have found the age to be 20.6 years. See Fogel and Engerman, *Time on the Cross*, 137–38; Richard Dunn, "The Tale of Two Plantations: Slave Life at Mesopotamia in Jamaica and Mount Airy in Virginia, 1799–1828," *William*

and Mary Quarterly 34 (1977): 58; Gutman, *Black Family,* 50, 75, 124, 171; James Trussell and Richard Steckel, "Age of Slaves at Menarche and Their First Birth," *Journal of Interdisciplinary History* 8 (1978): 504.

20. For examples, see n. 18.

21. Leith Mullings, "Women and Economic Change in Africa," in Nancy J. Hafkin and Edna G. Bay, eds., *Women in Africa: Studies in Social and Economic Change* (Stanford, 1976), 243–44; Karen Sacks, "Engels Revisited: Women, the Organization of Production, and Private Property," in Michelle Rosaldo and Louise Lamphere, eds., *Woman, Culture and Society* (Stanford, 1974), 213–22.

22. Guy Rocher, R. Clignet, and F. N. N'sougan Agblemagnon, "Three Preliminary Studies: Canada, Ivory Coast, Togo," *International Social Science Journal* 14 (1962): 151–52.

23. For an example of the privileges this occupation *could* involve, see Mary Bokin Chesnut, *A Diary from Dixie,* ed. Ben Ames Williams (New York, 1905), 24.

24. Rawick, *American Slave,* 17: 158; 2, pt. 2: 114; *White Hill Plantation Books (1817–1860)* (SHC, n.d.), 13.

25. See Rawick, *American Slave,* 10, pt. 5: 21. For other examples of midwives, see *ibid.,* 6: 256, 318; 16: 90–91; 10, pt. 5: 125. The job status of the midwife needs to be examined more closely than is possible here. Midwives were curers whose duty usually extended beyond delivering babies. Occasionally their cures spilled over into witchcraft or voodoo, and slaves who practiced these arts were often feared.

26. Rawick, *American Slave,* 2, pt. 2: 112. See also *ibid.,* 2, pt. 2: 55; 17: 174; Olmsted, *Journey in the Back Country,* 76.

27. Rawick, *American Slave,* 6: 297, 360.

28. *Ibid.,* 7: 315.

29. Sometimes pregnant women were made to weave, spin, or sew, in which case they usually did it with other women. The term "trash gang" was probably used only on very large plantations, but units of pregnant women, girls, elderly females, as well as boys and elderly men, probably worked together on a farm with twenty slaves. See n. 17.

30. See, for instance, Olmsted, *Journey in the Seaboard Slave States,* 423; Ulrich B. Phillips, *Plantation and Frontier Documents 1649–1863* (2 vols., Cleveland, 1909), 1: 127.

31. Rawick, *American Slave,* 2, pt. 1: 99.

32. Denise Paulme, ed., *Women of Tropical Africa* (Berkeley, 1963), 4.

33. Susan Carol Rogers, "Woman's Place: A Critical Review of An-

thropology Theory," *Comparative Studies in Society and History* 20 (1974): 152–62.

34. Nancy Tanner, "Matrifocality in Indonesia and Africa and among Black Americans," in Rosaldo and Lamphere, eds., *Woman, Culture and Society,* 146–50; Claire Robertson, "Ga Women and Socioeconomic Change in Accra, Ghana," in Hafkin and Bay, eds. *Women in Africa,* 115–32; Nancy B. Leis, "Women in Groups: Ijaw Women's Associations," in Rosaldo and Lamphere, eds., *Woman, Culture and Society,* 221–42.

35. Hughes, *Thirty Years a Slave,* 22.

36. Davis, *Plantation Life,* 191. Big Lucy thwarted all of the Barrows' instructions and her influence extended to the men also; see *ibid.,* 168, 173.

37. Elizabeth Hyde Botume, *First Days amongst the Contrabands* (Boston, 1893), 132. On a given plantation there could be a number of slave women recognized by other slave women as leaders. For instance, when Frances Kemble first toured Butler Island she found that the cook's position went to the oldest wife in the settlement.

38. J. E. Easterby, ed., *The South Carolina Rice Plantations as Revealed in the Papers of Robert W. Allston* (Chicago, 1945), 291.

39. Elizabeth Ware Pearson, ed., *Letters from Port Royal Written at the Time of the Civil War* (Boston, 1906), 210. Additional evidence that women quarreled can be found in a pamphlet stating the terms of an overseer's contract: "Fighting, particularly amongst the women . . . is to be always rigorously punished." Similarly, an ex-slave interviewed in Georgia noted that "sometimes de women uster git whuppins for fightin." See John Spencer Bassett, *The Southern Plantation Overseer, as Revealed in His Letters* (Northhampton, 1925), 32; Rawick, *American Slave,* 12, pt. 2: 57.

40. Gossip is one of many means by which women influence political decisions and interpersonal relationships. In Taiwan, for instance, women gather in the village square and whisper to each other. In other places, such as among the Marina of Madagascar, women gather and shout loud insults at men or other women. In still other societies, such as the black ghetto area studied by Carol Stack, the gossip network takes the form of a grapevine. See Michelle Rosaldo, "Woman, Culture and Society: A Theoretical Overview," in Rosaldo and Lamphere, eds., *Woman, Culture and Society,* 10–11, 38; Margery Wolf, "Chinese Women: Old Skill in a New Context," in Rosaldo and Lamphere, eds., *Woman, Culture and Society,* 162; Stack, *All Our Kin,* 109–15.

41. Blassingame, *Slave Community*, 77–103.

42. For instance, it is thought that Iroquois women obtained a high degree of political and economic power partly because of the prolonged absences of males due to trading and warfare. See John A. Noon, *Law and Government of the Grand River Iroquois* (New York, 1949), 30–31; Rosaldo, "Woman, Culture and Society," 36, 39.

43. See Blassingame, *Slave Community*, 92; Genovese, *Roll, Jordan, Roll*, 486. Of male slaves who provided extra food, John Blassingame wrote: "The slave who did such things for his family gained not only the approbation of his wife, but he also gained status in the quarters." According to Genovese, "the slaves would have suffered much more than many in fact did from malnutrition and the hidden hungers of nutritional deficiencies if men had not taken the initiative to hunt and trap animals."

44. Chesnut, *Diary from Dixie*, 348.

45. Frederick Douglass, *My Bondage and My Freedom* (New York, 1855), 27.

46. Rawick, *American Slave*, 11:53, 267.

47. Olmsted, *Cotton Kingdome* 26; Rawick, *American Slave*, 7:23.

48. Nancie Gonzalez, "Toward a Definition of Matrifocality," in Norman E. Whitten, Jr., and John F. Szwed, eds., *Afro-American Anthropology: Contemporary Perspectives* (New York, 1970), 231–43; Raymond T. Smith, *The Negro Family in British Guiana: Family Structure and Social Status in the Villages* (London, 1956), 257–60; Raymond T. Smith, "The Matrifocal Family," in Jack Goody, ed., *The Character of Kinship* (London, 1973), 125; Tanner, "Matrifocality in Indonesia and Africa and among Black Americans," 129–56.

49. Smith, "Matrifocal Family," 125.

50. *Ibid.*, 139–42.

51. Bassett, *Southern Plantation Overseer*, 31, 139, 141; Kemble, *Journal of a Residence*, 95, 127, 179; Phillips, *Plantation and Frontier Documents*, 1:109, 312.

52. Gutman, *Black Family*, 76.

53. Gutman suggests that the husband-wife and father-child dyad were as strong as the mother-child bond. I think not. It has been demonstrated that in most Western Hemisphere black societies, as well as in Africa, the mother-child bond is the strongest and most enduring bond. This does not mean that the fathers have no relationship with their children or that they are absent. The father-child relationship is of a

more formal nature than the mother-child relationship. Moreover, the conjugal relationship appears on the surface to be similar to the Western norm in that two-parent households prevail, but, when competing with consanguineous relationships, conjugal affiliations usually lose. See Gutman, *Black Family*, 79; Raymond T. Smith, "The Nuclear Family in Afro-American Kinship," *Journal of Comparative Family Studies* 1 (1970): 62–70; Smith, "Matrifocal Family," 129; Stack, *All Our Kin*, 102–5.

54. Genovese, *Roll, Jordan, Roll*, 465–66; Gutman, *Black Family*, 74, 117–18.

55. Charles S. Johnson, *Shadow of the Plantation* (Chicago, 1934), 66–70.

56. Smith, *Negro Family in British Guiana*, 109, 158, 250–51.

57. Egypt, et al., *Unwritten History of Slavery*, 10; Rawick, *American Slave*, 16:15.

58. Egypt, et al., *Unwritten History of Slavery*, 8; Rawick, *American Slave*, 16:25. See also *ibid.*, 7:3–24; 2:51–52.

59. Joyce Ladner, *Tomorrow's Tomorrow: The Black Woman* (New York, 1971), 177–263.

60. See Paulme, *Women of Tropical Africa*, 14; Tanner, "Matrifocality," 147; Mayer Fortes, "Kinship and Marriage among the Ashanti," in A. R. Radcliffe-Brown and Daryll Forde, eds., *African Systems of Kinship and Marriage* (London, 1939), 127.

61. Sylvia Leith-Ross, *African Women: A Study of the Ibo of Nigeria* (London, 1939), 127.

62. Frazier, *Negro Family*, 125.

63. Elkins, *Slavery*, 130.

Women's Perspective
on the Patriarchy in the 1850s

ANNE FIROR SCOTT

Anne Firor Scott is William K. Boyd Professor Emerita at Duke University. She has coauthored general works in American women's history, including Women and Men *(1977) and* One Half the People *(1975), and has published important volumes in southern women's history, including* The Southern Lady: From Pedestal to Politics *(1970) and* Unheard Voices: The First Historians of Southern Women *(1993). Her other works include* The American Woman: Who Was She *(1970) and* Making the Invisible Woman Visible *(1984). She has served as president of the Organization of American Historians.*

The essay that follows first appeared in the Journal of American History *in 1974.*

Southern women were scarcely to be seen in the political crisis of the 1850s. Historical works dealing with that crucial decade seldom mention a woman unless it is in a footnote citing a significant letter from a male correspondent. In women's own diaries and letters the burgeoning conflict between the North and South almost never inspired comment before John Brown's raid and rarely even then.

At the same time, women were a crucial part of one southern response to the mounting outside attack on slavery. The response was an ever more vehement elaboration of what has been called the "domestic metaphor," the image of a beautifully articulated, patriarchal society in which every southerner, black or white, male or female, rich or poor, had an appropriate place and was happy in it. "The negro slaves of the South are the happiest, and, in some sense, the freest people in the world," George Fitzhugh wrote, describing the happy plantation on which none were oppressed by care.[1] "Public opinion," he stoutly maintained, "unites with self-interest, domestic affection, and municipal law to protect the slave. The man who maltreats the weak and dependent, who abuses his authority over wife, children, or slaves is universally detested." Slavery, Fitzhugh thought, was an admirable educational system as well as an ideal society.[2]

What Fitzhugh argued in theory many planters tried to make come true in real life. "My people" and "my black and white family" were phrases that rolled easily from their tongues and pens. "I am friend and well wisher both for time and eternity to every one of them," a North Carolinian wrote to his slave overseer upon the death of a slave, expressing sorrow that he could not be present for the funeral.[3] This letter was one in a series of fatherly letters to that particular slave, and the writer, a bachelor, offered similar fatherly guidance to his grown sisters, as he doled out their money to them.

Even as planters tried to make the dream come true, they could not hide their fear and doubt. "It gave me much pleasure to see so much interest manifested," one wrote his wife, reporting that the slaves had inquired about her health and welfare, "and I am convinced that much of it was sincere."[4] Quick panic followed rumors of insurrection, and when the war came many planters took the precaution of moving their slaves as Yankee armies approached. For those who enjoy poetic justice there is plenty to be found in the pained comments of loving patriarchs when their most pampered house servants were the first to depart for Yankee camps.

Women, like slaves, were an intrinsic part of the patriarchal dream. If plantation ladies did not support, sustain, and idealize the patriarch, if they did not believe in and help create the happy plantation, which no rational slave would exchange for the jungle of a free society, who would? If women, consciously or unconsciously, undermined the image designed to convince the doubting world that the abolitionists were all wrong, what then?

Some southern men had doubts about women as well as slaves. This is clear in the nearly paranoid reaction of some of them to the pronouncements and behavior of "strong-minded" women in the North. Southern gentlemen hoped very much that no southern lady would think well of such goings-on, but clearly they were not certain.[5] Their fears had some foundation, for in the privacy of their own rooms southern matrons were reading Margaret Fuller, Madame de Staël, and what one of them described as "decided women's rights novels."[6]

Unlike the slaves, southern women did not threaten open revolt, and when the war came they did not run to the Yankees. Instead they were supportive, as they worked to feed and clothe civilians and the army, nurse the sick, run the plantations, supervise the slaves, and pray for victory. Yet even these activities were partly an indirect protest against the limitations of women's role in the patriarchy. Suddenly women were able to do business in their own right, make decisions, write letters to newspaper editors, and in many other ways assert themselves as individual human beings. Many of them obviously enjoyed this new freedom.[7]

Even before the war women were not always as enthusiastic in their support of the patriarchy as slavery's defenders liked to believe. To the assertion that "the slave is held to *involuntary service*," an Alabama minister responded:

So is the wife. Her relation to her husband, in the immense majority of cases, is made for her, and not by her. And when she makes it for herself, how often, and how soon . . . would she throw off the yoke if she could! O ye wives, I know how superior you are to your husbands in many respects—not only in personal attraction . . . in grace, in refined thought, in passive fortitude, in enduring love, and in a heart to be filled with the spirit of heaven. . . . I know you may surpass him in his own sphere of boasted prudence and worldly wisdom about dollars and cents. Nevertheless, he has authority, from God, to rule over you. You are under service to him. You are bound to obey him in all things. . . . you cannot leave your parlor, nor your bed-chamber, nor your couch, if your husband commands you to stay there![8]

The minister was speaking to a northern audience and intended, no doubt, to convince northern women that they should not waste energy deploring the servitude of the slave since their own was just as bad, but surely this Alabama man shaped his understanding of married life in his home territory.

The minister's perception is supported in a little volume entitled *Tales and Sketches for the Fireside,* written by an Alabama woman for the purpose of glorifying southern life and answering the abolitionists. Woman's influence, she wrote,

is especially felt in the home circle; she is the weaker, physically, and yet in many other respects the stronger. There is no question of what she can bear, but what she is obliged to bear in her positions as wife and mother, she has her troubles which man, the stronger, can never know. Many annoying things to woman pass unnoticed by those whose thoughts and feeling naturally lead them beyond their homes.

The writer added that since men were so restless, God in his wisdom designed women to be "the most patient and untiring in the performance . . . of duties." Weariness almost leaps from her pages. Not only is she bitter about the burdens of woman's lot, she also feels keenly the one-sidedness of those burdens and the failure of men even to notice.[9]

Personal documents provide even more detailed evidence of female discontent in the South of the 1850s. Unhappiness centered on women's lack of control over many aspects of their own sexual lives and the sexual lives of their husbands, over the institution of slavery which they could not change, and over the inferior status which kept them so powerless.[10]

The most widespread source of discontent, since it affected the majority of married women, was the actuality of the much-glorified institution of motherhood. Most women were not able to control their own fertility. The typical planter's wife was married young, to a husband older than herself, and proceeded to bear children for two decades. While conscious family limitation was sometimes practiced in the nineteenth century, effective contraception was not available, and custom, myth, religion, and men operated to prevent limitation. With the existing state of medical knowledge it was realistic to fear childbirth and to expect to lose some children in infancy.[11]

The diary of a Georgia woman shows a typical pattern of childbearing and some reactions to it. Married in 1852 at the age of eighteen to a man of twenty-one, she bore her first child a year later. In the summer of 1855, noting certain telltale symptoms, she wrote, "I am again destined to be a mother . . . the knowledge causes no exhilirating feelings . . . [while] suffering almost constantly . . . I cannot view the idea with a great deal of pleasure."[12] The baby was born but died in a few weeks, a circumstance which she prayed would help her live more dutifully in the future. A few months later she was happily planning a trip to the North because "I have no infant and I cannot tell whether next summer I will be so free from care, . . ."[13] but in four days her dreams of travel vanished abruptly when morning nausea led her to wonder whether she was "in a peculiar situation, a calamity which I would especially dread this summer."[14] Her fears were justified, and she had a miscarriage in August. There was no rest for the weary. By January 1857 she was pregnant again, and on her twenty-fourth birthday in April 1858 she was pregnant for the fifth time in six years, though she had only two living children. Diary volumes for the next two years are missing, but in December 1862 she recorded yet another pregnancy, saying, "I am too sick and irritable to regard this circumstance as a blessing *yet awhile*."[15] A year later with the house being painted and all in confusion she jotted the illuminating comment: "I don't wonder that men have studys which . . . I imagine to be only an excuse for making themselves comfortable and being out of the bustle and confusion of . . . housekeeping . . . and children."[16] She also expressed bitter opposition to the practice of sending pregnant slaves to work in the fields. By February 1865, after four years of war, she was writing that "unfortunately I have the prospect of adding again to the little members of my household. . . . I am sincerely sorry for it."[17] When the child was born prematurely in June the mother thanked God that it did not live. By 1869, this woman had managed to relegate her husband to a separate bedroom, and, for good measure, she kept the most recent infant in her bed, as effective a means of contraception as she could devise.[18] Later she reflected that she had never "been so opposed to having children as many women I know."[19]

The difference between the male and female angle of vision is illustrated in the life of a South Carolina woman, a niece of James L. Petigru, married to a cousin ten years her senior. She gave birth to six children in the first nine years of her marriage, and her uncle—normally a wise and perceptive human being—wrote to the young woman's mother: "Well done for little Carey!

Has she not done her duty . . . two sons and four daughters and only nine years a wife? Why the Queen of England hardly beats her."[20] If the uncle had had access to the correspondence between "little Carey" and her planter husband he might not have been so quick to congratulate her. It seems likely from the evidence of these letters that her three-month sojourns with her mother in the summers were partly motivated by a desire to prolong the time between babies, but no sooner did her lonesome husband come to visit than she was pregnant again.[21]

This woman had a faithful family doctor who moved into her household when time for her confinement drew near, but even his comforting presence did not prevent her fears of death each time. Mrs. Thomas, writer of the first diary, relied on a slave midwife, her mother, and a town doctor. Both these women loved their children and cared for them, though with ample assistance before the war. Yet each privately insisted that she would have preferred a much longer time between babies. As the Alabama minister quoted earlier suggested, however, a woman could not leave her bedchamber or her couch without her husband's permission.[22]

Women's private feelings about constant childbearing provide one example of unhappiness which was masked by the cheerful plantation image. The behavior of the patriarchs themselves in other realms of sexual life was another source of discontent. The patriarchal ideal which called for pure, gentle, pious women also expected a great deal of men: that they should be strong, chaste, dignified, decisive, and wise. Women who lived in close intimacy with these men were aware of the gap between the cavalier of the image and the husband of the reality, and they were also aware that those who had the greatest power were also—by women's standards—the most sinful. A diarist summarized an afternoon of sewing and conversation in Richmond County, Georgia: "We were speaking of the virtue of men. I admitted to their general depravity, but considered that there were some noble exceptions, among those I class my own husband. . . ."[23] The entry revealed a certain uneasiness even about the noble exception, since the writer added that if her faith in her husband should be destroyed by experience her happiness on earth would end, and added, "Between husband and wife this is (or should be) a forbidden topic." She was twenty-two.

This notation parallels one in a more familiar diary. Observing the goings-on of the lowcountry aristocracy, Mary Boykin Chesnut wrote: "Thank God for my country women, but alas for the men! They are probably no worse than men everywhere, but the lower their mistresses the more degraded they must be. . . ."[24] Chesnut's comment revealed the dual nature of male depravity: sexual aberration in general and crossing the racial barrier in particular. Concern on this topic was an insistent theme in the writings of southern women and continued to be so long after emancipation. It may be significant that they did not blame black women, who might have provided convenient scapegoats. The blame was squarely placed on men. "You have no confidence in men," wrote one husband; "to use your own phrase 'we are all humbugs,'" adding that he himself was a great sinner though he did not specify his sin.[25]

Miscegenation was the fatal flaw in the patriarchal doctrine. While southern men could defend slavery as "domestic and patriarchal," arguing that slaves had "all the family associations, and family pride, and sympathies of the master," and that the relationship between master and slave secured obedience "as a sort of filial respect," southern women looked askance at the fact that so many slaves quite literally owed their masters filial respect.[26] "There is the great point for the abolitionists," one wrote.[27] While some southern reviewers blasted "the fiend in petticoats" who wrote *Uncle Tom's Cabin*, southern women passed copies of the book from hand to hand.

Impressive evidence of the pervasiveness of interracial sex and its effects on the minds and spirits of white women, gathered thirty years ago, has recently found its way into print. James Hugo Johnston examined thirty-five thousand manuscript petitions to the Virginia legislature. Among these documents were many divorce petitions in which white women named slave women as the cause of their distress. In some petitions wives told the whole story of their marriages, throwing much light on what could happen to the family in a slave society. One testified that her husband had repeated connection with many slaves, another protested several black mistresses who had been placed in her home and had treated her insolently. Yet another recounted a complicated story in which her brother had tried to force her husband to send away his black mistress, without success. In several cases the husband's attention to his mulatto children, sometimes in preference to his legitimate children, was offered in evidence. The stories run on and on until one is surfeited with pain and tragedy from the white woman's point of view, pain which could doubtless be matched from the black woman's point of view if it had been recorded. Many petitioners candidly described their husbands' long attachment to black mistresses and their reluctance to give them up. Johnston also adduced evidence of the tortured efforts white men made to provide for their mulatto children, efforts corroborated by Helen Catterall's compilation of legal cases dealing with slavery.[28]

If so much evidence found its way into the official records of the state of Virginia, how much is there yet unexamined in the records of other slave states, and how much more was never recorded because women suffered in silence rather than go against religion, custom, and social approval to sue for divorce by a special act of the legislature? Johnston, from his close acquaintance with the documents, surmised that there must have been many women who calmly or sullenly submitted to becoming "chief slave of the master's harem," a phrase attributed to Dolley Madison.[29]

Even apart from miscegenation, the general sexual freedom society accorded to men was deeply resented by women. A thread of bitterness runs through letters describing marital problems, the usual assumption being that male heartlessness could be expected. The double standard was just one more example of how unfairly the world was organized:

As far as a womans being forever 'Anathema . . .' in society for the same offence which in a man, very slightly lowers, and in the estimation of some of his own sex rather elevates him. In this I say there appears to be a very very great injustice. I am the greatest possible advocate for womans purity, in word, thought or deed, yet I think if a few of the harangues directed to women were directed in a point where it is more needed the standard of morality might be elevated.[30]

Ten years later the same woman had not changed her mind: "It occurs to me that if virtue be the test to distinguish man from beast the claim of many Southern white men might be questionable."[31]

In addition to the widely prevailing skepticism with which women viewed the pretensions of their lords and masters (a label often used with a measure of irony), there was widespread discontent with the institution of slavery. "I never met with a lady of southern origin who did not speak of Slavery as a sin and a curse,—the burden which oppressed their lives," Harriet Martineau observed in her autobiography.[32]

In Virginia, after the Nat Turner rebellion, twenty-four women joined in a petition to the legislature, noting that though "it be unexampled, in our beloved State, that females should interfere in its political concerns," they were so unhappy about slavery that they were willing to break the tradition. They urged the legislature to find a way to abolish slavery.[33] An overseer of wide experience told Chesnut in 1861 that in all his life he had met only one or two women who were not abolitionists.[34] William Gilmore Simms, reviewing *Uncle Tom's Cabin* in the *Southern Quarterly Review*, made clear his understanding of the opposition to slavery among southern women.[35]

Of course Martineau and the overseer exaggerated to make a point, and the Virginia petitioners were unusual. Women of slaveholding families responded ambiguously to the life imposed on them. Some accepted it without question. Others, complaining of the burden of slavery, nevertheless expected and sometimes got a degree of personal service which would have been inconceivable to women in the free states.[36] It was also true that few were philanthropic enough to give up a large investment for a principle. It is further clear that most southern women accepted, with a few nagging questions, the racial assumptions of their time and place.

Even with these conditions many women of the planter class had strong doubts about either the morality or the expediency of slavery, as the following statements indicate. "Always I felt the moral guilt of it, felt how impossible it must be for an owner of slaves to win his way into Heaven."[37] "But I do not hesitate to say . . . that slavery was a curse to the South—that the time had come in the providence of God to give every human being a chance for liberty and I would as soon hark back to a charnel house for health inspiration as to go to the doctrines of secession, founded on the institution of slavery, to find rules and regulations."[38] "When the thunderbolt of John Brown's raid broke over

Virginia I was inwardly terrified, because I thought it was God's vengeance for the torture of such as Uncle Tom."[39] "I will confess that what troubles me more than anything else is that I am not certain that *Slavery is right*."[40] "When will it please our God to enfranchise both the holders and the slaves from bondage? It is a stigma, a disgrace to our country."[41] "In 1864 I read Bishop Hopkins book on slavery. He took the ground that we had a right to hold the sons of Ham in bondage. . . . Fancy a besotted, grinding, hardfisted slave driver taking up a moral tone as one of God's accredited agents!!"[42]

One doubter suggested that she would happily pay wages to her house servants if her husband would agree, and another thought slaves ought to be permitted to choose their own masters. Still another devoted all her time to teaching slaves to read and write, even though to do so was illegal, and to providing a Sunday school for slave children.[43]

Moral doubts were further complicated by strong personal attachments between white and black women. A South Carolina woman went into mourning in 1857 when her favorite slave died, and her sister wrote that "she loved Rose better than any other human being."[44] Another member of the same family insisted that her brother and brother-in-law keep promises made to slaves whom she had sold within the family. A Virginia woman, seeking permission to free her slave woman and keep her in the state, contrary to the law, testified to her "strong and lasting attachment to her slave Amanda."[45] Such phrases were not uncommon among southern women.

For every woman who held slavery to be immoral, or who simply loved individual slaves, there were dozens who hated it for practical reasons. "Free at last," cried one white woman when she heard of the Emancipation Proclamation. "If slavery were restored and every Negro on the American continent offered to me," wrote another, "I should spurn them. I should prefer poverty rather than assume again the cares and perplexities of ownership."[46] Such quotations could be multiplied. They are typified by a diary entry in the fall of 1866 expressing relief "that I had no Negro clothes to cut out this fall O what a burden, like that of Sinbad the Sailor, was the thought of 'Negro clothes to be cut out.'"[47]

Motherhood, happy families, omnipotent men, satisfied slaves—all were essential parts of the image of the organic patriarchy. In none of these areas did the image accurately depict the whole reality.

For women as for the slaves, open revolt was made difficult by many constraints. Though women had complaints, they shared many of the assumptions of men, and, at least intermittently, enjoyed the role and status of the landholding aristocracy. Discontent does not automatically lead to a clear idea of alternatives, and few, if any, southern women in the 1850s had visions of a multiracial society based on freedom, much less equality. Nor did they conceive of fundamental change in the patterns of marriage and family which bound them so tight. Some, to be sure, found widowhood a liberating experience.[48]

The ideology of woman's liberation, which was being worked out in the North by Sarah Grimké, Margaret Fuller, Elizabeth Cady Stanton, and others, had only begun to take shape in the minds of southern women, but signs of change can be found. A letter written from Yazoo, Mississippi, in 1849 to the *Southern Ladies Companion* complained about an article which seemed to imply that only men were part of mankind:

Woman is not, or ought not to be, either *an article* to be turned to good account by the persons who compose "this life" [men] nor a plaything for their amusement. She ought to be regarded as forming a part of mankind herself. She ought to be regarded as having as much interest of proprietorship in "this life" as anyone else. And the highest compliment to be paid her is that she is useful to herself—that in conjunction with the rest of mankind, in works of virtue, religion and morality, the sum of human happiness is augmented, the kingdom of the Savior enlarged and the glory of God displayed.[49]

By the 1850s some echoes of the woman's rights debate which had erupted in the North in 1848 began to reach southern ears. A violent attack on the Woman's Rights Convention held in Worcester, Massachusetts, in 1851 appeared in the *Southern Quarterly Review*, written by a distinguished southern woman, Louisa Cheves McCord.[50] A closer look at McCord's own history is instructive with respect to built-in constraints. Daughter of Langdon Cheves, she was outstandingly able both as a writer and as an

administrator. Yet she used her ability to defend the whole southern domestic metaphor, including slavery. One has only to imagine her born in Boston instead of Charleston to find in Louisa
McCord all the makings of a Margaret Fuller or an Elizabeth
Cady Stanton.

What was the significance of this widespread discontent? Public decisions are rooted in private feelings, and the psychological
climate in any society is one of the most important things a social
or political historian needs to understand. The South by 1860 was
in a high state of internal tension, as feelings of guilt and fear of
the future mounted. The part played by slaves themselves, as well
as by women, in exacerbating these tensions is just now beginning
to be examined. Speaking of the American Revolution, Charles
Francis Adams once remarked that it "drew its nourishment from
the sentiment that pervaded the dwellings of the entire population," and added, "How much this home sentiment did then, and
does ever, depend upon the character of the female portion of the
people, will be too readily understood by all to require explanation."[51] What Adams called "the home sentiment" was in the
South of 1860 an unstable and hence explosive mixture of fear,
guilt, anxiety, and discontent with things as they were. How much
this stemmed from the unhappiness of "the female portion of the
population" is not yet well understood, but it is worth a good deal
of study.

Notes

1. George Fitzhugh, *Cannibals All! or Slaves Without Masters* (Cambridge, Mass., 1960), 18.

2. *Ibid.*, 25.

3. William Pettigrew to Mose, July 12, 1856, Pettigrew Family Papers
(Southern Historical Collection, University of North Carolina [here-
after SHC]).

4. Charles Pettigrew to Caroline Pettigrew, Oct. 18, 1857, *ibid.*

5. Anne Firor Scott, *The Southern Lady: From Pedestal to Politics 1830–
1930* (Chicago, 1970), 20–21.

6. *Corinne,* Madame de Staël's famous feminist novel, appeared often
in lists of books read by southern women. Even Mary Wollstonecraft

was not entirely unknown in the South. See William R. Taylor, *Cavalier and Yankee: The Old South and the American National Character* (New York, 1961), 162–67, for discussion of a pervasive malaise among antebellum southern women.

7. See H. E. Sterkx, *Partners in Rebellion: Alabama Women in the Civil War* (Rutherford, N.J., 1970), for the most recent collection of evidence concerning the extraordinary vigor and range of southern women's activities during the war. It is important to note that this essay does not treat all classes of women. There were eight million southerners in 1860, of whom the largest part were ordinary farmer folk, slaves, and free blacks. This majority was ruled, politically, economically, and socially, by a small top layer, the large and medium-sized plantation owners who had money, or at least credit, slaves, and power. From their ranks came the proslavery philosophers, the mythmakers, the leaders of opinion. From their ranks came the most visible southerners, the minority which the rest saw and heard. It was members of this minority who consciously or unconsciously clung to the idea of the beautiful organic society so well described in George Fitzhugh, *Sociology for the South: or the Failure of Free Society* (Richmond, 1954). It was women of this minority who were called upon to play the appropriate role, to live up to the image of the southern lady. Other women, farmer's wives and daughters and illiterate black women, were part of society and in some inarticulate way doubtless helped to shape it, but historians have just begun to forge tools which may permit an examination of their role. For insights into southern society, see Steven A. Channing, *Crisis of Fear: Secession in South Carolina* (New York, 1970).

8. Fred A. Ross, *Slavery Ordained of God* (Philadelphia, 1859), 54–56.

9. R. M. Ruffin, *Tales and Sketches for the Fireside* (Marion, Ala., 1858).

10. For other sources of women's unhappiness, especially the desire for education, see Scott, *Southern Lady*. This essay concentrates on areas of complaint directly related to the patriarchal myth. Of course the education some women hoped for, had it been available, would have indirectly undermined the patriarchy.

11. See *Annual Report to the Legislature of South Carolina Relating to the Registration of Births, Deaths and Marriages for the Year Ending December 13, 1856* (Columbia, S.C., 1857). Though the report acknowledges grave deficiencies in its fact gathering, this early venture into vital statistics supports generalizations suggested here. For comparative purposes the report includes some statistics from Kentucky which are also sup-

portive. Of the deaths recorded in South Carolina in 1856, nearly one half were children under the age of five and nearly one fourth were children under one year. Of marriages in the same year, 5.7 percent were of men under twenty, while 40.4 percent of the women were under that age. Nearly one half of the men and three fourths of the women who married in 1856 were under twenty-five. One fourth of the men but only 9.4 percent of the women married between the ages of twenty-five and thirty. A cohort analysis of selected groups of southern women patterned on Robert V. Wells's study of Quakers might be useful, if data could be found. See Robert V. Wells, "Demographic Change and the Life Cycle of American Families," *Journal of Interdisciplinary History* 2 (Autumn 1971): 273–82. Analysis of the biographical sketches of 150 lowcountry planters prepared by Chalmers Gaston Davidson provides further evidence of the age gap between husbands and wives. Davidson's study is based on 440 South Carolinians who had 100 or more slaves on a single estate. (Although fifty of the planters were women—a somewhat startling fact—his information is always about the men these women married.) The majority of the men were one to ten years older than their wives in first marriage. For second marriages the age difference increased, as it did for third and fourth marriages. In cases where the woman was older than her husband (twenty-three in all), the age gap was usually up to five years, though three women were more than ten years older than their husbands. Chalmers Gaston Davidson, *The Last Foray: The South Carolina Planters of 1860: A Sociological Study* (Columbia, S.C., 1971), 170–267.

12. E. G. C. Thomas Diary, June 26, 1855 (Department of Manuscripts, Duke University).

13. *Ibid.*, May 26, 1856.

14. *Ibid.*, June 1, 1856.

15. *Ibid.*, Dec. 1862.

16. *Ibid.*, Dec. 31, 1863.

17. *Ibid.*, Feb. 12, 1865.

18. *Ibid.*, Jan. 29, 1869.

19. *Ibid.*, Nov. 29, 1870.

20. James Petigru Carson, *Life, Letters and Speeches of James Louis Petigru: The Union Man of South Carolina* (Washington, 1920), 441.

21. Letters of Charles and Caroline Pettigrew, 1856–1861, Pettigrew Family Papers.

22. The degree to which maternity shaped women's lives emerges

from any random examination of family histories. For example, Charles
and Mary Pratt Edmonston of North Carolina had their first child in
1812, their last in 1833. During those twenty-one years Mrs. Edmonston
bore eleven children, four of whom died in infancy. Mrs. Andrew Mc-
Collum of Louisiana bore ten children between 1840 and 1855, including
one set of twins. Three died in infancy. During 180 months of married
life, she spent ninety in pregnancy and seventy in nursing babies, since
she did not use wet nurses. Thus in all her married life there were twenty
months when she was neither pregnant nor nursing a baby. Margaret
Ann Morris Grimball, wife of South Carolinian John B. Grimball, married at twenty and had a child every two years for eighteen years. At
seventeen Varina Howell of Mississippi married Jefferson Davis, who
was thirty-five and a widower. Children were born in 1852, 1855, 1857, 1861,
and 1864. Georgian David Crenshaw Barrow married Sarah Pope, who
bore him nine children in seventeen years, then died. John Crittenden's
wife bore seven children in thirteen years. Robert Allston of South Carolina married Adele Petigru, ten years his junior. She bore ten children in
seventeen years, of whom five lived to maturity. Examples could be
multiplied indefinitely, but far more useful would be a careful demographic study of selected southern counties, tidewater and upcountry, to
give a firm underpinning to this kind of impressionistic evidence.

23. Thomas Diary, April 12, 1856.

24. Mary Boykin Chesnut, *Diary from Dixie,* ed. Ben Ames Williams
(Boston, 1949), 21–22.

25. Charles Pettigrew to Caroline Pettigrew, July 10, 1856, Pettigrew
Family Papers.

26. Quoted in Severn Duvall, "*Uncle Tom's Cabin:* The Sinister Side
of the Patriarchy," *New England Quarterly* 36 (March 1963): 7–8. This
perceptive article deserves serious attention from social historians.

27. Thomas Diary, Jan. 2, 1858.

28. James Hugo Johnston, *Race Relations in Virginia & Miscegenation
in the South 1776–1860* (Amherst, 1970); Helen Tunnicliff Catterall, *Judicial Cases concerning American Slavery and the Negro* (2 vols., Washington, 1926). See also Guion Griffis Johnson, *Ante-Bellum North Carolina:
A Social History* (Chapel Hill, 1937), 221, for evidence that cohabitation
with a Negro was the second most important cause for divorce in North
Carolina.

29. Johnston, *Race Relations in Virginia,* 237.

30. Thomas Diary, Feb. 9, 1858.

31. *Ibid.*, May 7, 1869.

32. Harriet Martineau, *Harriet Martineau's Autobiography: With Memorials by Maria Weston Chapman* (3 vols., London, 1877), 2:21.

33. Augusta County Legislative Petitions, 1825–1833 (Virginia State Library, Richmond).

34. Chesnut, *Diary from Dixie*, 169.

35. William Gilmore Simms, review of *Uncle Tom's Cabin, Southern Quarterly Review* 8 (July 1853): 216, 233.

36. Their expectations may be illustrated by the E. G. C. Thomas family in its poverty-stricken postwar phase still requiring, so they thought, a person to cook, a person to clean, a person to wash and iron, one to do the chores, and a carriage driver. See Thomas Diary, 1868–1869, as Mrs. Thomas details her search for reliable domestic help among the freedpeople. One complication was that it was considered unethical to hire fine servants who had once belonged to friends.

37. John Q. Anderson, ed., *Brokenburn: The Journal of Kate Stone 1861–1868* (Baton Rouge, 1955), 8.

38. Rebecca L. Felton, "The Subjection of Women," pamphlet 19, Rebecca L. Felton Papers (Manuscript Division, University of Georgia).

39. Mrs. Burton [Constance Cary] Harrison, *Recollections Grave and Gay* (New York, 1912), 42.

40. Thomas Diary, Sept. 23, 1854.

41. Martha E. Foster Crawford Diary, Feb. 7, 1853, Feb. 3, 1854 (Department of Manuscripts, Duke University).

42. Hope Summerell Chamberlain, *Old Days in Chapel Hill, Being the Life and Letters of Cornelia Phillips Spencer* (Chapel Hill, 1926), 93.

43. John Q. Anderson, "Sarah Anne Ellis Dorsey," in Edward T. James et al., eds., *Notable American Women 1607–1950: A Biographical Dictionary* (3 vols., Cambridge, Mass., 1971), 1:505–6. There were southern men who opposed slavery, too, but theirs was usually an economic, not a moral critique.

44. Jane P. North to Caroline Pettigrew, Nov. 16, 1857, Pettigrew Family Papers.

45. J. H. Easterby, ed., *The South Carolina Rice Plantation as Revealed in the Papers of Robert F. W. Allston* (Chicago, 1945), 149.

46. Caroline Merrick, *Old Times in Dixie* (New York, 1901), 19. Mary A. H. Gay of Georgia, quoted in Matthew Page Andrews, *Women of the South in Wartime* (Baltimore, 1920), 334.

47. Thomas Diary, Sept. 20, 1866.

48. A study of planter's widows would be interesting. Many of them conducted plantations with considerable success, and as they necessarily came in contact with the outside world in business they began to develop more forceful personalities and interest in politics as well. For example, Jane Petigru North, sister of the famous James L. Petigru, was widowed early and ran one plantation owned by her brother and then another owned by her son-in-law, Charles L. Pettigrew. She did not hesitate to take full responsibility, and like her brother she was an outspoken supporter of the Union down to the moment of secession.

49. *Southern Ladies Companion* 2 (1848): 45.

50. [Louisa Cheves McCord] L. S. M., *Southern Quarterly Review* 5 (April 1852), 322–41. See also Margaret Farrand Thorp, "Louisa Susannah Cheves McCord," in James et al., eds., *Notable American Women*, 2:451–52.

51. Charles Francis Adams, *Letters of Mrs. Adams with an Introductory Memoir by Her Grandson* (Boston, 1848), xix.

Of Lily, *Linda Brent, and Freud*

A NON-EXCEPTIONALIST APPROACH

TO RACE, CLASS, AND GENDER IN

THE SLAVE SOUTH

NELL IRVIN PAINTER

Nell Irvin Painter is Edwards Professor of American History at Princeton University. Her books include Exodusters: Black Migration to Kansas after Reconstruction, The Narrative of Hosea Hudson: His Life as Negro Communist in the South, *and* Standing at Armageddon: The United States 1877–1919.

The essay that follows is based on a paper delivered at the Berkshire Conference of Women Historians in 1990, which was first published in a special issue of the Georgia Historical Quarterly *(Summer 1992) devoted to southern women's history.*

In my work on sexuality in the nineteenth- and twentieth-century South, my mind returns often to what the late Herbert Gutman used to say about Karl Marx, but with application to Sigmund Freud: "He raises some very good questions." While I have plenty of feminist company in my turn toward psychoanalysis, the Freud I am using here is not quite the Freud who has been making recent appearances.[1] As a historian of the nineteenth- and early twentieth-century American South who remains tethered to a history project grounded in the archives, I find Freud is valuable mainly as an acute observer of nineteenth-century bourgeois society, as an analyst (no pun intended) who recognized the relationship between sexuality and identity. His writing permits unusually clear views into the ways in which social, economic, and ethnic hierarchies affected households and families, for he was accustomed to dealing with people in households that encom-

passed more than one economic class. Such vision enriches southern studies, which is still impoverished by exceptionalism and a
tendency to see race as an opaque obstacle that blocks feminist
investigation.

My subject is the family relations that affected the richest and
the poorest of antebellum southern daughters. The tragically tiny
number of black daughters who would have been actually or nominally free, and large cohort of white daughters who would have
lived beyond the reach of the aristocracy, belonged to families
who were able to shelter them from predatory wealthy men and
were more likely to escape the fate of the daughters under discussion here. But whether black or white, if young women lived in
households where men had access to the poorest and most vulnerable, these daughters ran gendered risks related to sexuality that
did not respect barriers of class and race.

It has been no secret, then or now, that in the plantation South,
owners and slaves lived on terms of physical closeness and often
engaged in sexual intimacy. Yet historians have followed the lead
of privileged nineteenth-century southerners who, though well
aware that sex figured among the services masters demanded of
slaves, briskly pushed the matter aside. Even psychoanalysts like
Abram Kardiner and L. Ovesey pass quickly over the repercussions of interracial sexuality in southern white families and hence
on southern society generally.[2] Virtually by default, the conclusion in southern history was that master-slave sex was a problem
for the slaves, not the master; thus as a social phenomenon, interracial, interclass sexuality has been relegated to African Americans alone. This is not the position I hold. Because intimate
relations affected white as well as black families, I argue that such
sexuality and its repercussions belong not to one race or the other,
but must reside squarely in southern history.[3]

One needs only to read the works of class- and gender-
conscious historians of Great Britain and Europe to recognize the
parallels between nineteenth-century European bourgeois societies and that of the antebellum South.[4] Such usefulness is not limited to historians' insights. Though very much in vogue with literary critics, Freudian psychoanalysis also offers thought-provoking
assistance to historians, particularly on the formation of individual identity. Specifically, Sigmund Freud's "Dora" case history

raises fundamental questions about the dynamics of elite families in a hierarchical society where the employment of servants (and here I concentrate on female servants) is routine. This essay addresses the pertinence of three pieces of Freud's writing to southern society, as reflected in two mid-nineteenth-century southern characters known as "Lily" and "Linda Brent."

Lily is the title character of an 1855 novel by Sue Petigru King (Bowen) (1824–1875). King was a daughter of the very respectable Charlestonian, Thomas Petigru. Having been educated in Charleston and New York, she had returned to South Carolina to pursue her career as a writer. Her Lily is the quintessential young plantation mistress: hyper-white, wealthy, and beautiful. Much better known today, thanks largely to the work of Jean Fagan Yellin and others, is "Linda Brent," who, in contrast to Lily, was a slave. Brent is both the central character and the pseudonym which the Edenton, North Carolina, fugitive slave, Harriet Jacobs (1813–1897), used in her autobiography, *Incidents in the Life of a Slave Girl*, originally published with the help of Boston abolitionists in 1861.[5]

If rich, white, and free Lily represents the top of the antebellum South's economic and racial hierarchies, then poor, yellow, and enslaved Linda Brent represents the near bottom. Linda, after all, has some free relations, and her grandmother, nominally enslaved, lives in her own house in town. Things could have been much worse for Linda Brent. Both Linda's and Lily's stories are about very young women and sex, and taken together with Freud's "Dora" they tell us a great deal about southern family dynamics in slaveholding households. As both texts are about sex and race, a word about the phenomenon of master-slave sex, as I discovered it in Gertrude Thomas's journal, precedes the discussion of Lily, Linda Brent, and "Dora."

Although historians have not begun to quantify its incidence, it is clear that sexual relations between male slavemasters and female slaves were exceedingly common in the antebellum South—as in any other slave society, as Orlando Patterson points out.[6] Nineteenth-century fugitive slave narratives, such as those of Frederick Douglass and Moses Roper, and the Fisk and WPA ex-slave narratives from the 1930s, are full of evidence that masters

did not hesitate to sleep with their women slaves, despite the
marital status of either. Although I have not had an opportunity to pursue this hunch, I suspect that about 10 percent of
masters also slept or wanted to sleep with their enslaved men and
boys; some mistresses possibly also regarded their female slaves
as objects of desire.[7] On the other side of the class and racial
continuums from the Frederick Douglasses and Moses Ropers,
white women—southerners and observers—penned and sometimes published criticisms of the institution of slavery based on
what they perceived as the demoralization of white men who
engaged in adultery and/or polygyny.

I began to draw my own conclusions as I concentrated on the
journal of Ella Gertrude Clanton Thomas (1834–1907), published
in 1990 as *The Secret Eye*.[8] Thomas, wealthy, educated, and white,
lived in and around Augusta, Georgia, for most of her life. She
began keeping a journal in 1848, when she was fourteen years old,
and stopped writing definitively in 1889, when she was fifty-five.
Although she was born into an immensely wealthy, slave-owning
family, Thomas married a man who was a poor manager. Her
husband, Jefferson Thomas, succeeded financially as a planter
before the Civil War, thanks to unpaid labor and continual financial help from Gertrude's father. But her father died in 1864
and their slaves were emancipated in 1865. After the war the
Thomases entered a long cycle of debt that sent Gertrude into the
paid labor force as a teacher. Her earnings kept the family afloat
economically, but poverty imposed great strains on the family.
This journal, therefore, chronicles a life of privilege before the
Civil War, the trauma of supporting the losing side, the loss of the
labor and prestige that slavery had assured her, and the chagrin
of downward mobility. Thomas joined the Woman's Christian
Temperance Union in the 1880s and became a suffragist in the
1890s. She died in Atlanta.

Initially I appreciated this journal for its value as a primary
source for the study of the social history of the South, for which
Thomas was an excellent witness. Extraordinary as her record is,
however, it works on yet another level, which psychoanalysis is
well equipped to explore. The journal contains a veiled text, characterized by the keeping of secrets, lack of candor, and self-
deception. Whereas the surface of this text presents a southerner

of a certain class at given historical junctures, a less straightforward message also emerges, though it is not so easy to glimpse. The veiled text, less bounded chronologically, is about families and gender, and it contains and reveals a great secret that is relatively timeless: adultery. I know from the "deception clues" and leakage in the journal that most certainly by the 1860s, probably by the 1850s, Thomas was painfully aware but unable to admit that her father had had children by at least one of his slaves.[9] By the 1870s, possibly as early as the 1850s, Thomas also knew that her husband had fathered at least one child by a woman who was not white.

This should come as no surprise. Harriet Martineau in the 1830s spoke of the plantation mistress as "the chief slave of the harem." Fredrika Bremer in the 1850s coined a famous phrase that Thomas quotes in her journal, "these white children of slavery." And Mary Chesnut wrote of the mulatto children in every slaveholding household.[10] Gertrude Thomas was far from alone.

Some of the most interesting evidence comes from fiction, which, considering the subject, should not be surprising. Most respectable nineteenth-century people retreated—or attempted to retreat—behind the veil of privacy, rather than reveal their actual patterns of sexuality. The very ability to conceal the rawer aspects of the human condition, an ability that we sum up in the term privacy, served as a crucial symbol of respectability when the poor had no good place to hide. Nonetheless the topic of interracial sexuality was of enough fascination to reappear in fiction under various disguises. Taking my cue from Gertrude Thomas, who was hypersensitive about sexual competition between women, I began to pursue sexuality through the theme of competition. Tracked in that guise, southern fiction reveals some interesting manifestations.

Sue Petigru King sounded themes that occur in the works of several white southern women writers, such as Caroline Lentz, Grace King, and Willa Cather. For example, Cather's final novel, *Sapphira and the Slave Girl* (1940), is precisely and openly about a white woman's perception of sexual competition between herself and a Negro woman. In its racial candor, *Sapphira* is exceptional. More often the competition between women is not about individuals with different racial identities, but about two white characters who are color-coded in black and white. While I realize that European writers such as Sir Walter Scott and Honoré de Balzac used light (blonde) and dark (*la belle juive*) female characters symbolically, Anne Goodwyn Jones, Mary Kelley, and Jane Pease, scholars familiar with southern writing, corroborate my view that nineteenth- and early twentieth-century white southern women writers were singularly fascinated by competition between light and dark women. While most publications by these women followed the usual theme of a young woman's quest for autonomy and her eventual marriage to a good man, they also very much echoed Gertrude Thomas's fixation on female rivalry.

Sue Petigru King is no longer very well known, but she loomed large in Gertrude Thomas's literary world and was known in Great Britain. William Thackeray, one of Britain's most celebrated authors, visited her on a trip to the United States. In the mid-nineteenth century King published several novels which repeatedly stressed themes of jealousy and competition between women, the best known of which is *Lily*.

Very briefly, *Lily* is the story of Elizabeth Vere, whom her father calls "Lily" because she is "as white as any lily that ever grew." Over the course of the novel's plot, Lily goes from age seven to seventeen. King described her heroine with words like "white," "pure," "innocent," "simple," and "lovely." The character with whom King paired Lily is her cousin, Angelica Purvis. Angelica is also a rich white woman, but King focused on the blackness of her dresses and the intense blackness of her hair. At one point, King contrasted Lily, who "seemed made up of light and purity," with Angelica, who "was dark, designing, distracting." Angelica is exotic; King described her as an "Eastern princess" and called her looks "Andalusian." Whereas Lily is pure, Angelica is passionate, evil, voluptuous. Angelica says of her attractiveness to men: "I am original sin."[11] At the age of seventeen, Lily is engaged to her first great love, Clarence Tracy, a childhood friend who is a graduate of Princeton University. Despite all her goodness, however, Lily is not rewarded with love, for Clarence is crazy in love with Angelica, who is married.

On the face of it, the most obvious theme in *Lily* is competition between two white women, which the less virtuous is win-

ning. But race hovers in the very near background. First, these
ostensibly white competitors are color-coded in black and white.
Then, as though to make the point unambiguously, King abruptly
introduces a new character, Lorenza, at the very end of the novel.
Lorenza is Clarence's Negro mistress. On the night before Lily's
wedding, Lorenza murders Lily out of jealousy over her impend-
ing marriage.

King left nothing to guesswork in this novel, and to hammer
home her message, she also addressed her readers directly. Her
point was the same made by Mary Chesnut in her Civil War diary:
that southern planter husbands repaid their wives' faithful virtue
with base infidelity. Wealthy southern men married young, pure,
rich, white girls like Lily, then left them for mistresses tinged by
blackness, whether of descent or intimation. King summed up
Mary Chesnut's conviction and Gertrude Thomas's fears: "It is
not the woman most worthy to be loved who is the most loved."
This conclusion is echoed in the writing of Sigmund Freud.

In 1912, Freud discussed exactly that phenomenon in his second contribution to the Psychology of Love: "On the Universal
Tendency to Debasement in the Sphere of Love." Freud ap-
praised the practical results of "civilized morality" and the sexual double standard from the standpoint of middle- and upper-
class men who were susceptible to psychosomatic impotence
with women of their own class. Freud said, making King's point:
"Where such men love they have no desire and where they desire
they cannot love."[12]

In *Lily*, the pure, young, rich, white daughter is the most dramatic loser in the southern sexual sweepstakes. In this interpretation of southern sexuality, the motif is competition between
women, and the victims are wealthy white women. Writers from
the other side painted a disturbingly similar, yet differently shaded
portrait.

While many ex-slave narratives discuss master-slave sexuality,
the most extended commentary comes from Harriet Jacobs, who,
writing under the pseudonym Linda Brent, told of being harassed
by her master for sex from the time she was thirteen. Her character, Linda, becomes the most literal embodiment of the slave as
sexual prey in the literature of slave narratives.

Harriet Jacobs depicted puberty as a "sad epoch in the life of a slave girl." As she became nubile, Linda Brent's master began to whisper "foul words in my ear," which is the kind of act whose consequences Freud understood. Jacobs generalized from Linda's predicament that "whether the slave girl be black as ebony or as fair as her mistress"—she, the slave girl, is sexually vulnerable.[13] This vulnerability robbed her of her innocence and purity. Hearing "foul words" from her master and angry and jealous outbreaks from her mistress, the slave girl, in Jacobs's phrase, became "prematurely knowing in evil things." The more beautiful she is, the more speedy her despoliation. Beauty, for Linda Brent and young women like her, was no blessing: "If God has bestowed beauty upon her, it will prove her greatest curse."[14]

Incidents is of great interest in this discussion because Jacobs confronted the sexual component of servitude so straightforwardly. She recognized, too, that slaves and owners interpreted the situation very differently. Jacobs dedicated an entire chapter of *Incidents in the Life of a Slave Girl* to "The Jealous Mistress." Here and elsewhere, Jacobs maintained that mistresses whose husbands betrayed them felt no solidarity whatever with their slaves.[15] Like other ex-slave narrators, Jacobs could ascertain the view of slaveowning women but emphatically did not share their conclusions. Writing as Linda Brent, Jacobs supplied the key word, "victim," and recognized that it was a matter of contention between slave and mistress.

White women, black women, and black men all resented deeply white men's access to black women. But the comments from the two sides of the color line are contradictory: where white women saw sexual competition—with connotations of equality—black men and women saw rank exploitation that stemmed from grossly disparate levels of power. Moses Roper, his master's child, relates the story of his near-murder, shortly after his birth, by his father's jealous wife. Frederick Douglass also noted that slaveowning women were distressed by the bodily proof of their husband's adulteries.[16]

For Jacobs, as for other ex-slave narrators, the prime victim was the slave woman, not the slaveowning woman, no matter how the latter perceived the situation. Slaveowners' sexual relations with their women slaves constituted one of several varieties of victimization by men whose power over them was absolute. Slaves of both sexes were opposed by class and by race, but women suffered a third, additional form of oppression stemming from their gender. Extorted sex was part of a larger pattern of oppression embedded in the institution of slavery.

Harriet Jacobs and Gertrude Thomas provide examples of the family dynamics of cross-class adultery. Located in very different places within the complicated families of slavery, each explicates the deleterious effects of adultery within their households. Like Jacobs and Thomas, Sigmund Freud, in his analysis of "Dora," recognized the damage that a father's adultery caused a daughter.[17]

"Dora" was eighteen-year-old Ida Bauer, whose father took her to see Freud in October 1900 after she threatened suicide. Phillip Bauer hoped that Freud would cure his daughter's mental and physical ailments and stem her wild accusations of sexual harassment. Ida had claimed that a close family friend, "Herr K" (Hans Zellenka), had made several sexual advances toward her, and she told Freud that in one instance "Herr K" had approached her with the same phrases he had used to proposition a servant woman. The entanglements ran deeper, for it was revealed that Herr K's young wife, "Frau K," was Phillip Bauer's lover. In this adulterous game between her father and the Ks, Ida felt as though she were a helpless pawn, attached emotionally to Frau K and the female servant, as well as to her estranged mother and father. Freud diagnosed the distraught young woman as hysterical and used her case to put certain theories to the test.

Freud had been thinking about hysteria for several years and had worked out his notions in letters to his close friend and regular correspondent, Wilhelm Fliess. These comments are exceedingly helpful to me, particularly in observations that Freud enclosed with a letter dated May 2, 1897. Here Freud noted that children, even very young babies, hear things that later become the raw material for fantasies and neuroses. Accompanying this letter was "Draft L," which includes a paragraph on "The Part Played by Servant Girls."[18]

In Draft L, Freud echoed his society's assumption that the poor young women who worked in bourgeois households were "people of low morals" because they were likely to become sexually involved with the men and boys of the household. Here Freud was echoing the most common of assumptions about black people in the South. But whereas Freud identified morals with class, white southerners saw low morals as a racial characteristic of African Americans. For my purposes, however, this is not the crucial insight that Freud took from his failed analysis of Ida Bauer. For me Freud's most useful observation relates to the critical importance of servants in the psychological and, hence, social dynamics of the families in which they work. Although Freud thought mainly of the ramifications of the situation on the family of the employers, as we saw in the case of Linda Brent, servants, too, felt the effects of adulterous—should I add incestuous?—family dynamics.

Freud wrote Fliess that in households in which servant women are sexually intimate with their employers, the children (here I believe he means female children) develop an array of hysterical fantasies: fear of being on the street alone, fear of becoming a prostitute, fear of a man hidden under the bed. In sum, said Freud, "there is tragic justice in the circumstance that the family head's stooping to a maidservant is atoned for by his daughter's self-abasement."[19]

Freud underscored the degree to which women in a household are emotionally intertwined. "Dora" identified with the servant that her would-be lover had tried to seduce. Observing situations in which race was not a factor, Freud understood that the very structure containing class and gender power dynamics is virtually Foucauldian in its leakiness. No class of women remained exempt from a degradation that aimed at the least of them. Just as Gertrude Thomas saw that her adulterous father and husband treated rich and poor and black and white women as interchangeable sexually, Freud saw there was a "part played by servant girls" and an object connection between "Dora" and her father's mistress. A recent Freud scholar, Hannah Decker, put her finger on the phenomenon that poisoned young women's lives in Freud's Vienna and that also characterized the nineteenth-century South: the careless sexual abuse of *das süsse Mädel*—the sweet young thing.[20]

Freud's letters to Fliess, "On the Universal Tendency to Debasement in the Sphere of Love," and especially the "Dora" case analysis show that "Dora's" predicament is reflected in both *Lily* and *Incidents in the Life of a Slave Girl,* but in somewhat different ways. Linda Brent is more directly comparable with "Dora," for she was the object of unwanted sexual advances, as was young Ida Bauer. The case of Lily Vere is less obvious, for she is the daughter of "Draft L," of "The Part Played by Servant Girls." Lily is the daughter whose affective value is lowered by the existence of the sexually vulnerable servant class and the allure of enticing dark/Negro women like Angelica and Lorenza. While Linda Brent is a clear victim of her society's hierarchies of race and gender, Lily, unloved by her fiancé and murdered by his servant lover, is victimized as well. Her fiancé, Clarence, is the very figure of the Freud patient suffering from psychically induced impotence.[21]

Examining these southern women's stories and taking Freud to heart leads to two conclusions: First, that historians of the United States South, sheltered too long in southern exceptionalism, have let an intellectual color bar obstruct their view of the complexity of gender roles within households that were economically heterogeneous. Lily and Linda Brent, two examples of a spoliation of young women that was no respecter of race or class, underscore both the sexual vulnerabilities and the psychological interrelatedness of southern daughters. Second, Freud contributed to our understanding that families and societies cannot designate and thereby set apart one category of women as victims. The victimization spread, in different ways and to different degrees. But where historians have been prone to construe southern family relations within watertight racial categories, the stories of these three daughters pose complicated new questions whose answers do not stop at the color line.

Historians have wanted to reach a single conclusion that would characterize the relationship between slaveowning and slave women in the antebellum South: *either* slave women were at the bottom of a hierarchical society, as the ex-slave narrators testify, *or* all southern women were, finally, at the mercy of rich white men. The relationship between black and white women through white men deserves to be named, for slavery often made women of different races and classes into co-mothers and co-wives as well as owners and suppliers of labor. The question is whether there should be one name or, reflecting the number of races involved, more than one.

So far no historian of southern women has given more than a chapter or its equivalent to interracial sexuality and the gender relations that flowed from it, but the work is coming along. Yet the older, full-length studies of race and gender in the antebellum South by Deborah Gray White, Catherine Clinton, and Elizabeth Fox-Genovese and the newer work that builds upon them all tend toward the use of one concept to characterize relations within extended southern households: oppression. Deborah Gray White, in *Ar'n't I a Woman,* stresses the "helplessness" and "powerlessness" of slave women vis-à-vis slaveowners and in American society in general. Conceding that white women and black men may have envied black women, White nonetheless views black women at the bottom of a malevolent system that disempowered all women, even those who were rich and white. She places slave women at the negative end of a continuum of power on which white women also occupied positions of relative powerlessness and exploitation.[22]

Viewing matters from the other side of the class/race divide, Catherine Clinton, in *The Plantation Mistress,* also acknowledges a "parallel oppression of women, both white and black." But where Deborah White cites instances of aggression on the part of white women against black, Clinton stresses plantation mistresses' roles as nurturers, mediators, and nurses. Clinton speaks of a patriarchy in which rich white men possessed slaves of both sexes as they possessed their own wives. In *The Plantation Mistress,* slaveowning women do not appear in hierarchical relationships with slave women. Rather than portray slaveowning women as rulers of their workers, Clinton sees white male masters as the font of all power and all evil.[23]

In *Within the Plantation Household,* Elizabeth Fox-Genovese departs from the view of black and white women's parallel exploitation that White and Clinton evoke. Stressing the spatial and emotional intimacy in which many slave and slaveholding women lived in plantation households, Fox-Genovese softens the domination of the master. She prefers the term "paternalism" to Clinton's "patriarchy," because paternalism carries an air of "legitimate domination," which was how slaveholding men viewed their role.

(Let us not quibble about whether slave owners should be allowed to choose the words we historians use to characterize them a century and a half later.)

But Fox-Genovese stiffens the authority of slave-owning women over their female slaves, providing theoretical and empirical arguments for a somewhat ambiguous but clearly hierarchical relationship between women of different races and classes. Rather than see masters as the proximate wielders of power, Fox-Genovese shows that slaveholding women and slave women were cognizant of who held the power between them and who could inflict the greatest violence with impunity. To make her point, Fox-Genovese enumerates instances of violence and minimizes slaveholding women's abolitionist leanings. For her, slaveholding women who saw themselves as victims of the kind of adultery that the slave system allowed were simply misguided.[24]

Clinton's more recent essays reveal the pathologies of planter families in which rape and adultery distort descent and parental attachment. While "Caught in the Web of the Big House" glimpses the ways in which owner-slave rape affected mistresses, the emphasis still falls mainly on the tragedy of the direct victim of assault: the slave woman. "Southern Dishonor," Clinton's spiked critique of both southern historiography and slavery's brutal system of reproduction, announces themes and works-in-progress in the study of sexuality and slavery.[25] Martha Hodes's 1991 dissertation and Mary Frances Berry's 1991 presidential address to the Organization of American Historians further enrich the historical literature by revealing the complexities of southern sexuality.[26]

So far this work, though intriguing, stops short of completing the investigation of the relationship between southern families, society, and history. If feminist history has taught us anything in the last two decades, it is that important private matters become important historical matters. The example of the South Carolina fire-eater, James Henry Hammond—whose emotional turmoil following his wife's desertion when he took a second slave wife so incapacitated him psychologically that he missed an important secessionist meeting that would have bolstered his sagging political career—makes the point.[27] Hammond's wife serves as a reminder that Gertrude Thomas's preoccupation—competition—

needs to reenter the equation, or historians risk missing much of the psychodrama of southern history. Focusing on one part of the picture, even if more compatible with present-day understandings of power relations, flattens out the inherent complexity of southern history. If historians do not acknowledge that wealthy white women saw themselves in competition with women who were black and poor and powerless, they miss a vital dimension of southern history that helps explain the thorniness of women's contacts across the color line well into the twentieth century. We must acknowledge the existence of two ways of seeing, even while we keep our eyes on fundamental differentials of power.

What my approach means for southern history is a renunciation of a "the South" way of thinking. For me there is seldom a "the South," for simple characterizations eliminate the reality of sharp conflicts over just about everything in southern culture, slavery most of all. Saying that "the South" was proslavery (or, later, prosegregation) equates the region with its ruling race and annihilates the position of at least one-third of its inhabitants. As a labor historian with a keen sense of the historical importance of all groups of people within a society (not simply the prestigious, published, and politically powerful), I insist on going beyond lazy characterizations in the singular. Recognizing the complex and contradictory nature of southern society, I can rephrase my conclusions about the study of southern history succinctly: Southern history demands the recognition of complexity and contradiction, starting with family life, and therefore requires the use of plurals; and though southern history must take race very seriously, southern history must not stop with race.

Notes

1. I am coming to Freud's writing from a different direction from that of literary critics and most Lacanians. Although Freud's work is the starting place for object relations theory, it, too, would be more useful to me than certain Lacanians (notably Jane Gallop, whose insights are valuable here) if object relations analysts were not so relentlessly mid-twentieth-century middle class. The family structure that objects relations scholars—such as Nancy Chodorow—envision is strictly nuclear,

whereas many nineteenth-century southern families included parental figures who were not related to children by birth.

2. Abram Kardiner and L. Ovesey, *The Mark of Oppression: Explorations in the Personality of the American Negro* (New York, 1951).

3. I should add that family relations also affect more than women and girls; men and boys deserve—and will ultimately receive—a far larger place in this piece of work in progress than they currently occupy.

4. See, for example, Lenore Davidoff, "Class and Gender in Victorian England: The Diaries of Arthur J. Munby and Hannah Cullwick," *Feminist Studies* 5 (Spring 1979):87–144; and Maria Ramas, "Freud's Dora, Dora's Hysteria," in Judith L. Newton, Mary P. Ryan, and Judith R. Walkowitz, eds., *Sex and Class in Women's History* (London, 1983), 72–113.

5. Sue Petigru King Bowen, *Lily* (New York, 1855) and Jean Fagan Yellin, ed., *Incidents in the Life of a Slave Girl Written by Herself, by Harriet A. Jacobs* (Cambridge, Mass., 1987). Although I am aware of the controversy surrounding the designation of genre of *Incidents,* I am treating it here as autobiography.

6. Orlando Patterson, *Slavery and Social Death: A Comparative Study* (Cambridge, Mass., 1982), 50, 229, 230, 261.

7. Hortense Spillers makes some tantalizing observations in this regard in "Mama's Baby, Papa's Maybe: An American Grammar Book," *Diacritics* 17 (Summer 1987):76–77.

8. Virginia Ingraham Burr, ed., *The Secret Eye: The Journal of Ella Gertrude Clanton Thomas, 1848–1880* (Chapel Hill, 1990).

9. Psychologists call cues that something is being withheld "deception clues" and the inadvertent disclosure of such material "leakage." Both deception clues and leakage are associated with the phenomenon of self-deception, which Gertrude Thomas practiced in regard to unpleasant personal truths that she did not want to confront.

10. Harriet Martineau, *Society in America* (3 vols., New York, 1837), 2:112, 118; Fredrika Bremer, *Homes of the New World: Impressions of America,* (2 vols., London, 1853), 1:382; C. Vann Woodward and Elisabeth Muhlenfeld, *The Private Mary Chesnut: The Unpublished Civil War Diaries* (New York, 1984), 42 (March 18, 1861).

11. Bowen, *Lily,* 206, 227–28. W. J. Cash also utilizes Spanishness to hint at the blackness within white southerners. See *The Mind of the South* (New York, 1941), 25.

12. Bowen, *Lily,* 278. *Sigmund Freud: Collected Papers,* trans. Joan

Riviere (New York, 1959), 4, 207. According to Freud, well-brought-up women who have been taught that sex is distasteful and who reject their sexuality tend to be inexperienced, inhibited, and frigid in marriage. This means that their husbands, who also regard the sex act as polluting, relate to their wives more as judges than as joyous physical partners. Hence only love objects who seem to these men to be debased—prostitutes and women of the lower class—can inspire in them full sensual feelings and a high degree of pleasure. This explains why these men keep lower-class mistresses (207, 210–11).

13. Yellin, *Incidents in the Life of a Slave Girl*, 27.

14. *Ibid.*, 28.

15. *Ibid.*, 27–28, 33.

16. Moses Roper, *A Narrative of the Adventures and Escape of Moses Roper from American Slavery*, 5th ed. (London, 1843), 9–10, quoted in Frances Smith Foster, *Witnessing Slavery: The Development of Antebellum Slave Narratives* (Westport, Conn., 1979), 78; and Frederick Douglass, *Narrative of the Life of Frederick Douglass an American Slave* (Boston, 1845), 4.

17. See Jane Gallop, "Keys to Dora," in *The Daughter's Seduction: Feminism and Psychoanalysis* (Ithaca, 1982), 137, 141–45, 147. Other commentators on the case include Elisabeth Young-Bruehl, ed., *Freud on Women: A Reader* (New York, 1990); Jim Swan, "Mater and Nannie: Freud's Two Mothers," *America Image* 31 (Spring 1974); Hannah S. Decker, *Freud, Dora, and Vienna 1900* (New York, 1991); Maria Ramas, "Freud's Dora, Dora's Hysteria," in Newton, Ryan, and Walkowitz, eds., *Sex and Class in Women's History;* and to a certain extent Mary Poovey, "The Anathematized Race: The Governess and *Jane Eyre,*" in Poovey, ed., *Uneven Developments: The Ideological Work of Gender in Mid-Victorian England* (Chicago, 1988).

18. Jeffrey Moussaieff Masson, *The Complete Letters of Sigmund Freud to Wilhelm Fliess, 1887–1904* (Cambridge, Mass., 1985), 241.

19. *Ibid.*

20. Decker, *Freud, Dora, and Vienna 1900,* 109.

21. See also Freud's "'Civilized' Sexual Morality and Modern Nervous Illness" (1908) and *Civilization and Its Discontents* (1930), in which he surveyed what he saw as the psychosexual dysfunctions associated with civilization. In "'Civilized' Sexual Morality" Freud makes some observations that might be useful in southern history: "In her [the girl's] mental feelings [as she marries] she is still attached to her parents, whose

authority has brought about the suppression of her sexuality; and in her physical behaviour she shows herself frigid, which deprives the man of any high degree of sexual enjoyment. I do not know whether the anaesthetic type of woman exists apart from civilized education, though I consider it probable. But in any case, such education actually breeds it. . . . In this way, the preparation for marriage frustrates the aims of marriage itself." Young-Bruehl, ed., *Freud on Women*, 176.

22. Deborah Gray White, *Ar'n't I a Woman: Female Slaves in the Plantation South* (New York, 1985).

23. Catherine Clinton, *The Plantation Mistress: Woman's World in the Old South* (New York, 1982).

24. Elizabeth Fox-Genovese, *Within the Plantation Household: Black and White Women of the Old South* (Chapel Hill, 1988).

25. Catherine Clinton, "Caught in the Web of the Big House: Women and Slavery," in Walter J. Fraser, Jr., R. Frank Saunders, Jr., and Jon L. Wakelyn, eds., *The Web of Southern Social Relations: Women, Family, and Education* (Athens, Ga., 1985), 19–34; Clinton, "'Southern Dishonor': Flesh, Blood, Race, and Bondage," in Carol Bleser, ed., *In Joy and in Sorrow: Women, Family, and Marriage in the Victorian South, 1830–1900* (New York, 1991), 52–68.

26. Mary Frances Berry, "Judging Morality: Sexual Behavior and Legal Consequences in the Late Nineteenth-Century South," *Journal of American History* 78 (December 1991):835–56. Martha Hodes, "Sex Across the Color Line" (Ph.D. diss., Princeton University, 1991); Eugene Genovese, "'Our Family, White and Black': Family and Household in the Southern Slaveholders' World View," in Bleser, ed., *In Joy and in Sorrow*, 69–87, grasped the reality of slaveholders' ideology of the family almost as though to substitute it for reality and without following its significance in family relations.

27. Drew Gilpin Faust, *James Henry Hammond and the Old South: A Design for Mastery* (Baton Rouge, 1982); and Carol Bleser, ed., *Secret and Sacred: The Diaries of James Henry Hammond, a Southern Slaveholder* (New York, 1988).

Radical Reconstruction and the Property Rights of Southern Women

SUZANNE D. LEBSOCK

Suzanne D. Lebsock is a professor of history at the University of North Carolina at Chapel Hill. In 1992 her work won her one of the highest accolades, a coveted MacArthur Award. Her first book, Free Women of Petersburg: Status and Culture in a Southern Town, 1784–1860 *(1985) won the Bancroft Prize and the Berkshire Conference of Women Historians Prize. Her second book,* A Share of Honor *(1989) was prepared in conjunction with a traveling exhibit honoring Virginia women. She is the coeditor of* Visible Women: New Essays on American Activism *(1993)—essays in honor of Anne Firor Scott.*

This essay first appeared in the Journal of Southern History *in 1977.*

In the summer of 1870 the editors of the *Revolution,* the New York–based woman-suffrage weekly, printed a buoyant letter from an unidentified Georgia feminist. "The cause of Woman's Rights in our state has undergone a wonderful reform within the last few years," she reported, and she went on to detail the property rights secured to married women under Georgia's Reconstruction constitution. A married woman was empowered to own property in her own name, and her husband could not sell it without her consent.[1] For northern feminists this was good news, proof that the southern states were not incorrigible where the rights of women were concerned.

Revisionist historians have likewise taken approving notice of the women's-rights measures that appeared in the Reconstruction constitutions, for here is evidence of Radical Republican sensitivity to yet another enlightened reform of the day. The reforms were in fact something less than enlightened, enacted by men who were hardly feminists. But on the face of it the Radical record was impressive. From late 1867 to early 1869 Radical-dominated conventions created new constitutions for ten states; in nine of them the "wonderful reform," the guarantee of property rights to married women, was made part of the fundamental law.[2]

For all their prominence in the Reconstruction constitutions, however, the place of these provisions in Reconstruction histories has been confined to honorable mention on running lists of those "other significant reforms" instituted by the Radicals. The meaning assigned the married-women's clauses in particular has thus hinged very much on the historian's interpretation of Radical reform in general. To James S. Allen, a Marxist who read Reconstruction as a bourgeois revolution, the women's provisions were added testimony to "the thoroughgoing nature of the democratic overturn" in the postwar South. A more moderate appraisal was offered by Kenneth M. Stampp, who placed the expansion of women's rights among the "modest" and "long overdue" reforms that appeared in "essentially conservative" constitutions. For Jack B. Scroggs the women's-property sections were instances of carpetbagger constitutional reform in the Atlantic seaboard states.[3]

Of the three, Stampp is nearest the mark. For the South as a whole the reforms were indeed modest, if modest is the proper term for constitutional provisions that in most places amounted to very little but in others meant a great deal. It was only in three of the older, eastern states that the married-women's clauses of 1868 made a difference. The *Revolution*'s Georgia correspondent was justifiably enthusiastic, for in Georgia, and in North Carolina and South Carolina as well, the Reconstruction constitutional conventions launched the women of their states on the road toward legal equality with men, at least on the matter of property rights and obligations. Farther to the west, however, the Reconstruction conventions did very little, partly because there was less to be done. In six states, Alabama, Arkansas, Florida, Louisiana, Mississippi, and Texas, some rights had been granted married women well before the Civil War, and with the exception of a minor revision in Louisiana, the 1868 conventions merely gave constitutional status to principles already firmly established in the statutory law. The Montgomery *Daily Advertiser* gave an apt assessment of the Alabama convention's work; the section containing the women's-property provision presented "nothing particularly worthy of notice."[4] As of 1868 the property rights granted women varied greatly among these six states. What they had in common was that few additional powers were granted women during the entire period of Republican rule.[5] Virginia, meanwhile, did not budge. A proposed women's-property section was tabled in the closing days of Virginia's 1868 convention, and nothing further was done until the General Assembly took action in 1877.[6]

The Reconstruction period, in other words, was but one phase of an ongoing process of reform that had begun in Mississippi in 1839 and continued by fits and starts in the southern states (and in the North as well, beginning in the 1840s) well into the present century.[7] The reforms enacted by the Radicals, significant as they were for the southeastern states, continued an established southern tradition of legislation, a tradition of progressive expansion of the property rights of married women for utterly nonfeminist purposes.

Feminists, not ones to quibble over the motivation behind the passage of the reforms, continued to hail each new property law as a victory for the cause. "Alabama has given married women equal property rights with their husbands," Kentuckian Mary B. Clay told the 1884 convention of the American Woman Suffrage Association. "I . . . recommend to the Southern women particularly the petitioning for property rights, because pecuniary independence is one of the most potent weapons for freedom, and because that claim has less prejudice [than woman suffrage] to overcome."[8] Southern feminists knew that property rights were far more easily secured than political rights, and they hoped to use economic equality as a stepping-stone to the more elusive right to vote.

Their optimism was ill founded, however. Married-women's-property reforms stood a chance for the same reasons that woman suffrage did not—there was something in them for men, and they had nothing to do with feminism. While it was true that a sequence of laws in any given state made wives the legal equals or near equals of their husbands, this equality was a by-product and not the intended object of reform. Southern women were granted property rights by virtue of chivalry, of familial self-interest, and of hard times. And this was as much the case in the Reconstruction constitutional conventions, carpetbaggers notwithstanding, as with any previous time and place.

South Carolina's 1868 constitutional convention was a showcase for chivalry. James M. Allen was the delegate who introduced the resolution calling for a married-women's-property clause, and as the measure's most vigorous spokesman, Allen set the terms of the debate: "I appeal to you who have lived here all your lives, and seen women suffer from the hands of the fortune hunters; the plausible villains, who, after securing the property of their wives, have squandered it in gambling and drinking; a class of men who are still going about the country boasting that they intend to marry a plantation, and take the woman as an incumbrance." Benjamin F. Randolph echoed Allen: "It is a common thing for men to talk about marrying rich wives, and to marry them for no other purpose than to squander their property." In the brief debate next to nothing was said about women. The discussion was rather a recital of the failings of men, a sequence of testimonials on the necessity of a law to prevent the "profligate," the "drunkard," the "villain," the "scoundrel," from raking off the fortunes of innocent women.[9]

Under the law as it then stood scoundrels had their opportunities. South Carolina, like most of the United States, had adopted the English common law as its basis for the legal relationships between husband and wife.[10] For single women the common law held no special restrictions on property ownership and control; a *feme sole* had the same rights as men. For married women it was a very different story. In theory marriage was a fair exchange in which the woman relinquished her property and her autonomy and received in return protection and support from her husband. The wife at marriage surrendered the control of her real estate and the ownership of her personal property to her husband. The wife's services, and therefore her wages if she were gainfully employed, also belonged to the husband. Although the wife was empowered to act in her husband's stead under certain circumstances, she had no standing as an independent economic agent.

She could make no contracts, she could not sue or be sued in her own name, and she could not execute a valid will. For his part, the husband was obliged to pay his wife's premarital debts, and he was instructed to support her and their minor children according to his means. Otherwise, the common law licensed the husband to do as he pleased with his wife's property. The law assumed that the husband would exercise his prerogatives for the couple's mutual benefit, but no legal remedy was available to the wife whose husband abused his power. A woman's property was at the mercy of her husband, and if he fell into debt her property was at the mercy of her husband's creditors.[11]

There were loopholes. Alongside the common law there had grown a second legal system, that of equity, which offered some relief to the cautious and wealthy few. By means of either a marriage contract or the establishment by will or deed of an estate in trust the property of a married woman could be freed from the control of her husband and from the claims of his creditors. If the terms of the settlement were liberal, the woman, acting through trustees, assumed all the powers ordinarily associated with property ownership. These equitable estates, however, required foresight and legal expertise, their administration was often complicated and expensive, and there was no absolute guarantee that the woman's rights would be upheld if her title were challenged in court. The vast majority of married women possessed no separate equitable estates; the minority who did lacked perfect security. Equity remained an uncertain escape route for the well-to-do.[12]

Most married women, therefore, took their chances under the common law. In the worst of circumstances the woman was the helpless victim of her husband's malevolence, incompetence, or plain bad luck in business. In the best of circumstances, at least as far as the law was concerned, she was economically passive. For some women this passivity was in itself exasperating. South Carolinian Mary Boykin Chesnut protested in a diary entry of 1862, "We had our share of my father's estate. It came into our possession not long after we were married, and it was spent for debts already contracted. . . . That being the case, why feel like a beggar, utterly humiliated and degraded, when I am forced to say I need money? . . . What a proud woman suffers under all this, who can tell?"[13]

The delegates to the South Carolina constitutional convention of 1868 were not, however, troubled by wounded female pride. They posed a simple problem—it was too easy for conniving men to exploit vulnerable women—and they proposed a simple solution: Permit the wife to retain title to her property; exempt that property from liability for the debts of her husband; let her sell her property should she need ready cash to support herself and her children; and let her bequeath it as she should see fit. Neither the problem nor the solution was that simple, as became apparent later, but the new married-women's-property provision did offer women some protection from fortune hunters and other varieties of unreliable manhood.

It also protected the blood relations of the woman, and this was no small matter. As long as women's hold on property was insecure delegates faced the prospect of having their own accumulations wasted or sold off to satisfy the claims of creditors. As Allen put it, "We are ourselves poor men now, but should we succeed in saving a little property, and leaving it to our wives, it is not a comfortable thought that when we are dead, some villain may marry our widows, and squander what we have saved for the care and comfort of those we love." Charleston representative Robert Carlos DeLarge added, "We also propose to secure the hard earnings that may be bequeathed by a mother on her death bed to a child, so that it cannot be taken and squandered by the husband or father of the child."[14] Men wanted their property to remain in the family. The protection of widows and daughters and granddaughters increased the odds that legacies would pass intact from one generation to the next.

Few of the South Carolina delegates opposed so well intended a measure on principle, although there were some reservations on details. DeLarge was afraid that the married-women's provision as proposed left too much room for fraud. If some men were so unscrupulous as to marry women strictly for their money, some would no doubt be unashamed to use the new law to elude creditors. A debtor might make an eleventh-hour transfer of property to his wife in order to defraud his creditors of their just claims to that property. DeLarge suggested the loophole be closed by requiring women to register with the local officials all property that was legitimately their own. Once DeLarge and other doubters were persuaded that a registration system was unnecessary, the married-women's-property section was approved with only eight dissenting votes.[15]

Although there was nothing in the speeches of the South Carolinians to indicate it, it appears that the married-women's provisions of 1868 were as much a response to the critically widespread indebtedness of the postwar years as to the evil designs of fortune hunters. There was, after all, nothing new about fortune hunting or in the awareness that it was a problem. "The impression now seems to prevail to a very great extent in South Carolina," a state senator had told his colleagues in 1855, "that protection of the property of the wife is due her, because, forsooth, there is a class of fortune hunters over the country. . . . I have been rather inclined to the opinion that there is a good deal of this in our State."[16] The South Carolina legislature was not sufficiently moved, however, to pass the married-women's bill of 1855. What seems to have made the difference in 1868 was not that the Radicals were more tender-hearted than their predecessors (although they may have been) but rather that in hard times a married-women's-property act became a significant new form of debtor relief. It was no coincidence that the first southern laws to secure the property of married women were enacted, from Florida to Texas, during and in the wake of the panics of the late 1830s and the severe depression that followed.[17] In Georgia and North Carolina, and initially in South Carolina, the married-women's-property provisions of 1868 were packaged with homestead exemptions in articles designed to relieve distressed property owners of both sexes.[18]

Homestead exemptions and the married-women's laws were functionally similar, for both protected families from the economic disaster that might, in the absence of the laws, stem from a husband's indebtedness. While the married-women's laws exempted whatever property the wife brought to the marriage from liability for her husband's debts, homestead provisions protected part of the property belonging to the head of the household, male or female. No matter how deep his or her indebtedness, a portion of shelter, land, and implements, amounting to a stipulated maximum value, was set aside for the continued use of the family. A creditor could not touch it. The family's assets might be considerably reduced, but its members could not be thrown out of their home, and the head of the household would remain in possession of sufficient property to allow the making of at least a meager living.

In the postwar South unscrupulous husbands presented a lesser danger to the fortunes of women than did the general economic crisis that threatened women and men together. Under the common law, of course, the property of married women was particularly vulnerable, and convention speakers did not hesitate to use the peculiar plight of married women to arouse sympathy for general measures of debtor relief. No story had more potential for evoking compassion and an outraged sense of justice than that of the woman who was impoverished by virtue of debts that she herself had not contracted. William L. Goodwin worked the story for all it was worth in urging a stay law on the Georgia convention: Fatherless children were "turned houseless and homeless on the charities of this cold-hearted world, forced from a once happy fireside, to roam our country over in search of daily labor, that their few scanty earnings may yet render comfortable that poor old silvery-headed mother. . . . She now is reduced to abject poverty, suffering not only for the luxuries, but for the actual necessaries of life. All for what?" Goodwin demanded. "To satisfy liabilities not of her own contraction—liabilities in the hands of that class of men which now holds our unhappy people in its grasp."[19] Married women, at least those who were married to debtors, had everything to gain from any general law that protected the indebted.

At the same time, the general demand for debtor relief probably did much to promote the approval of laws specifically for the protection of the property of married women. A married-women's law shielded the husband while it shielded the wife; a man who was about to lose his own holdings could rest in the knowledge that in the future his wife's property would be secure. And if given retroactive force, the married-women's-property provisions could function in the manner of a stay law. The provisions as written were models of ambiguity. Did they apply to women who were already married? Did they apply to property acquired by the wife before the provisions took effect? If a court answered yes on both counts, then here was a major new form of emergency economic relief; any creditor who had relied on a woman's property to satisfy her husband's debts would be left in the lurch. It is not clear whether any of the conventions intended the provisions to be interpreted in this way.

The Georgia convention, in any case, lost no time. No sooner were the major debtor-relief measures approved—a section to abolish imprisonment for debt and one to suspend most debts contracted before June 1865 as well as the homestead–married-women's article—than they were hurried off to military gover-nor George Gordon Meade with an urgent request that they be given immediate effect by the general's order. Meade complied.[20] Georgia Republicans evidently believed the homestead-married-women's article to be one of the most popular they had devised. As the day approached for the election to ratify the new constitu-tion the front page of Atlanta's Republican *New Era* carried the text of the article, issue after issue. Political considerations, it appears, had their part in the bestowal of property rights on mar-ried women.

The only relevant question that was not considered was what the new property laws might mean for the status of women. The makers of the 1868 constitutions of Georgia and the Carolinas leaped to provide the kind of protection that suited the immediate crisis. They did not stipulate what women might do with their property once they gained title to it. Future courts and legislatures were left to sort out the implications of constitutional clauses that were designed not to free the woman but to restrain the husband's creditors.

Elsewhere in the South the Reconstruction constitutional con-ventions exhibited the same protective impulse. With the excep-tion of Virginia the remaining southern states had long since exempted the property of the wife from liability for the hus-band's debts, and the Reconstruction conventions sealed the case by elevating the earlier laws to constitutional status. In addition, three states built safeguards for women into their homestead-exemption clauses. Men in Alabama, Florida, and Texas were forbidden from selling their homesteads without the wife's con-sent.[21] None of the conventions outside South Carolina, North Carolina, and Georgia granted married women any new powers over their property.

Indeed, few traces of feminism were evident in any of the conventions. James M. Allen, the chief sponsor of the married-women's-property provision in South Carolina, was asked point-blank whether he was also in favor of woman suffrage. "I am not," Allen declared, adding with some irrelevance, "nor do I believe in that class of persons who carry poodle dogs, and follow in the trail of mere fashion."[22] Allen demonstrated in that single sentence how simple it was for a delegate to be for women's property rights and against women's political rights, and in this he stood with the majority of delegates across the South. The treatment accorded woman-suffrage proposals in the constitutional conventions showed just how far removed the advocacy of married-women's-property laws could be from any sympathies with feminism.

The Arkansas convention was already in progress when Radical delegate Miles L. Langley wrote Susan B. Anthony of his intention to propose a woman-suffrage amendment. For this, he announced, "I expect to suffer reproach and slander, if nothing worse." What Langley suffered, when his time came, was ridicule. Jesse N. Cypert greeted Langley's proposal with a tongue-in-cheek proviso that "no man who has a wife shall be allowed to vote when the right is exercised by his wife." Cypert explained, "I hold, sir, that I am a Union man; and that, not only so far as the government is concerned, but as regards the relations of families. I do not wish to assist in inaugurating any system that will be likely to give rise to secession in families." Robert S. Gantt then rose in support of Cypert's proviso: "There are, in all families, two articles, neither of which more than one member of the family ought to wear; the one is, the breeches; I will not mention the other. (Laughter)." Hilarity fast turned to acrimony as the issue of woman suffrage was lost amid accusations and counteraccusations of disloyalty and ungentlemanly behavior. The entire matter was eventually tabled, and the convention took up other business. Langley wrote again to Susan B. Anthony to report the disaster. "The Democrats are my enemies because I assisted in emancipating the slaves. The Republicans have now become my opponents, because I have made an effort to confer on the women their rights. And even the women themselves fail to sympathize with me."[23]

In South Carolina and Virginia woman-suffrage spokesmen took more expedient approaches, arming themselves against derision with brief and cautious statements of principle. When William J. Whipper moved to strike the word *male* from the suffrage section of South Carolina's new constitution, he made it clear that he expected no support from his colleagues: "However lightly the subject may be treated; however frivolous you may think it, I tell you here that I know the time will come when every man and woman in this country will have the right to vote." The South Carolina delegates did not make light of Whipper's motion. Neither did they discuss it. The amendment was voted down without debate and without a roll call. Several weeks earlier John Curtiss Underwood had introduced a universal-suffrage resolution in the Virginia convention. Underwood spoke for nearly two hours in favor of enfranchising black men and the clergy before tacking on a final paragraph recommending woman suffrage. "But such is the prejudice of our people," he hedged, "and so little are we yet advanced beyond that savage state of society which makes conscientious and heaven-inspired woman the drudge or toy of her stronger and coarser companion, that I despair at this time of securing so desirable a progress." Underwood's speech provoked a lengthy rebuttal, but his adversary did not bother to address the issue of woman suffrage. In South Carolina, Virginia, and Louisiana woman suffrage got the silent treatment.[24]

Texas was the one state where the constitutional convention gave woman suffrage a hearing. A five-man majority of the Committee on State Affairs "earnestly" recommended the passage of a clause that would eliminate sex as a qualification for voters. This, the majority argued, would not only fulfill the principle of government by consent of the governed, but it would also give due recognition to woman's piety, her superior education, and her historic patriotism. The two authors of the minority report, meanwhile, took the classic "anti" position that woman in her proper sphere already exerted "an influence mightier, far, than that of the elective franchise." The report continued: "We believe that the good sense of every true woman in the land teaches her that granting them the power to vote is a direct, open insult to their sex, by the complication [*sic*] that they are so unwomanly as to desire the privilege." When copies of both reports reached the desk of the *Revolution* in New York, Elizabeth Cady Stanton pounced on the minority's prose as well as their reasoning. "We should think the men who penned the above bungling sentences had strayed out of their sphere," she noted acidly. Stanton went on: "Dearly beloved Texans, give your women at least a choice of *insults,* and rest assured they would prefer all these that flow from political equality to those they now enjoy in disfranchisement." It was not until several months later that the Texas convention made its final choice of insults. In January 1869 the woman-suffrage amendment failed by a vote of thirteen to fifty-two.[25] Stanton probably took the loss philosophically. No northern state had yet enfranchised women, and there was little reason to expect better from the South. "Say what you will about the rights of the conqueror and the duties of the conquered," she had written in 1868, "the safe and short way to reconstruction is for the North to lead in establishing a genuine republic in all her own borders. We cannot force on the South a higher civilization than we have ourselves."[26]

The conventions that so willingly gave married women constitutional rights to property ownership thus gave little serious consideration and less sympathy to woman suffrage. There was no paradox in this. The delegates regarded married-women's-property reform as a matter of debtors' rights rather than women's rights; apparently, no one worried that the granting of property ownership to wives would trigger "secession in families." Once the conventions of Georgia, North Carolina, and South Carolina had completed their work, however, subsequent lawmakers were obliged to decide just how much the legal status of women would be altered. The constitutional clauses were ambiguous. It was by no means clear whether the woman's new title to property carried with it any of the powers ordinarily associated with property ownership. Could a married woman mortgage her property? Could she enter into a business partnership? Could she bind her property as security for a loan acquired by some other person? By the default of the constitutional conventions the legislatures and the courts were given enormous interpretive latitude. They could, if they chose, remove in one stroke every disability the common law had imposed on married women. On the other hand, they could settle for minor repairs of the common law, giving the married woman the protection guaranteed her by the constitutions but leaving her as passive as ever.

No single approach was entirely satisfactory. Assuming that some husbands were incompetent, absent, or downright malicious, the wife would need some powers of disposal over her property in order to hold house and home together. But if she were given unqualified powers—meaning risks as well as rights—the protective function of the law would be lost; the husband and his creditors could no longer appropriate the wife's property, but she would be subject to exploitation by anyone with whom she had business dealings. The wife would have nothing to protect her but her own business wits, which at the time were held in no very great esteem. There was a middle ground. The lawmakers could aim for the best of both worlds, granting women some powers and denying them others. This, too, could spell trouble, for the resulting confusion might befuddle creditors and hence retard the conduct of business.

The dilemmas were not new. Antebellum legislators in all three states had foreseen some of the complications, and this was in part responsible for their persistent refusal to pass the married-women's-property bills introduced in the 1840s and 1850s.[27] A Georgia newspaper, for example, endorsed the "ladies bill" of 1845 in principle but urged caution, "lest in attempting to remedy acknowledged evils, it should lead to others of still greater magnitude."[28] Legislators evidently regretted that the law as it stood made for perpetual open season on the property of married women, but they hesitated to trade the familiarity and the simplicity of the common law for the uncertainties of some new system. "But here you propose to take a little civil law and tack it upon the common law," objected a South Carolina state senator in 1855. "But when you have done it, you will find that the work does not fit at all."[29] After 1868 legislators and justices no longer had a choice; they had to make the work of the constitutional conventions fit as best they could. In each of the three states the results were different.

The most dramatic turnabout came in Georgia by virtue of an 1869 supreme court decision. Prior to the Civil War, Georgia law was common law with a vengeance. "In this state," the code read, "the husband is the head of the family, and the wife is subject to him." Georgia statutes were harsher than the common law, for the wife's real estate as well as her personal property was made the absolute possession of her husband. The process of legal reform began during Reconstruction, but it did not originate with the

Radicals. In 1866 the Georgia legislature enacted a terse protective statute that, like most initial married-women's-property acts, gave the wife title to her separate property, real and personal, and exempted that property from liability for the debts of the husband. When the Radicals wrote the new constitution two years later they added nothing to the 1866 law.[30] The 1868 constitutional provision was a condensed version of the act of 1866, and neither suggested that married women could do anything with their property other than possess it.

The state supreme court nonetheless granted sweeping new powers to women in the 1869 decision in *Huff v. Wright*. Defendant C. A. Wright argued that her property was not liable for a debt she had contracted in 1866; she had been married at the time and contended that the promissory note she had signed was consequently void. The court disagreed and took the opportunity to spell out the new law of married-women's property in Georgia. The constitutional provision of 1868 made of the husband and wife "two distinct persons, with separate and distinct rights. In a word," the court declared, "the common-law rule upon this subject no longer prevails in this state." The abrogation of the common-law doctrine meant an end to woman's enforced passivity. The woman who married after 1868 retained, in the language of the court, "power to purchase, hold and convey property, contract and be contracted with, sue and be sued, as a feme sole."[31]

The new law was not everything a champion of strictly equal rights might have desired. The wife was still, for example, restrained from binding her property solely for the benefit of another person. And while the wife could control her property, she was not made responsible for the support of her family. The entire legal burden of family support remained the husband's, a sign, perhaps, that Georgia lawmakers for better or worse trusted mothers to take care of their own. The most glaring inequality was on the ownership of the wife's wages, which remained the absolute property of the husband. It was a long time before the needs of working-class women would command the attention already given those of the propertied. Georgia wives were not granted legal control over their earnings until 1943.[32]

Georgia had nevertheless conferred major new powers on its

women and, relative to other states, conferred them in record time. Progress was far slower in North Carolina, where the full potential of the 1868 constitutional provision was not realized until 1911. In the interim the guidelines for married-women's-property ownership were laid down in an 1872 act of the legislature and a state supreme court ruling of 1876. The 1872 statute, enacted by a legislature that was no longer under Republican control, did permit married women to become free traders, otherwise called sole traders or free dealers. That is, a wife with her husband's consent (or without it, if she were deserted or divorced) could file for exemption from her common-law disabilities in order to carry on a trade or business on her own account. Otherwise, married women remained under the tutelage of their husbands, for no contract made by a wife was valid unless her husband joined in it.[33] In 1876 the court added further restrictions. A wife's contract was good only if it referred specifically to her separate estate and if it was of direct benefit to her separate estate. North Carolina law, the court explained, "by no means converts a married woman into a *femme sole* in respect to her separate property." Rather, the constitutional provision was a blanket substitute for the old system of estates in trust under equity and, like all equitable settlements, "must be construed . . . as conferring on married women no powers beyond those expressly given or implied."[34]

The North Carolina court was as cautious as the Georgia court had been bold, and the apparent consequence was that North Carolina women increasingly ignored the law. By 1905 the supreme court was finding the gap between law and practice intolerable. "Married women today are the owners of property, both real and personal, worth millions of dollars," wrote Associate Justice Henry Groves Connor. "They employ tenants and croppers and cultivate thousands of farms, engage in merchandise, conduct hotels, boarding houses and almost every kind of business suited and sometimes unsuited to their mental and physical capacity." Connor estimated that nine-tenths of women's contracts for all these enterprises were "not enforcible in the courts." The court had in recent years expanded married-women's powers but felt it was time the legislature clarified and settled the issue by giving married women full contractual powers. It was six years more before the legislature complied. Except for the unavoidable continuation of the constitutional requirement that the husband join the wife in the sale of her property the Martin Act of 1911 freed women from their common-law disabilities.[35]

While Georgia hurried and North Carolina lagged, South Carolina seesawed. For more than a decade the law was liberal indeed, and this time feminism had an impact. In the heady reform atmosphere of Radical rule, feminism found a ready reception after 1868. Louisa Rollin broke the traditional public silence of South Carolina women in 1869 when she spoke for woman suffrage to a packed house of state representatives and senators. By late 1870 William Whipper was no longer the sole committed advocate of women's rights among Radical politicians. In December of that year Louisa Rollin's sister Charlotte Rollin presided at Columbia's first women's-rights convention. Those present organized an interracial woman-suffrage association, and among the officers were several high-ranking Republican officials and their wives.[36] Woman suffrage had become not only a debatable issue but, in Radical circles, a respectable one.

The General Assembly, meantime, had been at work on an enabling law to define with precision the property rights granted married women in the 1868 constitution. The debate was lengthy, the "Woman's Rights Question" was at its center, and the resulting legislation was powerful evidence of the new feminist face of South Carolina radicalism. The 1870 statute confirmed the powers stipulated in the constitution—to bequeath and convey property—and added a host of others. A married woman was empowered to make purchases, enter into contracts, and execute "all deeds, mortgages, and legal instruments of whatever kind" with the same force as a single woman. The wife would be solely responsible for the payment of her debts, although those contracted for her "necessary support" could still be charged to the husband.[37] With the act of 1870 the South Carolina General Assembly abandoned the protective posture that had prevailed just two years before.

The full implications of the new law were made clear some years later in the state supreme court's 1881 ruling in *Pelzer v. Campbell*. A married woman, Mary M. Campbell, had signed several notes as surety for her son's enterprises "without any advantage to herself or her estate." When her son's creditors sued the Campbells for payment Mrs. Campbell's attorneys argued that her property was not liable, as a married woman had no legal capacity to make any contract that endangered her separate property. The court held to the contrary that a married woman had such capacity under the statute of 1870 and that Mary Campbell's property was accordingly liable for the debt. The justices recognized that this ruling might be detrimental to some unwise women but reasoned that "when they take the right to control their separate estates they assume the risks of such control. . . . At first hardships may, in isolated instances, ensue from the inexperience of women in matters of business, but such hardships always arise upon any change in the rules of property or business."[38]

The South Carolina General Assembly, by then in Conservative hands, evidently did not look kindly on the court's interpretation. In 1882 the assembly trimmed the law of 1870, specifying that a married woman had no general power to contract. The court was thereafter an accomplice in the return to protectionism. In 1886 the court ruled that a married woman could not mortgage her property unless the mortgage was intended to benefit her directly. The year after, married women were deprived of the right to enter into business partnerships, for a partnership, the opinion read, "involves an obligation to contribute one's time and services, which a married woman has no right to control, and a personal liability for debts which she has no power to incur." Thus far no legal body had determined whether a wife's earnings were part of her separate estate. True to its policy of strict construction, the court ruled in 1887 that they were not. Until the legislature gave wives express power over their wages, the court insisted, husbands would retain their common-law possession of their wives' earnings. The decision had not yet gone to the printer when the General Assembly responded with an act that put married women in firm control of their wages. That much accomplished, the assembly made one final protective move in 1891, confirming by statute what the court had already established. The 1891 law prohibited married women from assuming responsibility for the debts of any other person and completed the legislature's attempt to take the risks out of property ownership for married women.[39]

Such a law would have rescued Mary Campbell in 1881, but in the 1890s it only seemed to compound the confusion over the precise rights of married women. When delegates gathered for South Carolina's 1895 constitutional convention a married-women's-property resolution was among the first to be introduced. The resolution did not call for a revision of the law; it asked for clarification of the law.[40] The Charleston *News and Courier* reported one delegate's comments on "the now much tangled issue": "Mr. Sheppard said that the Acts of the Legislature tinkering with the laws relating to the property of married women had caused more litigation and expense to the people of the State than any other one thing. He then pointed out in detail the dreadful botches the Legislature had made until now a Philadelphia lawyer could not tell what the law in this State on the subject was."[41] One of the "botches" Sheppard no doubt listed was that it was often impossible to guess when a contract was signed whether it endangered the woman's estate. In these marginal instances no party to the contract was assured of its validity until it was litigated. By then, of course, it was too late.

It was this conviction that the law had become unintelligible that inspired a movement to simplify the whole matter by giving married women the same powers as men. Failing that, one delegate suggested, it would be better to reimpose all of women's common-law disabilities than to let their property remain in a legal twilight zone.[42] No one in the convention seriously proposed that the common law be restored, however. The choice was between the preservation of the clumsy protective structure that had been constructed during the previous thirteen years and the elimination of all restrictions on married-women's contracts. The decisive vote came on an amendment that would have maintained the exemption of a married woman's property from liability for the debts of other persons. The simplifiers prevailed over the protectionists, seventy-six to forty-two, and the convention went on to approve the provision that freed the property of married women once and for all. There would be no more strings on married-women's contracts, and as to her separate property, the wife would possess "all the rights . . . to which an unmarried woman or a man is entitled."[43]

The passage of the constitutional provision marked a return to the principles first articulated in the Radicals' statute of 1870. The 1895 delegates, however, were evidently not moved by any egalitarian theory. As a result of the simplification of the law married women were emancipated, but, more to the point, their assets were emancipated for investment in all kinds of enterprises, their husbands' included. Moreover, the property of married women was once again subjected to the same predictable rules of trade that governed men. South Carolina had experimented with protective legislation and found it more trouble than it was worth. The 1895 grant of equal property rights was less a vote of confidence in married women than it was a reaction against legislation that had clogged the courts and impeded the flow of capital.

The Radicals of Georgia, North Carolina, and South Carolina had left highly variable legacies when they gave the married women of their states constitutional rights to property ownership. In this, the three states behaved very much like other states, that is to say, according to no set pattern, once the initial bills to reduce women's common-law vulnerability were enacted. Mississippi, Alabama, and Texas, for example, all passed laws to protect the wife's property from husband and creditors by 1848; forty years later Mississippi, always ahead of the pack, abrogated women's common-law disabilities altogether, Alabama retained some, and Texas retained them all.[44] The hit-or-miss quality of married-women's-property reform was likewise visible in the performances of the Reconstruction legislatures of the younger southern states. There was progress in Mississippi, where wages were defined as part of the wife's separate estate in 1871, and Arkansas enlarged the powers of married women with a comprehensive new statute in 1873.[45] But Alabama resisted innovation. From 1865 to 1871 the Alabama legislature was flooded with petitions from married women who wished to be made free dealers. The legislature could have taken the petitions as a mandate for a law that empowered all women to make business transactions. Instead, the petitions were regarded as a waste of precious legislative time, and power to grant free-dealer privileges was transferred to the local courts.[46] Major statutory changes in the law of married-women's property in Alabama, Mississippi, Florida, Louisiana, and Texas awaited the 1880s and beyond.

At century's end married-women's-property law in the South—and in the rest of the country, for that matter—was an odd assortment of powers, obligations, and disabilities, with the laws of each state different in detail, and sometimes in essentials, from those of any other. There were apparent inconsistencies within states as well. South Carolina in 1895, for example, had the dual distinction of having the most conservative divorce law in the United States (divorces were made unconstitutional in 1895), while its married-women's-property law ranked among the most progressive.[47] As an index to southern attitudes toward women, the law is completely unreliable.

There was, however, a kind of logic behind the diversity of the laws and the variable timing of their passage. Whatever status lawmakers might, in theory, have wished on women, some other consideration was always present to confuse—or to decide—the issue. All the initial married-women's-property acts were intended to insulate the wife from economic exploitation, but protection exacted its costs. For one thing, protective legislation often entailed a shift in the legal concept of marriage. The idealistic common-law assumption of a community of interests under the control of a benevolent husband was replaced by a rather cynical vision of masculine irresponsibility that made the interests of husband and wife separate and mutually antagonistic. This was clearest in the laws that prevented the wife from underwriting her husband's business ventures. Protection also required the maintenance of a legal system (or as the South Carolina case suggests, lack of system) that was more complicated and less certain than either the common law or the abrogation of the common law. And the more complex the law, the more inhibitions were placed on the mobilization of goods and services. The alternative, of course, was to abandon legal protection and let women fend for themselves.

Any significant change in the law of married-women's property thus amounted to a choice among evils, or among benefits, in the eyes of lawmakers. That being the case, it was no doubt possible for a small group of legislators with conviction to sway a much larger group of their ambivalent colleagues. The legal status of southern women hinged on the decisions of lawmakers for whom the status of women per se was rarely the paramount concern. The results, during Reconstruction and throughout the century, were correspondingly erratic.

Notes

1. *Revolution* 6 (July 7, 1870): 10.

2. The other major constitutional provision pertaining to the status of women was South Carolina's first legal provision for divorce. The legislature passed the divorce law in 1872. That law was repealed by the Redeemers in 1878, and divorces were made unconstitutional in 1895. Divorce was not again legalized in South Carolina until 1948. See John R. Millar, Jr., A Study of the Changes of Divorce Legislation in the State of South Carolina" (Ph.D. diss., Florida State University, 1954).

3. Allen, *Reconstruction: The Battle for Democracy (1865–1876)* (New York, 1937), 118–19; Stampp, *The Era of Reconstruction, 1865–1877* (New York, 1965), 172–73; Scroggs, "Carpetbagger Constitutional Reform in the South Atlantic States, 1867–1868," *Journal of Southern History* 27 (November 1961): 484–85. See also Robert Cruden, *The Negro in Reconstruction* (Englewood Cliffs, N.J., 1969), 99, 108; Rembert W. Patrick, *The Reconstruction of the Nation* (New York and London, 1967), 148.

4. *Montgomery Daily Advertiser,* December 13, 1867. The *Advertiser* was extremely hostile to the convention, however, and this statement should probably be read as "nothing inviting ridicule" or "something deserving of praise."

5. The exceptions are noted below.

6. Virginia, *Debates and Proceedings of the Constitutional Convention . . . 1867* (Richmond, 1868), 58–59, 554–55; *Richmond Dispatch,* April 14, 1868; Virginia, *Acts and Joint Resolutions . . . 1877–78* (Richmond, 1878), 333–34.

7. On the possible origins of the Mississippi law see Elizabeth G. Brown, "Husband and Wife—Memorandum on the Mississippi Woman's Law of 1839," *Michigan Law Review* 42 (June 1944): 1110–1121. Historical treatments of married-women's-property law are few. The best is Kay E. Thurman, "The Married Women's Property Acts" (LL.M. thesis, University of Wisconsin School of Law, 1966). See also Mary R. Beard, *Woman as Force in History: A Study in Traditions and Realities* (New York, 1946); John D. Johnston, Jr., "Sex and Property: The Common Law Tradition, the Law School Curriculum, and Developments Toward Equality," *New York University Law Review* 47 (December 1972): 1033–1092; Peggy Rabkin, "The Origins of Law Reform: The Social Significance of the Nineteenth-Century Codification Movement and Its Contribution to the Passage of the Early Married Women's Property Acts," *Buffalo Law Review* 24 (Spring 1975): 683–760.

8. Quoted in Elizabeth C. Stanton et al., eds., *History of Woman Suffrage* (6 vols., New York and Rochester, 1881–1922), 4:407–8. Alabama women, however, did not have equal property rights at that time.

9. South Carolina, *Proceedings of the Constitutional Convention of South Carolina . . . 1868* (2 vols. in 1, Charleston, 1868), 1:64–65; 2:783–88; quotations on pp. 785–86.

10. Texas, however, retained a few features of the Spanish civil law. Louisiana law, an adaptation of the Napoleonic Code, was entirely outside the common-law tradition. To reduce a very complex set of laws to a simple statement, in Louisiana the property inherited alone by either spouse remained her or his separate property, but any other property acquired during the marriage belonged to the community. The management of both the community property and the wife's property was assumed to be the husband's, although the wife could bring action to empower her to manage her separate estate. Louisiana law was known for the relative economic security it provided the wife. The 1868 constitutional provision outlawed the use of the "tacit mortgage," a loophole that had permitted the husband to evade creditors by claiming a prior, unrecorded debt to the wife. See Harriet S. Daggett, *The Community Property System of Louisiana, with Comparative Studies* (Baton Rouge, 1931).

11. For a detailed treatise on the legal status of women in the nineteenth century see Joel P. Bishop, *Commentaries on the Law of Married Women Under the Statutes of the Several States, and at Common Law and in Equity* (2 vols., Boston, 1873–1875).

12. Mary Ritter Beard in *Woman as Force*, 131–33, asserted that equity effectively mitigated the harshness of common-law doctrine and that statutory reform in the law of married women's property was therefore virtually unnecessary. More research is needed, but the current work of Carol Elizabeth Jenson of the University of Wisconsin–La Crosse, "Equity Jurisdiction and Married Women's Property: The Situation in Ante-Bellum America" (paper presented at the Conference on the History of Women, St. Paul, Minnesota, October 1975), suggests that Beard gave equity far too much credit. My own survey of Virginia wills and deeds indicates that equitable settlements were extremely rare before 1820. Thereafter, settlements were more commonplace, but they usually did not give the wife active control over her estate. Thurman, "Married Women's Property Acts," 12, suggests that the early statutory reforms were prompted in part by a Jacksonian desire to give poorer women the same kind of protection that had been available to wealthier women through equity. I have seen no direct evidence of this for the southern

states, but British reformers frequently pointed out the class bias of equity. See for example "The Property of Married Women," *Westminster Review* 90 (October 1868): 179–80. For a discussion of connections between the merger of common law and equity and married-women's-property reform in New York see Rabkin, "Origins of Law Reform."

13. Chesnut, *A Diary from Dixie,* ed. Ben Ames Williams (Boston, 1949), 186.

14. South Carolina, *Proceedings of the Constitutional Convention . . . 1868,* 2:786, 784.

15. *Ibid.,* 783–88. The new provision read: "The real and personal property of a woman, held at the time of her marriage, or that which she may thereafter acquire, either by gift, grant, inheritance, devise, or otherwise, shall not be subject to levy and sale for her husband's debts; but shall be held as her separate property, and may be bequeathed, devised, or alienated by her the same as if she were unmarried: *Provided,* That no gift or grant from the husband to the wife shall be detrimental to the just claims of his creditors." South Carolina, Constitution of 1868, art. 14, sec. 8, Francis N. Thorpe, comp., *The Federal and State Constitutions, Charters, and Other Organic Laws . . .* (7 vols., Washington, 1909), 6:3304; cited hereinafter as Thorpe, comp., *Constitutions.* Clyde and Sally Griffen have found evidence that husbands did at times use married-women's-property laws to defraud creditors. See their "Family and Business in a Small City: Poughkeepsie, New York, 1850–1880," *Journal of Urban History* 1 (May 1975): 328–30.

16. *Columbia, South Carolina, Legislative Times,* December 7, 1855.

17. Act of February 15, 1839, Mississippi, *Laws of the State of Mississippi . . . 1839* (Jackson, 1839), 72–73; Texas, Constitution of 1845, art. 7, sec. 19, Thorpe, comp., *Constitutions,* 6:3561; Act of March 6, 1845, Florida, *The Acts and Resolutions, Passed by the Legislative Council . . . 1845* (Tallahassee, 1845), 24–25; Act of December 8, 1846, Arkansas, *Acts and Resolutions . . . of the General Assembly . . . One Thousand Eight Hundred and Forty-Six* (Little Rock, 1846), 38–39; Act of March 1, 1848, Alabama, *Acts . . . of the General Assembly . . . 1847* (Montgomery, 1848), 79.

18. Georgia, *Journal of the . . . Constitutional Convention . . . 1867 and . . . 1868* (Augusta, 1868), 356–57; Georgia, Constitution of 1868, art. 7, Thorpe, comp., *Constitutions,* 2:838; North Carolina, *Journal of the Constitutional Convention . . . 1868* (Raleigh, 1868), 219–20, 249–50; North Carolina, Constitution of 1868, art. 10, Thorpe, comp., *Constitutions,* 5:2818–2819; South Carolina, *Proceedings of the Constitutional Con-*

vention . . . 1868, 1:64–65. In South Carolina the married-women's section was separated from the homestead-exemption clauses in committee.

19. *Charleston [S. C.] Daily Courier,* February 11, 1868.

20. Georgia, *Journal of the . . . Constitutional Convention,* 392–406, 603–5.

21. Alabama Constitution of 1868, art. 14, sec. 2, Thorpe, comp., *Constitutions,* 1:152; Florida, Constitution of 1868, art. 10, sec. 1, *ibid.,* 2:717; Texas, Constitution of 1868, art. 12, sec. 15, *ibid.,* 6:3613.

22. South Carolina, *Proceedings of the Constitutional Convention . . . 1868,* 2:785.

23. *Revolution* 1 (February 12, 1868): 84 (first quotation); Arkansas, *Debates and Proceedings of the Convention . . . 1868* (Little Rock, 1868), 701–24 (second quotation on p. 708, third quotation on p. 710); Stanton et al., eds., *History of Woman Suffrage* 3:806 (last quotation). Cypert and Gantt, it should be noted, were Conservatives, but Langley received no help from members of his own party.

24. South Carolina, *Proceedings of the Constitutional Convention . . . 1868,* 2:836–38 (quotation on p. 838); Virginia, *Debates and Proceedings of the Constitutional Convention,* 458–68 (quotation on p. 467); Louisiana, *Official Journal of the . . . Convention for Framing a Constitution . . . 1868* (New Orleans, 1868), 224.

25. Texas, *Journal of the Reconstruction Convention . . .* (2 vols., Austin, 1870), 1:245–46, 577–80 (first quotation on p. 579, second and third on p. 580); 2:413–14; *Revolution* 2 (September 3, 1868): 137–38 (last quotation).

26. *Revolution* 1 (May 14, 1868): 294.

27. The failure of the southeastern states to act at this time might also be attributed to the lesser severity of the depression or to the greater effectiveness of equity in the Southeast. Daniel J. Flanigan has noted a parallel east-west split on criminal procedure for slaves; see his "Criminal Procedure in Slave Trials in the Antebellum South," *Journal of Southern History* 40 (November 1974): 510 ff.

28. *Milledgeville Federal Union,* November 25, 1845.

29. *Columbia, South Carolina, Legislative Times,* December 8, 1855.

30. Georgia, *The Code of the State of Georgia* (Atlanta, 1861), secs. 1700, 1701, 1702. For a more detailed treatment of the legal status of Georgia women see Eleanor M. Boatwright, "The Political and Civil Status of Women in Georgia, 1783–1850," *Georgia Historical Quarterly* 25 (December 1941): 301–24.

31. *Huff v. Wright,* 39 Ga. 41 (1869), at 43.

32. Walter McElreath, *A Treatise on the Constitution of Georgia* (Atlanta, 1912), 166–68; Georgia, *Code of Georgia Annotated* (Atlanta, 1961), sec. 53–512.

33. North Carolina, *Public Laws . . . 1871–72* (Raleigh, 1872), 334–36.

34. *Pippen v. Wesson,* 74 N.C. 437 (1876), at 442–43, 445.

35. *Ball v. Paquin,* 140 N.C. 83 (1905), at 90; North Carolina, *Consolidated Statutes . . . 1919* (2 vols., Raleigh, 1919), sec. 2507; see also Guion G. Johnson, *Ante-Bellum North Carolina: A Social History* (Chapel Hill, 1937), 238–45.

36. *Charleston Daily Courier,* February 3, March 4, 1869; Stanton et al., eds., *History of Woman Suffrage* 3:828; Joel Williamson, *After Slavery: The Negro in South Carolina During Reconstruction, 1861–1877* (Chapel Hill, 1965), 338. The sources differ on whether it was Louisa Rollin or her sister Charlotte who addressed the legislature in 1869. The Rollin sisters, prominent in Charleston's free black society, were among Claude G. Bowers's favorite subjects, for an important part of the "tragic legend of Reconstruction" that Bowers did so much to popularize was, in his words, "the unprecedented prominence of women." A laudable insight, this, were it not for his leering approach. "Never," Bowers wrote, "had women lobbyists used their sex in securing legislative favors for selfish groups so brazenly—or so cleverly." *The Tragic Era: The Revolution After Lincoln* (Cambridge, Mass., 1929), vi.

37. *Charleston Daily Courier,* December 9, 1869; South Carolina, *Acts and Joint Resolutions of the General Assembly . . . 1869–70* (Columbia, 1870), pt. 1, 325–26.

38. *Pelzer v. Campbell,* 15 S.C. 581 (1881), at 582.

39. *Aultman v. Rush,* 26 S.C. 517 (1887); *Gwynn v. Gwynn,* 27 S.C. 525 (1887), at 526; *Bridgers v. Howell,* 27 S.C. 425 (1887); South Carolina, *The Revised Statutes of South Carolina* (2 vols., Columbia, 1894), secs. 2165, 2167.

40. South Carolina, *Journal of the Constitutional Convention of the State of South Carolina . . . Eighteen Hundred and Ninety-five . . .* (Columbia, 1895), 36.

41. *Charleston News and Courier,* October 1, 1895.

42. *Ibid.*

43. South Carolina, *Journal of the Constitutional Convention* (1895), 147–48, 251–52, 287–89.

44. Mississippi, *The Revised Code . . . 1880* (Jackson, 1880), sec. 1167.

The Mississippi constitution of 1890, art. 4, sec. 94, however, reserved the right of the legislature to regulate contracts between husband and wife. Thorpe, comp., *Constitutions,* 4:2100.

45. Mississippi, *The Revised Code . . . 1871* (Jackson, 1871), sec. 1778; Arkansas, *Acts of the General Assembly . . . 1873* (Little Rock, 1873), 382–85. The Arkansas law did not empower the wife to contract generally, but it did give her power to insure her husband's life for her benefit, to maintain her own savings account, to carry on a trade or business, to make transactions regarding her separate estate (provided a list of her property was duly registered), and to carry on litigation in her own name. The motives behind the passage of the act of 1873 are not discernible. It is clear, however, that the bill was not a party measure. In the Senate, where the bill originated, the Republicans split, ten in favor and eight against. The House approved the bill without debate in the closing hours of the session. Here party lines were more evident; the Republicans voted for the bill, thirty-three to five, the Democrats against, six to twelve. *Little Rock Daily Arkansas Gazette,* April 1, 25, 1873; Arkansas, "Journal of the House of Representatives, State of Arkansas, Session of 1873" (manuscript, 3 vols.), vol. 3, April 24, 1873.

46. At least twenty women were made free dealers by the legislature in the 1865–1866 session, thirty-eight in 1868, forty-one in 1869–1870, and eighty-four in 1870–1871. The 1868 free-dealer law eliminated the antebellum requirement that the husband be shown to be incompetent. The 1868 law required the husband's consent, and subsequent revisions prescribed remedies in cases in which the husband refused consent or the chancery court denied the woman's petition. Alabama, *Acts . . . of the General Assembly . . . 1845* (Tuscaloosa, 1846), 23; *ibid., 1868* (Montgomery, 1868), 546–47; *ibid., 1872–73* (Montgomery, 1873), 93–94; *ibid., 1874–75* (Montgomery, 1875), 194–95.

47. Given the belief that permitting divorce was a cause of marital conflict, there was a kind of consistency here; the outlawing of divorce and the emancipation of married-women's property both put the law on the side of cooperative marriages. On divorce in South Carolina see n. 2 above.

Bloody Terrain

FREEDWOMEN, SEXUALITY, AND

VIOLENCE DURING RECONSTRUCTION

CATHERINE CLINTON

Catherine Clinton is currently an associate of the W. E. B. DuBois Institute at Harvard University. Her first book, The Plantation Mistress: Woman's World in the Old South *(1982), was followed by* The Other Civil War: American Women in the Nineteenth Century *(1984). She is coeditor of two anthologies,* Portraits of American Women *(1991) and* Divided Houses: Gender and the Civil War *(1992). Her next volume,* Tara Revisited: Women, War and the Plantation Legend *(1995), includes over a hundred illustrations and traces the lives and images of black and white women in the nineteenth-century South.*

Her essay began as a paper delivered at the Organization of American Historians in 1987 and grew out of her ongoing work on southern women during the Civil War and Reconstruction. It first appeared in a special issue of the Georgia Historical Quarterly *(Summer 1992).*

We continue to unravel layers of evidence surrounding the cataclysmic episode in our past known as Reconstruction. It appears that after Appomattox the conquered Confederacy did not so much surrender as it refought old, familiar battles on the homefront. Conflict reconfigured: from the South's streets to its statehouses, in kitchens and courtrooms, terrain remained contested. Although Reconstruction has spawned a vital and prize-winning historical literature, many aspects of the era remain unexplored. And the African-American women of this and other generations remain buried beneath historians' disclaimers about sources and neglect, but buried nonetheless.[1]

Memoirs from this period *are* sparse. We have some black autobiographies, but most narratives by women are from the antebellum era or deal with the period following Reconstruction. Some manuscript material in southern archives offers evidence, but these traditional sources have severe limitations as most are written by whites and tell us more about white views than black lives. More valuable and indeed more exciting are the records of the Freedmen's Bureau. Three published volumes of edited documents offer scholars considerable insight into the power and possibilities afforded by this rich primary material.[2] Further, black newspapers are crammed with unexploited material. In Georgia alone, Augusta's *Colored American* and *Loyal Georgian,* and Atlanta's *Weekly Defiance* yield important insights into the struggles of this dynamic era, and women's rôles in them.[3]

The testimony of former slaves provides us with poignant images and, indeed, perhaps casts new light on the central dramas of this "dark and bloody" ground, as the era has been characterized. The suffering and violence experienced during this exceptionally savage era of racial realignment cannot be underestimated. George Wright and others have cautioned that the underreporting of both lynchings and murders, as well as beatings and threats, was notorious.[4] The problem is not to compare the violence against men to that against women in order to weigh in winners and losers, but rather to assess the scope of this violence and its role in the larger politics of Reconstruction.

African Americans had an enormous, sprawling agenda in the months and years following emancipation. Their concerns were titanic; and certainly political equality and economic justice headed the list. But it is equally clear that the integrity of the family and the protection of black women were top priorities for the leaders of the black community as well as the emancipated people at large. It is just as clear, if we confront the evidence which may sicken but nevertheless informs us, that white supremacists continued the exploitation of black women, clinging to the sexual tactics rampant during slavery as a means of maintaining racial control. The laws may have changed, but habits died hard.[5]

Before the war, Georgia, like other southern states, segregated its statutes into laws for whites and blacks, free and slave.[6] This triple-tiered system (with free blacks suffering partial but nevertheless significant legal disabilities) was explicit in matters of rape, a sex crime with which the white South was preoccupied. From 1770 on, Georgia law provided for capital punishment of those "slave, free negro, Indian, mulatto or mustizoe" defendants found guilty of rape or attempted rape of a white—while the death penalty was rarely applied to whites convicted of identical crimes.[7] An enslaved woman was classed as property by Georgia statute and could not charge rape under the law.[8] In 1861 the Georgia Code was amended: "Rape is the carnal knowledge of a female, whether free or slave, forcibly against her will." Despite this newly egalitarian definition of the crime, the punishment did not yield to this spirit of fairness: conviction for rape of free white females merited two to twenty years' imprisonment while "if committed upon a slave, or free person of color," the fine and imprisonment was left to "the discretion of the court."[9]

While statutory differential based on race diminished after the Civil War, extralegal means perpetuated the system of racial injustice. Postbellum appellate court opinions concerning rape in Georgia reveal forty-seven cases presented between 1865 and 1900, in virtually all of which the victims were white. In only nine cases were those convicted on rape charges black—six for attempted rapes and three for completed rapes, including an attack upon a prostitute. In only two cases were guilty verdicts overturned: a thirteen-year-old boy found guilty of rape was granted a new trial, and the court reversed a lower court conviction of a man with no evidence of attempted rape, holding him over for trial on robbery charges instead. Fitzhugh Brundage has noted that in Georgia, between 1880 and 1930, sixty-three victims of mob violence (lynched men) were accused of rape: sixty African Americans and three whites.[10] Although these numbers provide only partial and inconclusive statistical evidence, they nonetheless push us toward the logical conclusion that black men suspected of rape were given no day in court, but turned over to the mob. And what of black women during this period? Are we to assume that African-American women were spared the indignities which plagued their white southern sisters? The records of the Freedmen's Bureau indicate otherwise. Several annual state reports included a category of "Murders and Outrages" that chronologically cataloged rapes.

In the fall of 1868, sex crimes and murders appeared frequently in Louisiana records: Pamala Casillo accused Macrae of attempted rape and although he was arrested, authorities allowed him to escape from St. Martin's Parish.[11] In Franklin, a party of white men attacked a freedwoman and whipped her. The agent reported that "the negroes have not reported to the Bureau, as they fear to be seen about the Bureau office."[12] In Lafourche Parish, the daughter of James Heart was sexually assaulted by Collyer, a plantation overseer. Although the case was referred to a local judge, no action was taken.[13] In De Soto, Mariah Ramkly was brutally beaten by Frank Bell but no action was taken, leading bureau agent Michael Cary to complain, "Justice cannot be obtained in civil courts."[14] On August 30, in Winn County, a "colored girl" was raped by Victor Thompson. When Justice Curry issued a warrant, the accused was not arrested, as he was hiding in the woods, complained agent D. W. White.[15] By October over one hundred freedmen had been killed in Louisiana and the life of an agent in Bossier County threatened. On Halloween in Claiborne Parish, agent William Stokes grimly reported that nine or ten men armed and disguised had "ravished and severely beaten" a freedwoman. Stokes commented, "The freedpeople will not divulge anything for fear of death."[16] And so the patterns of racial violence and reprisals, echoes from the days of slavery, continued after emancipation.

Black leaders railed against these conditions and defiantly confronted the issue in speeches and editorials. The Rev. Henry McNeal Turner's oration celebrating the first anniversary of black freedom on January 5, 1866—published in local black papers across the South—included the following remarks: "Formerly there was no security for domestic happiness. Our ladies were insulted and degraded with or without their consent. Our wives were sold and husbands bought, children were begotten and enslaved by their fathers, we therefore were polygamists by virtue of our condition. But now we can marry and raise our children and teach them to fear God, O! black age of dissipation, thy days are nearly numbered."[17] Turner's optimism was premature, serving more as a rhetorical device to challenge white smears. He boldly asserted:

It was also said, and Southern fanatics rode that hobby everywhere, "That if you free the negro he will want to marry our daughters and sisters," that was another foolish dream. What do we want with their daughters and sisters? We have as much beauty as they. Look at our ladies, do you want more beauty than that? *All we ask of the white man is to let our ladies alone,* and they need not fear us. The difficulty has heretofore been, *our ladies were not always at our own disposal.*[18]

Freedpeople clearly understood the hypocrisy of sexual and racial relations in the wake of emancipation. Nearly twenty years later, little had changed. Some African Americans directly confronted these charges against black women. A letter from "Old Pelican," published in Atlanta's *Weekly Defiance,* countered the libel that "colored women are not moral and virtuous" by claiming that nine out of ten white/black liaisons are rape, and "there is no place of redress."[19] When a black man was charged with the rape of a white woman and sentenced to twenty years in prison, a Louisville paper complained: "Had the color of the parties been changed Rucker would now be a free man, such is justice in Kentucky."[20]

White observers condemned husbands who considered wife-beating a "right" and resisted bureau intervention. Ex-slaves reported that before emancipation masters prohibited slave men from striking their wives—and agents revealed that they assumed this paternalistic role after abolition. However, this is a much more complex dynamic when we consider that the very same masters who may have "protected" slave wives from being struck by their husbands might also have considered it *their own* right to strike the woman—to exert control and preserve authority on the plantation—a right they wished to maintain as employers.

Most freedwomen resisted bringing agents into domestic matters.[21] They recognized the limited role the bureau could play in their lives and the temporary nature of federal force. Indeed, former slaves more than Union troops probably sensed how short-lived this experiment of northern involvement would be. Reliance on bureau agents, allied by color with former masters, was dangerous for blacks in the short term and might result in long-term retaliation. The long arm of paternalism—clothed in blue uniform or tattered grey—was grasped only in utter desperation.

Women without alternatives sought assistance when frantic or destitute. In January 1867, a Madison, Georgia, petitioner asked the bureau to help a family with a "43 year old mother raising her six children (from 2 to 12 yrs. old) and keeping her sixty-five year old blind mother."[22] Equally common was the complaint of women run off the land just before getting paid. Some women complained about their husbands who left them in times of economic crises—but not to force apprehension or punishment, merely to justify their claims for assistance.[23]

Mothers were most severely affected by emancipation's adversities, as Jacqueline Jones has so eloquently demonstrated.[24] First and foremost, the care and feeding of children were responsibilities shouldered by women with few and rapidly depleting resources. A bureau agent reported from King Williams County, Virginia, that "there is little call for female help, and women with children are not desired."[25] This comment does not begin to convey the dimensions of this crisis. Among the thousands of freedpeople negotiating contracts and selling their labor, women with children were discriminated against and often "blackballed" by employers.

Mothers had few alternatives and little recourse. When Cornelia Whitley and her sick child were thrown out of the house of her employer, Allen Dickenson of Orange County, Virginia, in September 1865, she complained to the bureau. An agent reported that Mrs. Dickensen then assaulted Whitley for going to the agency for help.[26] Women were trapped and in some cases rendered senseless by the ordeal of survival.

A tragic tale from the records reveals the depths of one woman's despair. In October 1868, Polly Jennings of Halifax County, Virginia, was sentenced to hang for infanticide. The previous fall, her employer, a Mr. Jennings, had told her not to have any more children as she was unmarried and already supported five offspring. He threatened to dismiss her if she bore another child— pushing Polly and her children even further along poverty's downward spiral. She found herself pregnant again, and murdered her newborn in May, leaving it in the woods. A bureau officer attempted to get her death sentence for that crime commuted to life imprisonment. Polly Jennings' sacrifice of one child for the welfare of the five older ones was dramatic and unusual, but the fact that women were confronted with life and death issues on a daily basis was not.[27]

Whites often used children as weapons—to keep all workers, especially mothers, docile and submissive. A bureau agent reported in January 1866 that two freedwomen were bullied into signing a contract: the bonding of their children and possible separation were threatened if they failed to cooperate.[28] Scores of these accounts appeared annually in bureau records. And once women secured their children they would next have to figure out how to feed and educate them during times of decline and hardship.

We know that southern whites were unwilling to expand their prewar definitions of "manhood" and "womanhood" to include formerly enslaved persons. Although postwar law might recognize an African American woman as a person and a wife, and a black man as a citizen and a voter, Lost Cause ideologues promoted white supremacy with a vengeance. Emancipation and federal conquest created unprecedented levels of anxiety that spurred former Confederates into refighting the war on ideological grounds.

Within this new contest, gender and sexual roles were rewrought in a complex tangle of conflict and compromise. Certainly white supremacists intended to reassert their dominance by playing on antebellum themes—the "Sambo" incompetence of the black male and the "promiscuity" of black women. Both of these racist stereotypes were woven from white fears—that the black man might exact revenge against his oppressor for generations of inhumanity; and second, that the growing segment of the black population labelled "mulatto" might not be a result of slave women's licentiousness, but rather of white sexual coercion. Simultaneously, ex-Confederates, especially veterans, concocted new and important projections of their own fears—none more complex and potent than the "black rapist." Equally powerful within the ideological warfare was the defeminizing mythology launched at black womanhood during this era. Certainly Angela Davis, bell hooks, Deborah White, and Patricia Morton have made important inroads into this historical field embedded with landmines.[29]

Emancipation created few opportunities for African American women in the political economy beyond freedom. Women nevertheless seized the opportunity to express themselves, pioneering new avenues for individual and collective identity. In October 1866, Patience Thompson stated her case against a white man, Thomas Gross of Irwin County, Georgia. When she refused to sell him soap, Gross became verbally abusive and she replied in kind. He responded by beating her. When the case went to the grand jury, it refused to support her for fear of establishing a precedent of support for "every Negro who choose[s] to come before them." Thompson was forced to pay court costs and requested to "make up with Gross." She paid her fine but would not "make up" as the court had ordered.[30] Thompson was a strong example of this new model of freedwoman.

In July 1868, four black women in Prince Edwards County, Virginia, were in their own house singing when John Schofield, a white man, asked them to stop. When they refused he entered the house and beat them with his fists, then took out a knife and cut one of the women on the hand. Subsequently, Schofield was tried and fined, but "let go without reproof or caution from *Court*."[31] In Clinch County, Georgia, Viney Scarlett was arrested and given sixty-five lashes for verbally abusing a white woman.[32] Both the character and tone of black women's challenges shifted during Reconstruction, and were met with mighty resistance from white individuals and their legal system.

Black women, fighting against the labels attached to them by former slaveowners, not only challenged these stereotypes directly but some also retaliated violently against whites. One tragic outcome is revealed in the 1866 records of Culpepper County, Virginia, where Jane Twyman, working for Isaiah Perry and his son George, accused Perry's wife and daughter of sleeping with other men. Twyman made her accusations in front of other servants. Alerted, Isaiah Perry grabbed his gun and confronted the woman and then shot at her. After Twyman was wounded, Perry apologized—saying he did not mean to shoot her, only to frighten her. Twyman said she believed him in the presence of witnesses, and the two were reconciled. But while Twyman was having the bullet removed, Perry's son, in a drunken rage, pistol-whipped the wounded woman and "stomped" all over her. The case was reported, though not prosecuted, and ended when Isaiah Perry suddenly died, Jane Twyman died of her injuries, and two other witnesses to these attacks disappeared or died before George Perry could be brought to trial.[33]

It is difficult to fathom the fear created by a black woman fighting back—a force so strong that, in this particular case, it caused one white man to shoot at her and another to beat her to death. Such vocal and direct black female resistance, combined with the fear of male retaliation, fueled white hysteria during the postwar era.

The mechanism by which the nation was in physical reality linked by the end of the nineteenth century—the railroad—ironically supplied the means by which the country came to be divided ideologically: the railway coach.[34] An 1866 article in the *Loyal Georgian* asked: "Why is it that the wives and daughters of freedmen, though they be chaste as ice, and pay the same fare that white people do on railways, are put into filthy freight cars and compelled to submit to all kinds of vulgar and insulting language?"[35] Many distorted interpretations of this and other evidence have led some scholars to suppose that blacks were preoccupied with purity as a means of emulating white paragons. Perhaps models of white womanhood were cherished—but most likely to protect black women from errant white males whose techniques ranged from teasing to threats to gang rape. The status of "lady" was a plea for gentlemanly behavior from white males who had corrupted the status of slave women and intended to perpetuate this degradation past emancipation.

Few were able to challenge the hypocrisy of the sexual double standard explicitly, but African American women openly demanded the same protection and privilege afforded white women by law. Increasingly newspapers carried reports of exchanges where black women chided authorities for referring to them as "colored females," not because of the racial classification, but because they wished to be referred to as ladies. African Americans were forced to tackle the barriers imposed by labels and language, as well as physical impediments. In 1868, three "colored females" brought a case before the U.S. District Court because they were "put out of [the] ladies car" at Gordonsville, Virginia, by the railroad "on account of color."[36] Ida Wells-Barnett, only twenty-two, had her dress torn when ejected from the ladies' car and pushed off a train in Tennessee in 1884. Humiliated but not humbled, she struck back through the courts and was awarded $500 in damages (although a higher court reversed the verdict). This formative experience launched her on a career of reform and protest.[37]

Whites campaigned vigorously to insure that the image of black women remained tarnished after slavery. Southern white newspapers chronicled crime and ignorance among freedpeople, featuring any violence and depravity detected among African American women. This libel and certainly slander created a constant war of words and images. Both as assailants and assailed, black women were stereotyped in journalistic accounts. On July 30, 1867, the *Raleigh Register* reported:

Another Horrible Murder in Richmond—Richmond is excited over another horrible and mysterious murder. This time a colored woman is found dead in the suburbs of the city with signs of violence about her. At the coroner's inquest, strong circumstantial evidence was educed [sic], which implicates her paramour—a colored man—as the murderer, and he was arrested and committeed for examination.[38]

A week later another headline announced: "A Fiendish Nurse Poisons a Child" followed by: "On Saturday last a negro nurse employed by Mr. Wm. A. Pettaway in Richmond County, N.C. poured laudanum down the throat of his child, causing its death. On the previous day the female fiend had attempted to kill it by making it drink indigo. She was arrested."[39] During this same period the paper reported that a black wife had been shot through the head by a jealous husband, who then tried to conceal his crime by burning her body.[40] Whether victims or perpetrators, black women were involved in brutish horrors according to the sensational accounts reported by the white press. Rarely were they accorded the dignity of mention as clubwomen, churchwomen, educators or reformers.[41]

The message was clear and consistent. Before and during the Civil War black women were portrayed as aggressive, unrestrained, and pathological. In this way whites justified their custodial care—they were preventing African Americans from destroying one another. With emancipation, ex-Confederates lamented, former slaves were thrust into a free state for which they were unprepared.[42]

The white South spent time and energy discrediting freedwomen's campaigns for dignity. The courtesies or niceties afforded black women were the subject of parody. A copy of the *Black Republican and Office-Holder's Journal*, a handwritten and viciously racist lampoon of a Radical Republican newspaper, contained the following article:

WHITE OUTRAGE: Yesterday afternoon, in de ebening, about thirteen o'clock, a cupple ob colored ladies pushed a white gal off de sidewalk, when de purposterous white wench gib sass to dem two epectable colored ladies, and told dem dey ought to be ashamed!—We blush at the thought! We axes what was the police doing all dat time—where am de war power and de militia commission?[43]

This form of humor was both crude and effective. Indeed, these images filtered into the national press during Reconstruction, especially *Harper's Weekly*.

On the matter of the transformations wrought by freedom, many black men and women anticipated a strengthening of gender roles and conventional, if not puritanical, sexual morality within the black community once white coercion could be minimized. Black men hoped by establishing themselves as protectors of wives and daughters, they would lay claim to manhood while improving the lot of loved ones and kin. In 1865 Jenny Scott's husband stood up to soldiers who struck her and suffered a severe beating because of his heroism.[44] The following year a Georgia freedman complained to a bureau commissioner that his wife was accused by a "white lady" of "having intercourse" with another man. When the wife lashed back with verbal abuse, she was arrested, tried, sentenced to pay $16 in court costs and ordered sixty lashes. The husband wrote to the federal officer, "believing that the days for corporeal punishment of the colored race are past, and knowing that this is by far not an isolated case."[45]

The beating, whipping, abuse, and coercion of black women under slavery is, as I have argued elsewhere, underemphasized in historical accounts.[46] The casual way in which ex-slaves address these issues weighs in favor of its commonality. C. W. Hawkins of Little Rock, Arkansas, reported in the WPA narratives on coercion of slaves: "The women were beat and made to go to them. They were big fine men and the master wanted the women to have children by them. And there were some white men, too, who joined the slave women to do what they wanted to. Some of them

didn't want to stop when slavery stopped."[47] Indeed, many of
these attacks appear more violent and brutal in the postwar era.
Whether their motives were humanitarian or mercenary, planters
had a vested interest in keeping their slaves healthy and alive. As
ex-slaves, freedpeople could be maimed or killed with minimal
interference from the ruling elite. The violent response that befell
black resistance helped muzzle protest.

A Freedman's Bureau agent reported on September 10, 1866,
that Rhoda Ann Childs of Henry County, Georgia, was "taken
from her house, in her husband's absence, by eight white men who
stripped her, tied her to a log, beat and sexually abused her."[48] The
victim's own account of this incident appeared on October 13 in
the *Loyal Georgian:* "Myself and husband were under contract
with Mrs. Amanda Childs of Henry County and worked from
January 1, 1866 until the crops were laid by, or in other words until
the main work of the year was done without difficulty. Then (the
fashion being prevalent among the planters) we were called upon
one night." In Rhoda Childs's testimony, we have evidence of a
political conspiracy to deprive freedpeople of their share of their
labor. But far more chilling is her account of what followed. After
a severe beating, she was

thrown upon the ground on my back, one of the two men stood upon my
breast, while two others took hold of my feet and stretched my limbs as
far apart as they could while the man standing upon my breast applied
the strap to my private parts until they were satisfied that I was more
dead than alive. Then a man supposed to be an ex-Confederate soldier,
as he was on crutches, fell upon me and ravished me. During the whipping one of the men had run his pistol into me, and said he had a great
mind to pull the trigger. . . .[49]

In this and in many other cases, the wife of a former Union
soldier or the wife of a labor activist were victims of gang rape or
individual assault. In some ways such attacks might be viewed as
"symbolic," as a violation of the race—but regardless of the intent,
these acts of specific violence against individual women had human as well as political consequences. The black women who
suffered these brutal and dehumanizing attacks in this bloody
power struggle in the postwar South were not just symbols of
their race, but persons subjected to torture.

The attack upon the black wife or daughter provided a threat to communities as well as families. Hannah Travis recalled that "the Ku Klux never bothered us. They bothered some people about a mile from us. They took out the old man and whipped him. They made his wife get up and dance and she was in a delicate state. They made her get out of bed and dance, and after that they took her and whipped her and beat her, and she was in a delicate state, too."[50] For all the horror Hannah Travis's neighbor endured, she still escaped with her life, and we hope that of her unborn child. George Band's wife was not so lucky. Because her husband was a local leader, known as someone who could always defend himself, "the Klan came to his house, took his wife, hung her to a tree, hacked her to death with knives." Band sought revenge by killing fourteen of these vigilantes, surprising them with a Winchester rifle, but he was forced to flee the county.[51]

The ideological stand-off during Reconstruction included sexual as well as political dimensions. Myrta Lockett Avary's *Dixie After the War*, published in 1906, confidently claimed that "the rapist is a product of the reconstruction period."[52] Like most white southerners and most white Americans until the modern period, Avary did not bother to assign race to get her meaning across: she clearly expected readers to assume that the rapist was a black man and the victim a white female. Her explanation of the "Crime Against Womanhood" reflected popular ideology about the era: the ruin of innocent women by bestial blacks—a horror that justified lynching.[53] Further, Avary went on to argue that this crime "was a development of a period when the negro was dominated by political, religious and social advisors from the North and by the attitude of the Northern press and pulpit. It was practically unknown in wartime, when negroes were left on plantations as protectors and guardians of white women and children."[54] Avary, of course, damns the North for its indignation against southern lawlessness and "not one word of sympathy or pity for the white victim of negro lust."[55]

During Reconstruction these sexual libels and attacks upon the North were popular and frequent. An 1868 article in the *Atlanta Constitution* reported in earnest "that Mrs. Harriet Beecher Stowe is going to establish a school in Aiken, Ga., for the benefit of mulatto children that have been born in the South since its invasion by Yankee school-marms."[56] While these white supremacists smeared northern women, southern white women were exalted. Indeed the editors of the *Atlanta Constitution* even encouraged white women to fill the gallery of Georgia's Reconstruction legislature, commenting that "the ladies are welcome and we think their presence there will have a good effect upon that piebald body."[57] Much of this anxiety over blood, race, and sex reveals the torrents of hypocritical rage among white southerners at this juncture.

Unfortunately for southern black women, emancipation escalated the degree of sexual violence to which they might be subjected. Freedwomen struggled to avoid the daily harassment imposed by white men. The so-called withdrawal of women from the labor force were actually attempts by black women to shift their productive roles into the family economy whenever possible, escaping white overseers and employers who proved an enduring threat. Freedwomen did not have the luxury of being interested in the status assigned to women ensconced in the domestic realm; they required protection. Black women wanted respectability and the public image of virtue, first for survival and then as a foundation for their own and their family's prosperity.

Ironically, African American women's strategies and struggles in the nineteenth century have created bitter debate in the twentieth century as we attempt to reconcile the matrifocality of black households with racist and sexist assumptions about the role of families within modern culture. Further, the abolition of slavery shifted notions of appropriate sexual conduct and gave black women, if not more opportunities to resist coercion, at least the hope that their horizons could expand while sexual abuse diminished. Reconstruction in many ways offered black women their rights, but little means to exercise those new legal privileges. It afforded women a voice, but denied African Americans a forum within which to speak and be heard without reprisals.

The sexual terrorism of race politics during Reconstruction is evident. White women's bodies became sacred territory over which ex-Confederates organized and battled, refighting the war and reexerting regional and race pride. Black women's bodies were just as critical. For too long shame and silence cloaked their sexual violation. Almost all the scholarly literature published on the topic of rape in the South deals exclusively with white victims, even the works devoted to interracial rape. This reflects racism pervasive within both the academy and society at large. But indictments are finally emerging—as there is no statute of limitations for historians. Voices ring loud and clear—compelling us to listen, to examine our shortcomings, and to incorporate critical issues of gender and sexuality into our reconstructions of freedwomen.

Notes

1. Despite historians' sensitive and extensive treatment of questions of race, region, and class in most comprehensive studies—especially Eric Foner, *Reconstruction: America's Unfinished Revolution, 1863–1877* (New York, 1988); Leon F. Litwack, *Been in the Storm So Long: The Aftermath of Slavery* (New York, 1979); and equally compelling, Clarence Mohr, *On the Threshold of Freedom: Masters and Slaves in Civil War Georgia* (Athens, Ga., 1986); and George C. Rable, *But There Was No Peace: The Role of Violence in the Politics of Reconstruction* (Athens, Ga., 1984)—these works rarely focus on women and provide little or no mention of sexual coercion and rape. This conspicuous neglect of the topic is not due to a lack of evidence, as Gerda Lerner's *Black Women in White America: A Documentary History* (New York, 1972); Jacqueline Jones's *Labor of Love, Labor of Sorrow: Black Women, Work, and the Family from Slavery to the Present* (New York, 1985); and Leslie Schwalm's "The Meaning of Freedom: African-American Women and Their Transformation from Slavery to Freedom in Lowcountry South Carolina" (Ph.D. diss., University of Wisconsin, Madison, 1991), demonstrate. Rather mainstream historical literature consistently ignores these issues. The author would like to thank the American Council of Learned Societies for their support.

2. Ira Berlin et al., eds., *Freedom: A Documentary History of Emancipation*, series I, vols. 1–3 (New York, 1982–1990).

3. I would like to thank David Katzman for calling my attention to the black newspaper collection at Widener Library, Harvard University.

4. George Wright, *Racial Violence in Kentucky, 1865–1940: Lynchings, Mob Rule, and "Legal Lynchings"* (Baton Rouge, 1990).

5. See Catherine Clinton, "Southern Dishonor: Flesh, Blood, Race and Bondage," in Carol Bleser, ed., *In Joy and Sorrow: Women, Family, and Marriage in the Victorian South, 1830–1900* (New York, 1991), 52–68;

Herbert Gutman, *The Black Family in Slavery and Freedom* (New York, 1976), 83–84, 395–99; and Sara Rapport, "The Freedmen's Bureau as a Legal Agent for Black Men and Women in Georgia: 1865–1868," *Georgia Historical Quarterly* 73 (Spring 1989):39–41.

6. Peter Bardaglio, "Families, Sex and the Law: The Legal Transformation of the Nineteenth Century Southern Household" (Ph.D. diss., Stanford University, 1987.

7. *Digest of the Laws of the State of Georgia* (Savannah, 1802), 430.

8. See Clinton, "Southern Dishonor," 65–66.

9. *The Code of the State of Georgia* (Atlanta, 1861), art. 4248, sec. 33, p. 824.

10. See Fitzhugh Brundage, *Lynching in the New South: Georgia and Virginia, 1880–1930* (Champaign-Urbana, Ill. 1993).

11. The Bureau of Refugees, Freedmen and Abandoned Lands (hereinafter cited as BRF&AL), National Archives, record group 105, entry 1322, vol. 30, La., Murders and Outrages, W 226, W 238, and W 248, St. Martin's Parish, May 20, 1868.

12. *Ibid.*, R 466, Franklin County, June 14, 1868.

13. *Ibid.*, B 317, Lafourche Parish, July 31, 1868.

14. *Ibid.*, C 142, DeSoto County, June 20, 1868.

15. *Ibid.*, W 390, Winn County, August 30, 1868.

16. *Ibid.*, S 507, Claiborne Parish, November 10, 1868.

17. *Colored American*, January 13, 1866.

18. *Ibid.*

19. *Weekly Defiance*, February 24, 1883.

20. *The Bulletin*, September 24, 1881. But such a sentence was of course less brutal than the lynch mobs to which most "black rapists" were consigned.

21. See Rapport, "The Freedmen's Bureau as a Legal Agent," 39–41.

22. BRF&AL, Letters Received, microfilm, M798, reel 15, Madison, Ga., January 2, 1867.

23. Rapport, "The Freedmen's Bureau as Legal Agent," BRF&AL, Letters Received, microfilm, M1048, reel 26, 0516, Gordonsville, Va., May 17, 1867, and M798, reel 17, Greensboro, Ga., August 15, 1867.

24. Jones, *Labor of Love, Labor of Sorrow.*

25. BRF&AL, Letters Received, microfilm, M1048, reel 10, 0580, King Williams County, Va., June 30, 1866.

26. *Ibid.*, reel 12, 0073, Gordonsville, Va., January 6, 1866.

27. *Ibid.*, reel 33, 0827–30, Halifax County, Va., October 29, 1868.

28. *Ibid.*, M826, reel 13, 0513–17, Jackson, Miss., January 11, 1866.

29. Angela Y. Davis, *Women, Race & Class* (New York, 1981); bell hooks, *Ain't I a Woman: Black Women and Feminism* (Boston, 1981); Deborah Gray White, *Ar'n't I a Woman?: Female Slaves in the Plantation South* (New York, 1985); Patricia Morton, *Disfigured Images: The Historical Assault on Afro-American Women* (Westport, Conn., 1991).

30. BRF&AL, Murders and Outrages, M798, reel 13, Irwin County, Ga., October 15, 1866.

31. *Ibid.*, M1048, reel 59, Prince Edwards County, Va., July 1868.

32. *Ibid.*, M798, reel 13, Clinch County, Ga., August 8, 1866.

33. *Ibid.*, Letters Received, M1048, reel 12, 0220–0240, Culpepper County, Va., February 1866.

34. Segregation legislation began in Tennessee in 1881 with a railway case and *Plessy v. Ferguson* (1896), which also stemmed from a railway discrimination suit.

35. *Loyal Georgian,* February 17, 1866.

36. BRF&AL, Murders and Outrages, microfilm, M1048, reel 59, Gordonsville, Va., February 21, 1868; *ibid.*, Letters Received, M1048, reel 31, Gordonsville, Va., February 21, 1868.

37. See Paula Giddings, "Ida Wells-Barnett," in G. J. Barker-Benfield and Catherine Clinton, eds., *Portraits of American Women* (New York, 1991), 367–85.

38. *Raleigh Register,* July 30, 1867.

39. *Ibid.*, August 8, 1867.

40. *Ibid.*, July 30, 1867. This incident anticipated Richard Wright's *Native Son* (New York, 1940) by over half a century.

41. See also *Richmond Enquirer,* July 24, 1864.

42. See Mrs. N. B. De Sassure, *Old Plantation Days: Being the Recollections of Southern Life Before the Civil War* (New York, 1909), 18.

43. *Black Republican and Office-Holder's Journal,* August 1865. Available at Widener Library, Harvard University.

44. BRF&AL, Murders and Outrages, microfilm, M1048, reel 59, 0120–0123, Richmond, Va., June 8, 1865.

45. *Ibid.*, M798, reel 13, Clinch County, Ga., July 2, 1866.

46. See Clinton, "Southern Dishonor."

47. George P. Rawick, ed., *The American Slave: A Composite Autobiography* (19 vols., Westport, Conn., 1972), 9:218.

48. BRF&AL, Letters Received, microfilm M798, reel 14, September 10, 1866.

49. *Loyal Georgian,* October 13, 1866.

50. Rawick, *The American Slave*, 10:350.

51. *Ibid.*, 6, pt. 2: 134–36.

52. Myrta Lockett Avary, *Dixie After the War* (New York, 1906), 377.

53. Even women reformers like Jane Addams and Frances Willard were unwilling to denounce the lynching of "rapists."

54. Avary, *Dixie After the War*, 384.

55. *Ibid.*

56. *Atlanta Constitution*, June 27, 1868.

57. *Ibid.*, July 18, 1868.

Scarlett O'Hara

THE SOUTHERN LADY AS NEW

WOMAN

ELIZABETH FOX-GENOVESE

Elizabeth Fox-Genovese is Eleanore Raoul Professor of the Humanities at Emory University. Her first book was The Origins of Physiocracy: Economic Revolution and Social Order in Eighteenth Century France *(1976), which was followed by a coauthored volume,* Fruits of Merchant Capital: Slavery and Bourgeois Property in the Rise and Expansion of Capitalism *(1983). Her* Within the Plantation Household: Black and White Women of the Old South *(1988) won the Julia Cherry Spruill Prize. Her most recent book,* Feminism Without Illusions, *appeared in 1992.*

Fox-Genovese has contributed extensively to literary journals and anthologies and is published widely in the fields of feminist theory, women's studies, and American studies. The essay that follows is reprinted from American Quarterly, *where it first appeared in 1981.*

If *Gone with the Wind* has become something of an American classic, it has done so as much by its popular appeal as by any aesthetic merit. The components of its record-breaking success include all the classic ingredients of popular romance wrapped in the irresistible trappings of historical adventure and glamour—the hurtling saga of sectional catastrophe and rebirth, the nostalgia for a lost civilization, the green Irish eyes of a captivating and unruly miss, and the langorous, steel-sprung dynamism of her Rhett Butler. But, if the novel fails to transcend its indebtedness to popular culture and to a sentimental female tradition, it nonetheless betrays a complexity that distinguishes it from the standard mass-market historical melodrama.[1]

The extraordinary overnight success of *Gone with the Wind* testifies to the immediacy with which it engaged the American imagination. Critical acclaim, which likened it to *Vanity Fair* and *War and Peace,* as well as popular sales, rapidly established the saga of Scarlett O'Hara as a significant addition to the national culture.[2] Scarlett and her world entered the mainstream of American life, thereby incorporating the Old South, its beauties and its travails, firmly into the prevailing myth of the American past. In this respect, *Gone with the Wind* celebrated, even as it contributed to, the restoration of the South to the nation and the nation to the South.

Like so many spontaneous cultural manifestations, the appearance of *Gone with the Wind* had been carefully engineered. In the 1930s the American public was showing a taste for historical fiction and southern fiction. When Harold Latham acquired the manuscript for Macmillan in 1935, he was on a trip through the South looking for southern material—looking, in fact, for *Gone with the Wind,* had he only known it existed.[3] So Mitchell's novel fit into the demand of a popular sensibility that, as Warren Susman has argued, had taken a conservative turn. The American people, in Susman's view,

entered an era of depression and war somehow aware of a culture in crisis, already at the outset in search of a satisfactory American Way of Life, fascinated by the idea of culture itself, with a sense of some need for a kind of commitment in a world somehow between eras.[4]

The First World War looms as the critical experience of cultural transformation. There was an element of strain and unreality in the prosperity and "liberation" of the twenties—a glossing over of problems unresolved. This link between the war and the two postwar decades provided the context for the drafting and reception of *Gone with the Wind.* Its compelling dynamism derived as much from its implicit engagement with the America of the 1920s as from its outward concern with the Civil War and Reconstruction. Never just another historical romance of magnolias and moonlight, *Gone with the Wind* grappled with the nature of the New South, with twentieth-century problems of social change and tension, and with the dilemmas of female identity in the modern world.

The story of Scarlett O'Hara, which opens and closes the novel and organizes the intervening flood of historical cataclysm, drew countless readers through the collapse of one civilization and the birth of another. Scarlett engaged a special identification from her readers by simultaneously mobilizing and obscuring the tensions of female being and passion that plagued Mitchell and her contemporaries. The appeal of *Gone with the Wind* has proved so broad and enduring as to defy any single explanation. Surely every female reader will always cherish her own Scarlett. And the novel's attraction for men can be traced to Rhett's special qualities, in particular that tough and ferocious romanticism so reminiscent of Hemingway's heroes or Humphrey Bogart's roles. Yet any possible explanation of the novel's appeal should take account of Mitchell's special ability to render Scarlett's experience at once immediate and distant. Holding a careful line between mystification and autobiographical realism, Mitchell casts Scarlett's tale neither as a gothic fantasy nor a portrait of the modern woman. Instead, Mitchell chooses to wed Scarlett to the death and rebirth of the South, but she also uses that historical specificity to veil altogether contemporary concerns. *Gone with the Wind,* in short, rests on a series of displacements that both bind the reader with an illusion of psychological immediacy and mask the immediacy of social issues. Mitchell's decision to weigh equally Scarlett and the agony of social upheaval, the individual and historical process, forces us to consider both strands of the novel together, however complex the reading.

Like any text, *Gone with the Wind* must be taken on its own terms, as a discrete entity with rules, logic, and meaning of its own. Yet, also like any text, it must be read in full historical and cultural context. We gain nothing from insisting on a radical purity that severs the text entirely from its production and reception, from the motivations—open and buried—of its author or from the predispositions of its readers. The full complexity of Margaret Mitchell's personal relation to her novel exceeds the scope of this essay, but no reading of the novel should dismiss the relation as insignificant. Mitchell, who had not assumed her own adult female identity without detours, wrote a single novel that, whatever its scope and range of compelling characters, focused upon a female adolescent's passage to womanhood. And her account of Scarlett's passage raises all the questions of female identity, role, and sexuality that figured in American consciousness during the first three decades of the twentieth century.[5]

If Mitchell did not write the *bildungsroman* of a twentieth-century southern female adolescence and young womanhood, she nonetheless understood female being as historically specific.[6] By displacing Scarlett's career historically while simultaneously confronting her with contemporary dilemmas, she relies upon history and social conventions to complete the silences she leaves in her exploration of female identity, just as she relies upon them to contain, in however contradictory a fashion, the painful and confusing desires of the female self. Indeed, by emphasizing history and social order, which she merges with the idea of civilization, she obscures the measure of her personal rebellion against prescribed female roles. In *Gone with the Wind,* she offers a rationalization of middle-class American values, especially white middle-class social domination. Yet the rationalization depends on establishing a historical pedigree for a national ruling class in a period of advanced capitalism and perceived social change. This rationalization, moreover, is laced with veiled challenges to the prevailing gender system, even as it proclaims that gender system as the cornerstone of social order. At its core lies a psychological exploration of the place of women within the ruling class and of the tensions between their subjective desires and their assigned objective role.

Mitchell invests Scarlett with the conscious and unconscious conflicts that inform the transition from explosive and tense girl-hood to socially determined womanhood under conditions in which that transition is open to reinterpretation. By casting the dilemmas of her own generation in the context of the Civil War, Mitchell prohibited an autobiographical reading of her text. She intended to distance herself from the most pressing emotional conflicts, to protect herself as well as her privacy from curious readers. The one-to-one relationship between Mitchell and Scarlett, even if it could be established, matters little, and is certainly less important than the kind of female identity that attracted so many female readers. The point, after all, is less to understand the personal case history of Margaret Mitchell than to understand its mediation through a fictional character that responded to the fantasies of so many American women. Only in this sense does the 1920s substratum that underlies the Civil War foreground become significant. But, in this sense, it matters that the roots of *Gone with the Wind* lie in the imagination and experience of a woman who came to maturity with, as she frequently insisted, the generation of flappers.

Born in 1900, Margaret Mitchell lived most of her life in the Atlanta of the New South. The preliminary biographical materials available and her own *Gone with the Wind Letters* portray a young woman torn by the claims of family traditions, conventional behavior, an independent career, and a strong streak of social and sexual rebellion. Her correspondence exudes contradictions in her self-perception—or, better, her preferred self-presentation—which can only be captured by that generally misused term, ambivalence. Her epistolary style reminds one of nothing so much as her own descriptions of Scarlett: "She knew how to smile so that her dimples leaped, how to walk pigeon-toed so her wide hoop skirts swayed entrancingly, how to look up into a man's face and then drop her eyes and bat the lids rapidly so that she seemed a-tremble with gentle emotion. Most of all she learned how to conceal from men a sharp intelligence beneath a face as sweet and bland as a baby's" (59).[7] Or, "At sixteen, thanks to Mammy and Ellen, she looked sweet, charming and giddy, but she was, in reality, self-willed, vain and obstinate. She had the easily stirred passions of her Irish father and nothing except the thinnest veneer of her mother's unselfish and forebearing nature" (59). Although Scarlett has nothing but contempt for the simpering girls who live out the prescriptions of southern ladyhood, she nevertheless adopts the conventions when she wants to attract men.

Although *Gone with the Wind* cannot be reduced to a simple reading of Scarlett O'Hara as Margaret Mitchell, bits of Mitchell's attitudes can be found scattered among various characters, and Scarlett herself does contain attributes which Mitchell possessed. Mitchell's psychological complexities emerge from the structure of the novel as a whole, from the interactions among characters and their allotted rewards or punishments. Mitchell's own ambivalence becomes clearest in the gaps that separate the affects with which she invests a character—the sympathy or admiration she makes the character invite—and the destiny she assigns to the character. The historical setting further permits Mitchell both to distance her readers from the psychological drama and to bind them to it. For she uses history as a specific series of events—a drama in its own right—and as a common, nostalgic memory of a lost agrarian world.

Hers was the last generation to grow up with minimal exposure to the new cultures of radio and film. Her experience of vicariously living the histories of grandparents, parents, and communities through the telling and retelling of tales must have been common throughout the country. "I was about ten years old," she wrote, "before I learned that the war hadn't ended shortly before I was born."[8] In the South, the stories of fathers and the lullabies of mothers ensured a widespread and living engagement with the events of the Civil War and Reconstruction; similarly, elsewhere, historical events and interpretations probably became intertwined with the personal identities of many Americans. But, given the emergence of a national industrial and indeed corporate economy, that familial and local identity was becoming more a private and less a public matter. In this respect Mitchell wrote for a generation that increasingly recognized regional identities as distinct, yet in some sense interchangeable, strands in a national history. Even the special legacy of southerners was becoming ever less a source of divisiveness and defensiveness under the influence of the proponents of the New South creed.[9] The arrival of Woodrow Wilson in the White House opened a new stage in the vindication of southern concerns: with him came the racial segregation of public buildings and his personal endorsement of D. W. Griffith's racist film *Birth of a Nation*.

As social commentary, *Gone with the Wind* moves between a historical treatment of the 1860s and general statements about civilization as a universal category. But the oscillation between the particular and the general invites contemporary identification. To the extent that the readers' identification bridges the past and present, the statements about society proffered by the novel function as commentaries on contemporary problems. Mitchell's psychological realism, however complex, ensures the appeal of her work far more than does her faithful depiction of social types. It is the combination of contemporary psychological power and historical verisimilitude that commands attention. For Mitchell's accuracy and realism of detail can be compatible with a number of conflicting, broad patterns. To put it differently, the precision in detail does not necessarily tell us anything about the argument, commitments, or world view which the detail is marshalled to serve. What did Mitchell hope to accomplish in telling the tale of Scarlett O'Hara, and in writing a novel of the Civil War and Reconstruction?

The historical setting of *Gone with the Wind* cannot be reduced to a simple displacement of Mitchell's era, for that era, the 1920s, required special historical foundation.[10] For Mitchell, the New South, of which she was trying to make sense as a setting for female life, needed to be understood in the mainstream of American life. The middle-class values which were being challenged by the ferment of the 1920s had to be anchored in a national culture, not limited to sectional idiosyncrasies. In *Gone with the Wind* Mitchell reread southern history through a prism of conservative progressivism. If she indeed effected a certain displacement from the 1920s to the earlier period, she did so not to jettison it entirely, nor to reduce it to a simple case study of the present, but literally to reconstruct it. She sought to fashion a history appropriate to the national concerns and destiny of the New South.

Gone with the Wind as a whole transforms a particular regional past into a generalized national past. In this respect, it contributes to integrating southern history into national history even as it reestablishes the South, with all its idiosyncrasies, as an only slightly special case of an inclusive national destiny. Mitchell's antebellum South manifests features characteristic of the nation as a whole. Even prior to the war, the cavalier tradition is shown as infused with the blood of Irish immigrants. As W. J. Cash does in *The Mind of the South,* Mitchell emphasizes the assimilation of the various gradations of the white elite—specifically excluding poor "white trash"—into a rural precursor of the industrial middle class.[11]

Throughout the novel, Mitchell explicitly underscores her interest in the rise of Atlanta and the emergence of a business culture in the South. She returns regularly to the excitement and importance of Atlanta as a raw, growing, bustling city, the outgrowth of the railroads. She directly points to the similarities between Atlanta and Scarlett: "Atlanta was of [Scarlett's] own generation, crude with the crudities of youth and as headstrong and impetuous as herself." The two were roughly the same age and grew up together. During Scarlett's first seventeen years, Atlanta developed from a stake in the ground into a "thriving small city of ten thousand that was the center of attention for the whole state. The older quieter cities were wont to look upon the bustling new town with the sensations of a hen which has hatched a duckling." The maternal reference should be noted. In the eyes of the staid Georgia towns, Atlanta had little to recommend it save some railroads "and a bunch of mighty pushy people . . . Scarlett always liked Atlanta for the very same reasons that made Savannah, Augusta, and Macon condemn it. Like herself, the town was a mixture of the old and the new in Georgia, in which the old often came off second best in its conflicts with the self-willed and vigorous new" (141–43).

Atlanta, not the "old days," emerges as the victor in *Gone with the Wind.* Tara, which initially figures as a dynamic, frontier plantation—the locus of vitality—ends as a place of retreat. In the early pages of the novel, Gerald O'Hara confidently points to the land as the only reliable source of wealth. Even during the war, Scarlett recalls and echoes his view. But by the war's end, Scarlett must turn to the city to raise the money to pay the taxes on Tara. And the section of the novel devoted to Reconstruction takes place in the city. When, at the conclusion, Scarlett thinks of returning to Tara, she thinks only of a temporary refuge. With only the slightest exaggeration, it could appear as the typical house in the country to which busy city dwellers repair for rest and refreshment. In this sense, it blends imaginatively with those New England farm houses that had also once encompassed productive labor. In Mitchell's rendition, the Civil War becomes a national turning point in the transition from rural to urban civilization. And this reading permits her to incorporate the South into a shared national drama.

This vision of Atlanta as symbol of a general urban vitality conflates the destiny of the city with the defense of middle-class values. Mitchell reserves her endorsement for an enterprising, indigenous, southern bourgeoisie—for those who can adapt to the times without sacrificing the essence of their values. Her merciless depiction of the Yankees as rapacious, dishonest, political parasites identifies them as predators, not true capitalists. Yankees are those who manipulate and stir up Negroes and poor whites. She reserves her rage for those who came South to milk the victim. She never denies the possibility of honest Yankee businessmen, comparable to their southern counterparts. But she does intend to make the country as a whole understand "what the South endured in the days of Civil War and Reconstruction."[12]

Atlanta stands for the dynamism of the New South. At the core of the novel lies Mitchell's fascination with the way in which a new world emerges from the ashes of the old. Time and again, she returns to the problem of a dying civilization in confrontation with one being born. How, she asks, does one make money from the collapse of a society? Who makes the money? How does one survive, adapt, and prosper in the wake of a major social up-heaval? Historically, economically, and socially, Atlanta provides the lynchpin of *Gone with the Wind.* By the novel's close, all of the major characters have tied their destinies to that of the city. Similarly, the character of Scarlett provides the novel's identificatory core. For against the collapse of the Old South and the birth of the New, the novel chronicles Scarlett's coming of age—her painful assumption of the burdens of southern womanhood. The historical cataclysm, however, transforms Scarlett's saga from the account of establishing a personal identity as a woman into an investigation of how to become—or whether to become—a lady.

The terms "woman" and "lady" evoke mature female identity, but in different forms. "Woman" suggests at once a more inclusive and more private female nature, whereas "lady" evokes the public representation of that nature. To be a lady is to have a public presence, to accept a public responsibility. But the essence of that presence and that responsibility consists in recognizing and maintaining a sexual division of labor that relegates any proper woman to the private sphere. No lady would admit that she, and not her husband, ran the plantation. No lady would admit to being hungry in public. No lady would admit to sexual desire or pleasure.

In Mitchell's account, the Civil War and Reconstruction forced the issue of how one remains a lady under new historical conditions. Changing times permit and even require new modes of behavior. At the same time, no society would survive did not its female members internalize certain standards and responsibilities.

In *Gone with the Wind* the special case of appropriate female behavior and values in the collapse of a civilization is overdetermined by the private drama of a girl who grows to womanhood under tumultuous conditions. Mitchell provides ample evidence that Scarlett would have had trouble with or without the war. But without the war, social structures and norms would have provided a corset for her unruly impulses. It is Mammy who embodies those shattered structures and norms, and who struggles in vain to tighten the laces of the corset.

What a young miss could do and what she could not do were as different as black and white in Mammy's mind: there was no middle ground of deportment between. Suellen and Carreen were clay in her powerful hands and harkened respectfully to most of her warnings. But it had always been a struggle to teach Scarlett that most of her natural impulses were unladylike. Mammy's victories over Scarlett were hard-won and represented a guile unknown to the white mind. (76–77)

Scarlett stands apart in *Gone with the Wind,* not merely because she is the central character, but because for her alone among the female characters do the years of the war and its aftermath render problematical the question of appropriate gender role—the definition of being, the aspiration to become, a lady. Any understanding of Scarlett's personality must take account of the other characters who, by responding to the pressures of the times, relate to her and provide both the context and the measuring stick for her responses. Mitchell once claimed that her novel had been written entirely "through Scarlett's eyes. What she understood was written down; what she did not understand—and there were many things beyond her comprehension, they were left to the reader's imagination."[13] Mitchell's claim will not withstand even a cursory reading of her text. Possibly she believed that she had written from Scarlett's point of view. But if so, she confused her own identification with Scarlett and had trouble differentiating her function as presenter of Scarlett's vision from her function as commentator on Scarlett. In any event, whatever the source of Mitchell's ambivalence about sexuality, gender identity, and gender role, it reaches schizophrenic proportions. Her relationship with Scarlett, her own creature, exemplifies her dilemma of identification and judgment.

Scarlett O'Hara is not beautiful. Nor is she a lady, although in her idiosyncratic way, she sentimentally aspires to be one, provided that it does not cost too much. Her adored mother Ellen had been a lady; Melanie Hamilton Wilkes is a lady; Aunt Pittypat Hamilton, Mrs. Merriwether, Mrs. Meade, India Wilkes, and the other Atlanta worthies pride themselves on being ladies. Her sisters, Suellen and Carreen, suffering like Scarlett from Ellen's saintly distance, are pale shadows of ladies. Belle Watling, to be sure, is not a lady, but the classic whore with a heart of gold, a shrewd and successful business woman in her own right, has a far deeper sense than Scarlett of the essential qualities that informed true ladyhood. But however splendid her personal qualities, the code cannot admit her as a lady. Scarlett, for her part, has no time for irrelevant niceties, and no understanding of the deeper meanings. Raw like the burgeoning city of Atlanta, determined and grasping like her Irish immigrant forebears. Scarlett has never been nice and, with the advent of the war, commits herself whole-heartedly to surviving. Scarlett's survival tactics include marriage without love hastily entered into for spiteful reasons, manslaughter, the theft of her sister's fiancé, flagrant disregard of proper female behavior to the point of risking the lives of her own menfolk, and the mindless sacrifice of her husband's life. The same arsenal houses such lesser sins as dancing while in mourning, offering herself for cold cash to pay the taxes on Tara, parading around town while pregnant, flaunting a disconcerting talent for business, and otherwise violating all accepted conventions that defined the southern lady. In Scarlett's judgment, the Yankees, in all other respects so despicable, were right "on this matter. It took money to be a lady" (610). The times, the grim days of the war and Reconstruction, demanded harsh stratagems of those who would survive them. Survival assured, the times would permit the resumption of ladylike graces. Let others retain, at the risk of destruction, the inner sense of being ladies, or assume the mask, whatever their inner feelings of despair. She was different. And "she knew she would never feel like a lady again until her table was weighted with silver and crystal and smoking with rich food, until her own horses and carriages stood in her stables, until black hands and not white took the cotton from Tara" (609).

Mitchell makes scant effort to redeem Scarlett from the stark

self-interest and greed of her chronicled behavior. On the contrary, from the opening pages of the novel, in which upland Georgia basks in the glow of antebellum serenity, she establishes the
fundamental contours of Scarlett's grasping personality. The self-
conscious manipulation with which Scarlett pursues her prey
foreshadows precisely the resources she will muster in her pursuit of financial security during Reconstruction. Her marriage to
Rhett Butler and the ensuing hold on material security do not
suffice to transform her into a real lady. But then Scarlett lacks any
vital understanding of what it is to be one.

Through Scarlett, Mitchell exposes the hypocrisy of being a
lady or a gentleman. Time and again, she shows Scarlett chafing
under the constraints of correct behavior and utterance. No one,
in Scarlett's view, could believe the phrases that govern po-
lite interchange. Repeatedly, she mentally dismisses Melanie as
"mealy-mouthed." Yet Mitchell also shows Scarlett raging because Rhett cannot be counted on to be a gentleman. In the scene
of the charity bazaar in Atlanta, Scarlett worries that Rhett cannot be trusted to observe the gentleman's code and keep his
mouth shut. A few pages later, during the same scene, Scarlett
flares up at the hypocrisy of required ladylike conduct. Finally, in
the name of the Cause, Rhett bids for Scarlett as his partner to
lead the opening reel. Scarlett, aching to dance, furious at the
imprisonment of her mourning, joins him, feet tapping "like cas-
tenets," green eyes flashing. This one scene captures all the contradictions of Mitchell's attitudes. For the codes against which
Scarlett rebels also provide her protection; she festers at their
demands, but fears a world that will not provide her the respect
the codes are designed to ensure. If she does not always wish to
meet the requirements of being a lady, she should not wish to be
treated like one.

Mitchell thus remains ambivalent about Scarlett's difficulties.
She regularly calls attention to Scarlett's natural vibrancy. "There
was no one to tell Scarlett that her own personality, frighteningly
vital though it was, was more attractive than any masquerade she
might adopt. Had she been told, she would have been pleased but
unbelieving. And the civilization of which she was a part would
have been unbelieving too, for at no time before or since, had
so low a premium been placed on female naturalness" (80). Here,

Mitchell seems to hold civilization responsible for repressing healthy and attractive female vitality, but her novel as a whole offers a more complex reading of the relation between female vitality and civilization. Vitality serves as a code word for sexuality, and Mitchell harbored conflicting attitudes towards the proper relation between sexuality, gender identity, and gender role.

Her confusion on this matter endows the novel with a complexity that transcends Scarlett's stereotypical features. For indisputably, if in an occasionally perverse way, Scarlett invites identification. The dynamics of that identification turn upon Scarlett's proximity to young bourgeois women of the twenties and thirties. Her career raises questions of appropriate female behavior in a changing world. Her internal life reverberates with overtones of the early twentieth-century crisis in the bourgeois family and the received notions of fitting female behavior.[14] Much of the force of the novels as an affirmation of acceptable, middle-class social attitudes depends upon Scarlett's psychological plausibility. Scarlett herself is caught in a war between the socially ordained role into which she is expected to fit and her own natural impulses. The war in Scarlett, as perhaps in Mitchell herself, is fierce, for she lacks that solid bridge between the two—a strong identity as a woman—which might permit her to weather the storms of social change. But the acceptance of herself as a woman, Mitchell implies, would have required a resilient identification with another woman, presumably her mother, that would have nurtured her initiation into female sexuality and generativity.

As Scarlett herself comes to understand at the close of the novel, the only women she has ever loved and respected are her mother and Melanie. Tellingly, Scarlett omits Mammy from this company despite compelling claims. As Rhett (who along with Ashley represents the voice of objective judgment) categorically affirms, both Ellen and Melanie were genuinely great ladies. Scarlett's tragedy lies in her inability to understand the meaning of being a lady. Scarlett is correct in her criticisms of the hypocrisies of the pseudo-ladies, although even here, she underestimates their strengths. Surviving the war and its aftermath calls for more than forms of gentility. Scarlett fails to realize that the prevailing etiquette represents a social effort to codify, institutionalize, and reproduce the deeper qualities of the lady and the fabric of an entire society. Having never grasped the depth and meaning of the informing spirit, she confuses it with its forms. So deeply does she miss the point that until the moment of Melanie's death she remains unaware that Melanie believes in the words she uses and the standards she observes, and that those words and standards derive from strength rather than weakness. Only at Melanie's deathbed does she recognize that Melanie too would have killed the Yankee who threatened them—or would have died in the attempt.

Ellen and Melanie are presented as attractive and admirable, albeit highly self-disciplined and possibly repressed. The interpretation adopted depends upon one's angle of vision and the relative weight accorded to Scarlett's perceptions, as against an independent reading that derives from the actions and words of the characters themselves. Thus, Scarlett reveres Ellen even though the reader has ample evidence that Ellen may have failed decisively as a mother. Ellen's most direct address to Scarlett comes in the form of a letter, written as soon as Ellen receives word of Scarlett's shameless dancing at the Atlanta charity bazaar. That letter, with its cold feelings, could have been written by any one of the Atlanta worthies. Melanie, on the same occasion, insists on believing the best of Scarlett and defends her. Yet Scarlett persists in seeing Melanie as pale, fragile, and lacking in womanly warmth and charm—in a word, asexual. The reader, however, having seen Melanie's plain face flare into beauty with the passion of her love for Ashley, has every reason to appreciate her special strength. Both Melanie and Ellen lack that raw undisciplined sexuality that pulsates in Scarlett herself, but Mitchell makes less than clear whether she regards sexuality as a male or female trait. Time and again, she links Scarlett's exuberance to her paternal inheritance. She establishes Scarlett's early preference for the activities of boys over those of girls. She proclaims Scarlett's repugnance for and failure at motherhood. Although she leaves no doubt about Scarlett's attractiveness to men, she links Scarlett's success as a belle to her unseemly ambition.

Mitchell remains preoccupied with those features of being a lady that survive social upheaval. If the role of lady is constructed and carries serious responsibilities, how much of that role can be taken to persist through change? Or, to put it differently, does being a lady possess an essence that remains constant as manners change? The sections of the novel that describe Scarlett's early forays into the world of business betray what could be interpreted as a strong feminist approval of the self-reliance, business skills, and survival abilities of the heroine. By Mitchell's day, the South had a tradition of resilient women who, with or without their menfolk, had seen their families through the difficult postbellum decades and had reestablished family fortunes. Scarlett's economic success need not have contravened her standing as a lady. Scarlett runs into trouble not for adapting to new times, nor for displaying a vigorous individualism, but for transgressing those boundaries at which individualism becomes greed and adaptation a threat to any viable social order. For Mitchell, those limits seem to have come with the employment of convicts, the systematic betrayal of business's own standards of probity, and female intrusion—however inadvertent—into the political domain. But if Mitchell shows Scarlett's irresponsible actions as bearing heavy consequences, she does not show Scarlett experiencing pain or guilt as a result of them. The social dimensions of superego sanctions are delineated, but Scarlett has not internalized them. Her own responses remain determined by whether she gets what she wants: at the center of Scarlett, the apparent woman, lingers a demanding and frightened child. In presenting Scarlett as emotionally immature and willful, Mitchell validates the legitimacy of social constraints on female lives. In presenting Scarlett as so personally immune to the normal emotional responsibilities for her socially inappropriate behavior, Mitchell questions the psychological foundations for socially prescribed roles. She remains, in short, deadlocked on the social possibilities for and the social legitimacy of the free expression of female nature.

Mitchell's strategy highlights a gap between the desire and its object, between the act and its emotional resonance. The formal account of Scarlett's actions and behavior is shadowed by unstated psychological considerations. The central flaw in Scarlett's character, the source of her egoism, derives from the relationship with her mother that purportedly furnishes her standards of being a lady. All explicit references to Ellen in the novel, including Scarlett's own, are positive. Yet all indirect evidence suggests that

Scarlett never attained that psychological identification with her mother that would have provided the bedrock for becoming her mother's successor. At the center of the novel, at the end of the devastating road back from the destruction of Atlanta, falls Ellen's death. For Scarlett, that road "that was to end in Ellen's arms" ended in a "blank wall," in "a dead end." Scarlett had believed that she was fleeing to "the protection of her mother's love wrapped about her like an eiderdown quilt." With Ellen dead, the hope of that love had vanished. From her despair and abandonment, Scarlett wrests the determination to survive. Somewhere "along the road to Tara, she had left her girlhood behind her." The scene that marks her assumption of womanhood ends with her vow: "As God is my witness, I'm never going to be hungry again" (418). That night, she first dreams what is to become her recurrent nightmare, of being lost in the fog. On this occasion, Melanie comes to her bedside. Later in the novel, Rhett would comfort her, promising to feed and spoil her like a treasured child. But she still passes on to Bonnie, her daughter, a fear of the dark.

The first appearance of the dream underscores the psychological dimension of her fight against hunger. The scene in the fields of Tara conflates, in a manner that persists throughout the novel, the elements of ladyhood that derive from social structure and those that derive from intrapsychic identification—especially from the mother-daughter relationship. Scarlett's willfulness, graspingness, and jealousy of other women, including her own sisters, have been present from the opening pages. Her admiration of and love for her mother have also there. But her mother emerges as distant and preoccupied, as having never recovered from an early passion, as having little of her emotional substance to give to those she so dutifully cares for. Scarlett germinated the need for love and nurture from her childhood. The crisis of her adulthood consolidates a persisting need. The social and historical circumstances of that crisis merely determine the form and intensity of her adult behavior. The underlying longing remains to be wrapped in the quilt of her mother's love. The hunger she determines to appease harks back to a longstanding unconscious feeling of deprivation.

Richard King has recently argued, in *A Southern Renaissance*, that the southern family romance, which "placed the father-son relationship at its center," left only the role of mother to the white woman who, as mistress of the plantation, was to care for the "wants and needs of her family both white and black." In King's view, this "queen of the home" was denied erotic appeal and, in "extreme form," was "stripped of any emotional nurturing attributes at all. Eventually, she came to assume a quasi-Virgin Mary role." Interestingly, Mitchell does state that Scarlett perceives her mother as the Virgin Mary. But she also provides the reader with information that supports a more complex interpretation.[15]

Ellen Robillard O'Hara had, as an adolescent, experienced an intense passion for a young cousin whom her family prevented her from marrying. After his death, in a barroom brawl in New Orleans, the young Ellen cried all night and then dried her tears and closed her heart. Her marriage to Gerald O'Hara is presented simply as an alternative to entering a convent for the rest of her life. This renunciation of her own passionate self crippled Ellen's ability to provide nurture to her own daughters and bequeathed, at least to Scarlett, contradictory attitudes toward men as objects of sexual and emotional desire. On the surface, Mitchell affirms Ellen's goodness and Scarlett's love for her. But Mitchell also shows that Scarlett managed to hide much of her impetuous, passionate self from Ellen, that in crucial ways Ellen did not know—perhaps did not want to know—Scarlett. Mitchell also informs us that Ellen had never told Scarlett that "desire and attainment were two different matters" (73). These clues and others invite the reader to criticize Ellen from Scarlett's perspective, much in the manner that Lillian Smith would criticize her own mother. Yet they do not commit Mitchell to an open critique of the mother's (her own mother's) failure vis-à-vis the daughter.[16]

If Ellen's death forces Scarlett to assume a womanhood for which she is not emotionally prepared, Melanie's death, at the novel's close, provides her with an opportunity to relive and rework that earlier loss. The parallels between Ellen and Melanie are deep and numerous. Most important, however, in psychological terms, is Melanie's marriage to Ashley, whom Scarlett loves. Scarlett's failure to understand the nature of Ashley and Melanie's love for each other, her attempt to fathom the secrets of that love through reading Melanie's letters from Ashley, her resentment of Melanie in the face of Melanie's maternally unselfish love for her, all evoke the attitudes of a female Oedipal crisis, of an adolescent girl who loves her father and hates her mother. Melanie and Ashley permit Mitchell to explore that crisis because they are not Scarlett's parents. Yet the emotional logic of the situation forces the reader to take it as evidence of Mitchell's using Melanie as a double for Ellen. And whatever Scarlett's conscious feelings, her relationship with Melanie permits her to come to terms with her ambivalent feelings about her mother. Only at Melanie's death-bed does Scarlett begin to see clearly, to arrive at some measure of self-understanding. Only at Melanie's death does she recognize the true object of longing in her recurring nightmare of cold and hunger. Throughout the novel we are told that Scarlett loves Ellen; as the novel progresses, we come to know that Melanie loves Scarlett. That love, as Rhett asserts, may indeed be Scarlett's cross, but it may also be her salvation. For at the end, the loss of Rhett may have to be weighted against her recognizing Rhett as the object of her desire.[17]

Ellen had endowed Scarlett, the child, with a hunger for herself, a longing for maternal love. That longing colors Scarlett's choice of men. Both consciously and unconsciously, Scarlett perceives Ashley Wilkes to be cut from the same cloth as Ellen. Aristocratic and self-controlled, he possesses self-knowledge and acts according to principles that she cannot fathom. Until the final scenes of the novel, Scarlett misunderstands and misevaluates Ashley: she understands neither his strength nor his weakness. Least of all does she understand his love for Melanie, or that his love could coexist with an altogether different love for herself. In comparable fashion, Scarlett misperceives Rhett: only in the final pages of the novel does she recognize her love for him (although the reader has known of that love since the early sections of the novel on the war years in Atlanta), but by then she has (apparently) lost him. Scarlett's woeful inability to fathom her own desires or those of the men in her life has its roots in her inability to arrive at a mature female identity—to become a woman. Or so Mitchell would seem to be suggesting. Scarlett fails to integrate her needs and her desires, her understanding of love—the longing of romantic love—with her sexual feelings. There are persisting hints that Scarlett, the erstwhile tomboy, would, on some level, prefer to be a man. Mitchell never fully resolves these tensions.

For although she allows Scarlett a clearer perception of herself and her desires, she deprives her of the objects of that desire. In the end, Scarlett has only herself. Even Tara will provide only a temporary retreat, not a full life.

Mitchell's ambivalent attitudes towards female sexuality, gender identity, and gender role—desire, womanhood, and ladyhood—informed her own life, as well as the life of her heroine. The discrete components of this ambivalence include uncertainty as to whether sexuality is compatible with womanhood, mixed feelings about motherhood and its relationship to sexuality, and the possibility for wedding female individualism to ladyhood. The core of Scarlett's dilemma remains whether she can transform her need for her mother into love for a man and children. And this basic psychodynamic pattern is faithful to an increasingly typical early twentieth-century pattern. Ellen could be read as a positive rendition of Philip Wylie's "Momism." Gerald O'Hara could qualify as the absent father. Scarlett herself could be recast as a 1920s flapper.[18] Mitchell mediates, rather than invites, these transpositions. But the compelling popularity of her novel may have turned on her readers' effecting the identifications for themselves. Even the resonances that bind contemporary identifications to the historical plot do not clarify Mitchell's own attitudes toward the appropriate meaning and responsibilities of womanhood and ladyhood, especially toward female destiny relative to that of men.

Historians such as Anne Firor Scott and A. Elizabeth Taylor have demonstrated the interdependence of the position of southern women and the southern social system as a whole, and have argued that southern women themselves criticized southern patriarchy.[19] Mitchell understands these arguments, but on the surface, her own critique is more narrowly focused on men as men and is more indirect in its expression. For Mitchell does not so much criticize men as display their weaknesses and, too often, kills them off. At the same time, she endows men with the objective view of history and the nature of civilization. Despite the constant juxtaposition of Rhett and Ashley in Scarlett's mind, Mitchell presents them as one in their grasp of historical process. Thus, even as individual men fall by the wayside, men as a group emerge as the custodians of objective knowledge. The problem is to identify Mitchell's own ultimate attitude toward the claims of female independence. That problem is complicated by her play with transsexual identifications: "But Scarlett, child of Gerald, found the road to ladyhood hard" (58). Ellen's early passion suggests that sexuality cannot simply be classified as masculine. Mitchell nonetheless underscores Scarlett's inheritance from her unruly Irish father and portrays raw sexuality as masculine and inherently dominating—to wit, the famous scene in which a drunken Rhett carries Scarlett off to bed. Mitchell also considers the relations between sexuality and generativity problematical: Scarlett miscarries the baby conceived in her and Rhett's mutual passion; Ellen, reproducing without passion, lost all of her sons; Melanie dies in childbirth; Bonnie, beloved of both Scarlett and Rhett, dies perhaps as a result of her inherited Irish recklessness, perhaps as a result of her father's delight in her unladylike high spirits, perhaps as a result of the Oedipal confusions that inform Scarlett's own life, perhaps in testimony to Scarlett's and Rhett's failed communication—their inability to reproduce.

Any of these readings is compatible with one or another female critique of patriarchy and the toll it exacted from women. Any is compatible with a severe judgment on women who rebel against their ordained role. Mitchell, like Scott and Taylor, stresses the interdependence of female role and social system. If she, consciously or not, resented the constraints that the role of lady imposed on women, she remained attached to the class basis of the social system—to the class and race relations within which that role was essential. But Mitchell's strategy is complicated by her interest in social change and her commitment to establishing the Old South as a special case of a general national past. Her treatment of the Old South brilliantly blends a nostalgia for a lost social order, a more stable agrarian world, with a specific evocation of southern culture. She eschews any defense of slavery as a coherent social system in favor of evoking a harmonious agricultural order reminiscent of that evoked in *I'll Take My Stand*.[20] Her early discussion of Tara, resting upon a detailed rendition of upland Georgia, establishes the specificity of time and place, but none of the description bears any relation to the slave system. Mitchell brings her readers to accept a particular world without including any of the social features that structure it. By this mar-

velous sleight of hand, she invites a national audience to accept
the Old South as a direct antecedent of its own American civilization. The lost antebellum civilization is validated for the South
even as it is absorbed into the loss of an earlier American order.

Similarly, Mitchell recasts southern slavery to conform to a
national class system. Her attitudes toward blacks resemble those
of Howard Odum in their social Darwinism and in "the racist
transformation of social 'facts' into natural givens." Yet, as Odum
did in his later works, Mitchell also allows for the development of
a black leadership under white guidance. Her attitudes remain
contradictory, all the more because she draws upon black characters to provide psychologically revealing doubles of whites, but
she is wedded to conservative class and racial attitudes. Her attitudes toward contemporary issues shape her depiction of slavery
which, in her treatment, disappears as a coherent social system.[21]

Mitchell distinguishes between house and field slaves. In an
authorial intervention, she explains that "the house negroes and
yard negroes" despised "these lowly blacks." For the position of
the house slaves rested upon merit and effort. "Just as Ellen had
done, other plantation mistresses throughout the South had put
the pickanninies through courses of training and elimination to
select the best of them for the positions of greater responsibility.
Those consigned to the fields were the ones least willing or able to
learn, the least energetic, the least honest and trustworthy, the
most vicious and brutish. And now this class, the lowest in the
black social order, was making life a misery for the South" (654).
Mitchell here echoes the prevailing capitalist ideology of work,
schooling, and the promotion of merit, tempered by a harsh attitude toward crime.

Mitchell also describes even the good, deserving blacks as
"monkeyfaced" and "childlike." The former fieldhands, whom
the Yankees had so irresponsibly promoted to positions of responsibility, "conducted themselves as creatures of small intelligence
might naturally be expected to do. Like monkeys or small children turned loose among treasured objects whose value is beyond
their comprehension, they ran wild—either from perverse pleasure in destruction or simply because of their ignorance." Not
naturally malicious, they were, "as a class, childlike in mental-
ity" (654). Mitchell thus combines racism as a justification for

black subordination with a commitment to individual betterment through the work ethic. Blacks, she believes, can rise in the social ladder to the extent that they accept and profit from the tutelage of their white betters.

Mitchell cannot resist some nostalgic pronouncements on the ties binding the black and white family, but her star characters in this category—Mammy, Uncle Peter, Sam, and, with special reservations, Prissy—all relate to the white family as individuals rather than as members of families of their own. And the personal loyalties that transcend class and racial lines all have roots in the lost agrarian civilization. When the blacks remain true to those roots and reject their chance for independence they fare well, and even have the freedom to chastise their masters. The moment they cut loose from the restraining bonds, their inferiority becomes a crippling disadvantage. By thus substituting racism for slavery as the basis for domination, Mitchell endorses precisely the process that historically established the grounds for a reconciliation between the North and the South.

Mitchell's harsh attitude towards blacks collectively does not prevent her from valuing individual blacks on the basis of their personal attributes. Mammy especially, but also Uncle Peter, Sam, and even Prissy are shown as genuine characters in their own right. Mitchell in fact uses them as psychological doubles for important white characters. Uncle Peter functions as a double for Ashley and, beyond him, for the white gentlemen of the antebellum South. Uncle Peter embodies all the manners, bearing, and respect for convention that purportedly characterized the antebellum aristocracy. From this perspective, Uncle Peter's finicky timidity reflects on Ashley and alerts the reader to those weaknesses which Scarlett refuses to see, or at least to interpret correctly. Sam, in contrast, throws into relief the solidity and dependability that underlie Rhett's unconventional and disturbing surface behavior. Prissy illuminates Scarlett's own failure to achieve an internal sense of female generativity: "Laws, Mis Scarlett, I doan know nothing 'bout birthin babies." And, in this case, since Prissy has claimed to have precisely that knowledge, her failure underscores the gap between Scarlett's external appearance as a grown woman and her internal identity as a needy child.

In this context, Mammy plays the most complex role of all.

The life of the character almost escapes Mitchell's control, and assuredly escapes Mitchell's racist convictions. For Mammy, the compelling double for Ellen, comes close to providing Scarlett with everything that Ellen could not. Mammy's knowledge of Scarlett and her acceptance of her could have provided the foundations for Scarlett's gender identity. Mammy neither sees nor experiences any contradictions between understanding Scarlett and loving or forgiving her. Lacing Scarlett into her corset, forcing her to eat before a barbecue so she will not disgrace herself by eating at it, are to Mammy the unavoidable requirements of correct behavior. Scarlett's recalcitrance elicits disciplinary action but not condemnation. Mammy could have molded Scarlett into a lady, precisely because Mammy would have felt no need to repudiate Scarlett the needy child and the sensual woman. Ellen, having repudiated those qualities in herself, could not afford to recognize them in Scarlett and, therefore, could not help her deal with them. Mammy, swishing proudly in her red petticoat, knows as much about sexuality as Belle Watling. Mammy also knows that you wear your red satin where it does not show. But if Mitchell could, consciously, allow Mammy to lay bare Ellen's failures as a woman and as a mother, she could not surmount her class and racial attitudes in order to allow Mammy's knowing nurture to provide Scarlett's maternal identification. Herein, perhaps, lies her most devastating, if unintended, condemnation of the values she sought to support.

Gone with the Wind originated in and spoke to a particular moment in American culture. Its very status as a novel, straddling the worlds of elite and mass culture, captured the dilemma of a bourgeois society that struggled to preserve its own values against internal rebellion and to engage the allegiance of a broad and heterogeneous popular base. Not unlike the new languages of radio, film, and advertising, it appeared to offer Americans an image of themselves at once specific enough to invite identification and general enough to encompass national diversity.[22] Mitchell's re-creation of the 1860s, so faithful in its historical detail, bound the destruction of an ordered world to the birth of modern America. Structurally equated as the two great opportunities for making a fortune, the building up and breaking up of civilizations emerge as cyclical recurrences in human affairs. That philosophical distance in no way detracts from the poignancy and drama of the carefully documented tale. Nor does it ever soar to encompass the full range of human destinies. Rather, it subsumes a purportedly traditional society under the aegis of bourgeois norms. And this fusion, in turn, promises the persistence of those norms in a world that is outstripping its original social base.

No one more compellingly portrayed the relation between the past and the future of the nation and the South than Mitchell. But, for her, the binding up of wounds required a shared bourgeois ethic and could ill afford the luxury of mourning a "feudal" past. Under the bourgeois rubric, the nation could be understood as the destiny of the South and the South as a generalized, rural, national past. Perhaps it is a final, fitting irony that the magnetic core of Mitchell's vision of a revitalized bourgeois order lay in the unconscious life of a most disorderly girl.

Notes

I would like to thank Thomas Africa, Herbert Aptheker, Sarah Elbert, Duncan Rice, Lewis Rubin, Sterling Stuckey, and, as always, Eugene D. Genovese.

1. The problem of genre merits particular attention with respect to *Gone with the Wind,* but transcends the scope of this essay. As a novel, *Gone with the Wind* falls somewhere between the great bourgeois novels and recent mass-market melodramas or gothics, and blends features of all. Less programmatic, at once historically more accurate and psychologically more complex than the classic melodrama, it nonetheless approaches the melodrama in that its "universal moral order validates current social attitudes." And, like the social melodrama, it basically affirms a connection between traditional middle-class domestic morality and "the operative principles of the cosmos." See John G. Cawelti, *Adventure, Mystery, and Romance* (Chicago, 1976), on these questions of genre. *Gone with the Wind* also owes much to the tradition of the historical novel analyzed by Georg Lukacs, *The Historical Novel* (Boston, 1963).

2. David O. Selznick's spectacular film only extended its impact. Among many, see Roland Flamini, *Scarlett, Rhett, and a Cast of Thousands: The Filming of Gone with the Wind* (New York, 1975); and Jack Temple Kirby, *Movie-Made Dixie: The South in the American Imagination* (Baton Rouge, La., 1978).

3. Finis Farr, *Margaret Mitchell of Atlanta* (New York, 1974), 110–13.

See also Richard Gray, *The Literature of Memory: Modern Writers of the American South* (Baltimore, 1977), 93, 151.

4. Introduction in Susman, ed., *Culture and Commitment, 1929–1945* (New York, 1973); and his "The Thirties," in Stanley Coben and Lorman Ratner, eds., *The Development of an American Culture* (Englewood Cliffs, N.J., 1970).

5. Among many, see James McGovern, "The American Woman's Pre–World War I Freedom in Manners and Morals," *Journal of American History* 55 (1968):315–33; Estelle Freedman, "The New Woman: Changing Views of Women in the 1920's," *Journal of American History* 61 (1974):372–93; Gerald E. Critoph, "The Flapper and Her Critics," in Carol V. R. George, ed., *Remember the Ladies: Essays in Honor of Nelson Manfred Blake* (Syracuse, N.Y., 1975).

6. Cf. Dawson Gaillard, "*Gone with the Wind* as Bildungsroman, or Why Did Rhett Butler Really Leave Scarlett O'Hara?" *Georgia Review* 28 (1974):9–18.

7. Farr, *Margaret Mitchell,* is the most comprehensive treatment available. See also *Atlanta Historical Bulletin: Margaret Mitchell Memorial Issue* 9 (1950); Robert L. Grover, "Margaret Mitchell, The Lady From Atlanta," *Georgia Historical Quarterly* 52 (1968):53–69; and Richard Harwell, ed., *Margaret Mitchell's Gone with the Wind Letters, 1936–1949* (New York, 1976). All references to *Gone With The Wind* will be to the first edition (New York, 1936).

8. Harwell, ed., *Letters,* 3.

9. Paul Gaston, *The New South Creed: A Study in Southern Mythmaking* (New York, 1970). See also Michael O'Brien, *The Idea of the American South, 1920–1941* (Baltimore, 1979); Daniel Aaron, *The Unwritten War: American Writers and the Civil War* (New York, 1973); and Gray, *Literature of Memory.*

10. Mitchell's work may, in this respect, be compared to that of Ulrich Bonnell Phillips, *Life and Labor in the Old South* (1929; rpt. Boston, 1963). See also Eugene D. Genovese, "Ulrich Bonnell Phillips: Two Studies," in his *In Red and Black: Marxian Explorations in Southern and Afro-American History* (New York, 1968), 259–98.

11. Cash, *The Mind of the South* (New York, 1941). Mitchell recognized the similarity between her views and those of Cash and warmly praised his book when it appeared.

12. Harwell, ed., *Letters,* 57.

13. *Ibid.,* 41.

14. See among others John C. Burnham, "The Progressive Era Revolution in American Attitudes toward Sex," *Journal of American History* 59 (1973):885–908; and references in n. 5 above. For changing southern attitudes, see John Ruoff, *Southern Womanhood, 1865–1920: An Intellectual and Cultural Study* (Ann Arbor, 1980); Anne Firor Scott, "The 'New Woman' in the New South," *South Atlantic Quarterly* 65 (1962):473–83. Cf. Ellen Glasgow, *In This Our Life* (New York, 1941).

15. King, *A Southern Renaissance: The Cultural Awakening of the American South, 1930–1955* (New York, 1980), 35.

16. Lillian Smith, *Killers of the Dream*, rev. ed. (New York, 1961).

17. This reading suggests that the years between the death of Ellen and that of Melanie constitute, in part, an extended period of mourning for Scarlett. See Sigmund Freud, "Mourning and Melancholia," in James Strachey, ed., *The Standard Edition of the Complete Psychological Works of Sigmund Freud, 1914–1916* (London: Hogarth Press, 1957), 14:243–58. For the general problems of female psychological development, see J. Chasseguet-Smirgel et al., *Female Sexuality* (Ann Arbor, 1970); Harold P. Blum, ed., *Female Psychology: Contemporary Psychoanalytic Views* (New York, 1977).

18. Philip Wylie, *A Generation of Vipers* (New York, 1942).

19. Scott, "Women's Perspective on the Patriarchy in the 1850's," *Journal of American History* 61 (1974):52–64; Taylor, "The Last Phase of the Woman Suffrage Movement in Georgia," *Georgia Historical Quarterly* 43 (1959):11–28.

20. Twelve Southerners, *I'll Take My Stand: The South and the Agrarian Tradition* (New York, 1930).

21. Odum, *The Social and Mental Traits of the Negro* (New York, 1910), 52 ff.; and King, *Southern Renaissance*, 41.

22. For example see Lary May, *Screening Out the Past* (New York, 1980.)

Disorderly Women

GENDER AND LABOR MILITANCY IN

THE APPALACHIAN SOUTH

JACQUELYN DOWD HALL

Jacquelyn Dowd Hall is Julia Cherry Spruill Professor of History at the University of North Carolina at Chapel Hill. Her most recent book, which she coauthored, Like a Family: The Making of a Southern Mill World *(1990), won the Albert J. Beveridge Prize, the Merle Curti Prize and the Philip Taft Prize. Her first book,* Revolt Against Chivalry: Jessie Daniel Ames and the Women's Campaign Against Lynching *won the Lillian Smith Award and the Frances B. Simkins Prize when it appeared in 1979. A revised edition was reissued in 1993.*

Hall's article won a prize from the Berkshire Conference of Women Historians. It first appeared in The Journal of American History *in 1986.*

The rising sun "made a sort of halo around the crown of Cross Mountain" as Flossie Cole climbed into a neighbor's Model-T and headed west down the gravel road to Elizabethton, bound for work in a rayon plant. Emerging from Stony Creek hollow, the car joined a caravan of buses and self-styled "taxis" brimming with young people from dozens of tiny communities strung along the creek branches and nestled in the coves of the Blue Ridge Mountains of East Tennessee. The caravan picked up speed as it hit paved roads and crossed the Watauga River bridge, passing beneath a sign advertising Elizabethton's newfound identity as a "City of Power." By the time Cole reached the factory gate, it was 7:00 A.M., time to begin another ten-hour day as a reeler at the American Glanzstoff plant.[1]

The machines whirred, and work began as usual. But the reeling room stirred with anticipation. The day before, March 12, 1929, all but seventeen of the 360 women in the inspection room next door had walked out in protest against low wages, petty rules, and high-handed attitudes. Now they were gathered at the factory gate, refusing to work but ready to negotiate. When 9:00 A.M. approached and the plant manager failed to appear, they broke past the guards and rushed through the plant, urging their co-workers out on strike. By 1:40 P.M. the machines were idle and the plant was closed.[2]

The Elizabethton conflict rocked Carter County and made national headlines. Before March ended, the spirit of protest had jumped the Blue Ridge and spread through the Piedmont. Gastonia, Marion, and Danville saw the most bitter conflicts, but dozens of towns were shocked by an unexpected workers' revolt.[3]

The textile industry has always been a stronghold of women's labor, and women were central to these events. The most well-known protagonist in the 1929 strikes was, and remains, Gastonia's Ella May Wiggins, who migrated from the mountains, composed ballads for the union, and became a martyr to the workers' cause. But even Ella May Wiggins has been more revered than explained. Memorialized in proletarian novels but slighted by historians, she has joined a long line of working-class heroines who served with devotion and died young. Elizabethton too had its heroines, cast from a more human mold. They were noted by contemporaries sometimes as leaders, more often as pathetic mill girls or as "Amazons" providing comic relief. In historical renditions they have dropped out of sight. The result has been thin description: a one-dimensional view of labor conflict that fails to take culture and community into account.[4]

Elizabethton, of course, is not unusual in this regard. Until recently, historians of trade unionism, like trade unionists themselves, neglected women, while historians of women concentrated on the Northeast and the middle class. There were few scholarly challenges to the assumption that women workers in general and southern women in particular were "hard to organize" and that women as family members exercised a conservative pull against class cohesion. Instances of female militancy were seen and not seen.[5] Because they contradicted conventional wisdom, they were easily dismissed.

Recent scholarship has revised that formulation by unearthing an impressive record of female activism.[6] But our task is not only to describe and celebrate but also to contextualize, and thus to understand. In Elizabethton the preindustrial background, the structure of the work force and the industry, the global forces that impinged on local events—these particularities of time and place conditioned women's choices and shaped their identities. Equally important was a private world traditionally pushed to the margins of labor history. Female friendships and sexuality, cross-generational and cross-class alliances, the incorporation of new consumer desires into a dynamic regional culture—these, too, energized women's participation. Women in turn were historical subjects, helping to create the circumstances from which the strike arose and guiding by their actions the course the conflict took.

With gender at the center of analysis, unexpected dimensions come into view. Chief among them is the strike's erotic undercurrent, its sexual theme. The activists of Elizabethton belonged to a venerable tradition of "disorderly women," women who, in times of political upheaval, embody tensions that are half conscious or only dimly understood.[7] Beneath the surface of a conflict that pitted workers and farmers against a new middle class in the town lay an inner world of fantasy, gender ideology, and sexual style.

The melding of narrative and analysis that follows has two major goals. The first is a fresh reading of an important episode in southern labor history, employing a female angle of vision to reveal aspects of the conflict that have been overlooked or misunderstood. The second is a close look at women's distinctive forms of collective action, using language and gesture as points of entry to a culture.

The Elizabethton story may also help to make a more general point. Based as it is on what Michel Foucault has termed "local" or "subjugated" knowledge, that is, perceptions that seem idiosyncratic, naive, and irrelevant to historical explanation, this study highlights the limitations of conventional categories.[8] The women of Elizabethton were neither traditionalists acting on family values not market-oriented individualists, neither peculiar mountaineers nor familiar modern women. Their irreverence and inventiveness shatter stereotypes and illuminate the intricacies of working-class women's lives.

In 1925 the J. P. Bemberg Company of Barmen, Germany, manufacturer of high-quality rayon yarn by an exclusive stretch spinning process, began pouring the thick concrete floors of its first United States subsidiary. Three years later Germany's leading producer of viscose yarn, the Vereinigte Glanzstoff Fabriken, A.G., of Elberfeld opened a jointly managed branch nearby. A post–World War I fashion revolution, combined with protective tariffs, had spurred the American rayon industry's spectacular growth. As one industry publicist put it, "With long skirts, cotton stockings were quite in order; but with short skirts, nothing would do except sheer, smooth stockings. . . . It was on the trim legs of post-war flappers, it has been said, that rayon first stepped out into big business." Dominated by a handful of European giants, the rayon industry clustered along the Appalachian mountain chain. By World War II over 70 percent of American rayon production took place in the southern states, with 50 percent of the national total in Virginia and Tennessee alone.[9]

When the Bemberg and Glanzstoff companies chose East Tennessee as a site for overseas expansion, they came to a region that has occupied a peculiar place in the American economy and imagination. Since its "discovery" by local-color writers in the 1870s, southern Appalachia has been seen as a land "where time stood still." Mountain people have been romanticized as "our contemporary ancestors" or maligned as "latter-day white barbarians." Central to both images is the notion of a people untouched by modernity. In fact, as a generation of regional scholars has now made clear, the key to modern Appalachian history lies not in the region's isolation but in its role as a source of raw materials and as an outlet for investment in a capitalist world economy.[10]

Frontier families had settled the fertile Watauga River Valley around Elizabethton before the Revolution. Later arrivals pushed farther up the mountains into the hollows carved by fast-falling creeks. Stony Creek is the oldest and largest of those creek-bed communities. Two miles wide at its base near Elizabethton, Stony Creek hollow points fourteen miles into the hills, narrowing almost to a close at its upper end, with only a little trail twisting toward the Tennessee–North Carolina line. Here descendants of the original settlers cultivated their own small plots, grazed live-stock in woods that custom held open to all, hunted and fished in an ancient hardwood forest, mined iron ore, made whiskey, spun cloth, and bartered with local merchants for what they could not produce at home.[11]

In the 1880s East Tennessee's timber and mineral resources attracted the attention of capitalists in the United States and abroad, and an era of land speculation and railroad building be-gan. The railroads opened the way to timber barons, who stripped away the forests, leaving hillsides stark and vulnerable to erosion. Farmers abandoned their fields to follow the march of the logging camps. Left behind, women and children did their best to pick up the slack. But by the time Carter County was "timbered out" in the 1920s, farm families had crept upward to the barren ridge lands or grown dependent on "steady work and cash wages." Meanwhile, in Elizabethton, the county seat, an aggressive new class of bankers, lawyers, and businessmen served as brokers for outside developers, speculated in land, invested in homegrown factories, and looked beyond the hills for their standards of "push, progress and prosperity."[12]

Carter County, however, lacked Appalachia's grand prize: the rush for coal that devastated other parts of the mountains had by-passed that part of East Tennessee. Nor had county farmers been absorbed into the cotton kingdom, with its exploitative credit system and spreading tenancy. To be sure, they were increasingly hard pressed. As arable land disappeared, farms were divided and redivided. In 1880 the average rural family had supported itself on 140 acres of land; by 1920 it was making do on slightly more than 52 acres. Yet however diminished their circumstances, 84.5 percent still owned their own land. The economic base that sustained traditional expectations of independence, production for use, and neighborly reciprocity tottered but did not give way.[13]

The coming of the rayon plants represented a coup for Eliza-bethton's aspiring businessmen, who wooed investors with prom-ises of free land, tax exemptions, and cheap labor.[14] But at first the whole county seemed to share the boomtown spirit. Men from Stony Creek, Gap Creek, and other mountain hamlets built the cavernous mills, then stayed on to learn the chemical processes that transformed the cellulose from wood pulp and cotton linters (the short fibers that remain on cotton seeds after longer, spinnable fibers are removed) into "artificial silk." Women vied for jobs in the textile division where they wound, reeled, twisted, and inspected the rayon yarn. Real-estate prices soared as the city embarked on a frenzied improvement campaign and private developers threw up houses in subdivisions of outlying fields. Yet for all the excitement it engendered, industrialization in Carter County retained a distinctly rural cast. Although Elizabethton's population tripled (from 2,749 in 1920 to 8,093 in 1930), the rayon workers confounded predictions of spectacular urban growth, for most remained in the countryside, riding to work on chartered buses and trains or in taxis driven by neighbors and friends.[15]

Women made up a large proportion of the 3,213 workers in the mills. According to company sources, they held 30 percent of the jobs at the Bemberg plant and a full 44 percent at the larger Glanzstoff mill—where the strike started and the union gained its firmest hold. Between 75 and 80 percent of those female employees were single and aged sixteen to twenty-one. But these figures underestimate the workers' youth, for the company ignored state child-labor laws and hired girls as young as twelve or, more commonly, fourteen. By contrast, a significant proportion of male workers were older, married men. Since no company records have survived, it is impossible to describe the work force in detail, but its general character is clear: The work force was white, drawn predominantly from Elizabethton and Carter County but also from contiguous areas of North Carolina and Virginia. Adult married men, together with a smaller number of teenage boys, dominated the chemical division, while young women, the vast majority of whom commuted from farm homes, processed the finished yarn.[16]

Whether married or single, town- or country-bred, the men who labored in the rayon plants followed in the footsteps of fathers, and sometimes grandfathers, who had combined farming with a variety of wage-earning occupations. To a greater extent than we might expect, young women who had grown up in Elizabethton could also look to earlier models of gainful labor. A search of the 1910 manuscript census found 20 percent (97/507) of women aged fourteen and over in paid occupations. The largest proportion (29.6 percent) were cooks and servants. But close behind were women in what mountain people called "public work": wage-earning labor performed outside a household setting. Most of these (25.1 percent) worked in the town's small cotton and garment mills. Clerks, teachers, and boardinghouse keepers rounded out this employment profile. But a few women pursued more exotic careers. A widowed "authoress—historical" headed a comfortable ten-member household. Living in a boardinghouse with her husband were a thirty-two-year-old woman and her twelve-year-old daughter, apparently members of a traveling theater troupe, their place of business listed as "on the road."[17]

For rayon workers from the countryside, it was a different story. Only 5.2 percent of adult women on Stony Creek were gainfully employed (33/638). Nineteen of these were farmers. The rest—except for one music teacher—were servants of washerwomen.[18] Such statistics, of course, are notorious for their underestimation of women's moneymaking activities. Nor do they reflect the enormous amount of unpaid labor performed by women on Carter County farms. Still, the contrast is telling, and from it we can surmise two things. The first is that industrialization did not burst upon a static, conflict-free "traditional" world. The women who beat a path to the rayon plants came from families that had already been drawn into an economy where money was a key to survival. The second is that the timber industry, which attracted Carter County's men, undermined its agricultural base, and destroyed its natural resources, created few opportunities for rural women. No wonder that farm daughters in the mills counted their blessings and looked on themselves as pioneers. For some the rayon plants offered another way of meeting a farm daughter's obligations for the family economy. But others had more complex motivations, and their route to the factory reflected the changing configuration of mountain women's lives.

Flossie Cole's father owned a tiny farm on Stony Creek, with a gristmill built from stones he had hauled over the mountain in an ox-drawn sled. When Flossie was "two months and twelve days old," he died in a coal-mining accident in Virginia, leaving his wife with seven children to support. The family kept body and soul together by grinding corn for their neighbors and tending the farm. Cole may have been new to factory labor, but she was no

stranger to women's work. While her brothers followed their father's lead to the coal mines, she pursued the two most common
occupations of the poorest mountain girls: agricultural labor and
domestic service in other people's homes. "We would hire out and
stay with people until they got through with us and then go back
home. And when we got back home, it was workin' in the corn or
wash for people." When Cole lost her job after the strike, she
went back to domestic service, "back to the drudge house," as she
put it.[19]

Bessie Edens was the oldest of ten children in a family that had
been to Illinois and back before the rayon mills arrived. Her father
had found a job in a brickyard, but her mother missed the mountains and insisted on coming home. Edens dreamed of an education and begged to go to nursing school. But her parents opposed
her plan. At fifteen she too went to work as a servant. "Then I'd
come back when Momma had a baby and wait on her, and help if
she needed me in any way." When asked fifty years later about a
daughter's place on a hardscrabble farm, Edens replied: "The girls
were supposed to do housework and work in the fields. They were
supposed to be slaves." By the time the rayon plants opened,
Edens was married and the mother of two. She left the children
with her mother and seized the chance to earn her own money
and to contribute to her family's support.[20]

Nettie Reece's father worked for Elizabethton's Empire Chair
Company while her mother kept up a seven-acre farm on the
outskirts of town. Mrs. Reece also kept four or five cows, ten
to fifteen hogs, and one hundred chickens—all that while giving birth to ten children, eight of whom survived. Nettie Reece
earned her first fifty cents pulling weeds in a wealthy family's yard.
When the German factory managers arrived, she waited on tables
at their boardinghouse (although her father was indignant when
she brought home "tips" and almost made her quit). At fourteen
she got a reeling job at the Bemberg plant. To her, work seemed
an extension of school, for she was surrounded by girls she had
known all her life. "We grew up together," she remembered. "We
used to be called the dirty dozen. [When we went to work] it
looked like the classroom was walking down the street." Movies,
Chautauqua events, and above all the opportunities for courting
presented by the sudden gathering of so many young people in the

town—these were Nettie Reece's main memories of the eight months she spent at Bemberg before the strike began.[21]

Whether they sought employment out of family need, adventurousness, or thwarted aspiration—or a combination of the three—most saw factory labor as a hopeful gamble rather than a desperate last resort. Every woman interviewed remembered two things: how she got her first job and the size of her first paycheck. "I'll never forget the day they hired me at Bemberg," said Flossie Cole. "We went down right in front of it. They'd come out and they'd say, 'You and you and you,' and they'd hire so many. And that day I was standing there and he picked out two or three more and he looked at me and he said, 'You.' It thrilled me to death." She worked fifty-six hours that week and took home $8.16.[22]

Such pay scales were low even for the southern textile industry, and workers quickly found their income eaten away by the cost of commuting or of boarding in town. When the strike came it focused on the issue of Glanzstoff women's wages, which lagged behind those at the older Bemberg plant. But workers had other grievances as well. Caustic chemicals were used to turn cellulose into a viscous fluid that was then forced through spinnerets, thimble-shaped nozzles pierced with tiny holes. The fine, individual streams coagulated into rayon filaments in an acid bath. In the chemical division men waded through water and acid, exposed all day to a lethal spray. Women labored under less dangerous conditions, but for longer hours and less pay. Paid by the piece, they complained of rising production quotas and what everyone referred to as "hard rules."[23]

Women in particular were singled out for petty regulations, aimed not just at extracting labor but at shaping deportment as well. They were forbidden to wear makeup; in some departments they were required to purchase uniforms. Most galling of all was company surveillance of the washroom. According to Bessie Edens, who was promoted to "forelady" in the twisting room, "men could do what they wanted to in their own department," but women had to get a pass to leave the shop floor. "If we went to the bathroom, they'd follow us," Flossie Cole confirmed, "'fraid we'd stay a minute too long." If they did, their pay was docked; one too many trips and they lost their jobs.[24]

Complaints about the washroom may have had other meanings as well. When asked how she heard that a strike was brewing, Nettie Reece cited "bathroom gossip."[25] As the company well knew, the women's washroom where only a forelady, not a male supervisor, could go might serve as a communications center, a hub of gossip where complaints were aired and plans were formulated.

The German origins of the plant managers contributed to tension. Once the strike began, union organizers were quick to play on images of an "imported Prussian autocracy." The frontier republicanism of the mountains shaded easily into post–World War I Americanism as strikers demanded their rights as "natural born American citizens" oppressed by a "latter day industrialism." In that they had much in common with other twentieth-century workers, for whom the democratic values articulated during the war became a rallying cry for social justice at home. The nationality of the managers helped throw those values into sharp relief.[26]

Above all, the fact that the plant managers were newcomers to the region made them unusually dependent on second- and third-line supervisors, few of whom could be drawn from established hierarchies of age and skill. The power that shop-floor supervisors thus acquired could cut two ways. If used arbitrarily to hire and fire, it could provoke resentment. At the same time, men and women whose primary concern was the welfare of family and friends might act more as shop stewards than as enforcers of the company will. Reduced to promoting the likes of Bessie Edens to authority over seventy-five young women from her own mountain coves, the managers strengthened their opposition.[27]

Efforts to organize the plants by local American Federation of Labor (AFL) craft unionists had begun at least as early as 1927.[28] But the strike was initiated on March 12, 1929, by women in the Glanzstoff inspection department, by what one observer called "girls in their teens [who] decided not to put up with the present conditions any longer." For weeks Margaret Bowen had been asking for a raise for herself and the section she supervised. That morning she had asked again and once more had been turned away. Christine Galliher remembered the moment well: "We all decided in that department if they didn't give us a raise we wasn't going to work." One by one the other sections sent word: "We are more important than any other department of the plant. . . . Why don't you walk out and we will walk out with you?" At 12:30 the inspectors left their jobs.[29]

On March 13 the women returned to the plant and led the rest of the work force out on strike. Five days later Bemberg workers came out as well. By then the Carter County Chancery Court had handed down two draconian injunctions forbidding all demonstrations against the company. When strikers ignored the injunctions, plant managers joined town officials in convincing the governor to send in the National Guard. The strikers secured a charter from the AFL's United Textile Workers (UTW). Meeting in a place called the Tabernacle, built for religious revivals, they listened to a Baptist preacher from Stony Creek warn: "The hand of oppression is growing on our people. . . . You women work for practially nothing. You must come together and say that such things must cease to be." Each night more workers "came forward" to take the union oath.[30]

Meanwhile, UTW and Federal Conciliation Service officials arrived on the scene. On March 22 they reached a "gentlemen's agreement" by which the company promised a new wage scale for "good girl help" and agreed not to discriminate against union members.[31] The strikers returned to work, but the conflict was far from over. Higher paychecks never materialized; union members began losing their jobs. On April 4 local businessmen kidnapped two union organizers and ran them out of town. Eleven days later a second strike began, this time among the women in the Glanzstoff reeling room. "When they blew that whistle everybody knew to quit work," Flossie Cole recalled. "We all just quit our work and rushed out. Some of 'em went to Bemberg and climbed the fence. [They] went into Bemberg and got 'em out of there." With both plants closed by what workers called a "spontaneous and complete walkout," the national union reluctantly promised its support.[32]

This time the conflict quickly escalated. More troops arrived, and the plants became fortresses, with machine guns on the rooftops and armed guardsmen on the ground. The company sent buses manned by soldiers farther up the hollows to recruit new workers and to escort them back to town. Pickets blocked narrow mountain roads. Houses were blown up; the town water main was

dynamited. An estimated 1,250 individuals were arrested in con-
frontations with the National Guard.[33]

As far as can be determined, no women were involved in barn
burnings and dynamitings—what Bessie Edens referred to as the
"rough . . . stuff" that accompanied the second strike. Men "went
places that we didn't go," explained Christine Galliher. "They had
big dark secrets . . . the men did." But when it came to public
demonstrations, women held center stage. At the outset "hundreds of girls" had ridden down the main street "in buses and
taxis, shouting and laughing at people who watched them from
windows and doorsteps." Now they blocked the road at Gap
Creek and refused soldiers' orders that they walk twelve miles to
jail in town. "And there was one girl that was awful tough in the
bunch. . . . She said, 'No, by God. We didn't walk out here, and
we're not walking back!' And she sat her hind end down in the
middle of the road, and we all sat down with her. And the law
used tear gas on us! . . . And it nearly put our eyes out, but we still
wouldn't walk back to town." At Valley Forge women teased the
guardsmen and shamed the strikebreakers. In Elizabethton after
picket duty, women marched down the "Bemberg Highway . . .
draped in the American flag and carrying the colors"—thereby
forcing the guardsmen to present arms each time they passed.
Inventive, playful, and shrewd, the women's tactics encouraged a
holiday spirit. They may also have deflected violence and garnered community support.[34]

Laughter was among the women's most effective weapons. But
they also made more prosaic contributions, chief among which
was taking responsibility for the everyday tasks of the union. In
this they were aided by the arrival of middle-class allies, a series of
extraordinary women reformers who provided new models of or-
ganizational skill and glimpses of a wider life.

After World War I national women's organizations long interested in working women had looked with increasing concern on
the relocation of the female-intensive textile industry to a region
where protective legislation was weak and unions were weaker.
The National Women's Trade Union League (NWTUL) launched
a southern educational campaign. The Young Women's Christian
Association (YWCA) strengthened its industrial department and
employed a series of talented southern industrial secretaries. In

1927 Louise Leonard left her YWCA post to found the Southern Summer School for Women Workers in Industry. The convergence of interest in the South's women workers intensified with the 1929 strikes. The strikes, in turn, raised reformers' expectations and lent substance to their strategies. Leonard, for instance, visited Elizabethton, recruiting students for the Southern Summer School. Some of those who went returned again and again, and for them the school offered an exciting political education. But the benefit ran both ways. For Leonard the strike confirmed in microcosm the school's larger hopes: the nature of southern industrialization made women the key to unionization; women had led the way at Elizabethton; once reached by the Southern Summer School (and a trade-union movement more sensitive to their needs), women would lead the way throughout the South.[35]

Unlike the YWCA-based reformers, the NWTUL was a newcomer to the region, and to most of its executive committee the South was literally "another nation." Dependent on the writings of journalists and sociologists, NWTUL leaders concluded that southern workers were crippled by poverty and paternalism and that only a roundabout approach through southern liberals would do. The Elizabethton strike persuaded them to take a fresh approach. The NWTUL's twenty-fifth anniversary convention, held in 1929, featured a "dramatic and moving" speech by Margaret Bowen and a historical tableau linking the revolt of the Lowell, Massachusetts, mill girls with "the revolt of the farmers' daughters of the new industrial South today." Matilda Lindsay, director of the NWTUL's southern campaign, became a major presence at Elizabethton and at subsequent conflicts as well.[36]

Within a week after the inspectors' walkout, Matilda Lindsay set up shop in Elizabethton and began coordinating women's union support activities. Women gave out union food vouchers at L. G. Bowles's boardinghouse, where Margaret Bowen lived. They helped to run the union office. Teams of "pretty young girls" distributed handbills and took up contributions at union "tag days" in Knoxville and Asheville. A similar contingent tried to see Gov. Henry H. Horton in Nashville. Failing, they picketed his home. When the strike dragged on, the union leased a boardinghouse for young women and put Lindsay in charge. At the Tennessee Federation of Labor's 1929 convention, UTW officials acknowledged Lindsay's contributions: "She was speaker, adviser, mother, sister, bookkeeper, secretary and stenographer . . . and we are happy to say she did them all without protest and without credit." But the tribute said less about Lindsay than about the distance between the vision of women reformers and the assumptions of trade-union leaders. Whether workers or reformers, women were seen as supporting players, not the best hope for cracking the nonunion South.[37]

In any event, it was workers, not organizers or reformers, who bore the brunt of the struggle and would have to live with its results. And beneath high spirits the terms of battle had begun to change. The militancy of Alfred Hoffmann, the utw's chief organizer at Elizabethton, matched the strikers' own. But he was hobbled by a national union that lacked the resources and commitment to sustain the strike. Instead of translating workers' grievances into a compelling challenge, the utw pared their demands down to the bone. On May 26, six weeks after the strike began, the union agreed to a settlement that made no mention of wages, hours, working conditions, or union recognition. The company's only concession was a promise not to discriminate against union members. The workers were less than enthusiastic. According to the strike's most thorough chronicler, "It took nine speeches and a lot of question answering lasting two and a half hours to get the strikers to accept the terms."[38]

The press, for the most part, greeted the settlement as a workers' victory, or at least a satisfactory resolution of the conflict. Anna Weinstock, the first woman to serve as a federal conciliator, was credited with bringing the company to the bargaining table and was pictured as the heroine of the event. "SETTLED BY A WOMAN!" headlined one journal. "This is the fact that astounds American newspaper editors." "Five feet five inches and 120 pounds of femininity; clean cut, even features"—and so on, in great detail. Little was made of Weinstock's own working-class origins. She was simply a "new woman," come to the rescue of a backward mountain folk. The strikers themselves dropped quickly from view.[39]

Louise Leonard had visited Elizabethton only weeks before the utw capitulated. With her was the left-wing journalist Mary

Heaton Vorse. Both were heartened by what they found. In her years of labor reporting, Vorse "had never seen anything to compare with the quality of courage and determination of the Elizabethton strikers." Leonard was impressed not only by the women's leadership but also by the strike's community support.[40] As it turned out, neither "courage and determination" nor community support was sufficient to the strikers' needs. The contest at Elizabethton was an unequal one, with a powerful multinational corporation backed by the armed force of the state pitted against workers who looked to an irresolute national union for support. But it was not so unequal in contemporary eyes as hindsight would have it. To the strikers, as to Vorse and Leonard, the future seemed up for grabs.

Observers at the time and historians since saw the Elizabethton strike as a straightforward case of labor-management strife. But the conflict appeared quite different from within. Everyone interviewed put the blame for low wages on an alliance between the German managers and the "leading citizens" of the town. Preserved in the oral tradition is the story of how the "town fathers" promised the company a supply of cheap and unorganized labor. Bessie Edens put it this way: They told the company that "women wasn't used to working, and they'd work for almost nothing, and the men would work for low wages. That's the way they got the plant here." In this version of events the strike was part of an ongoing tug-of-war. On one side stood workers, farmers, and small merchants linked by traditional networks of trade and kin. On the other, development-minded townspeople cast their lot with a "latter day industrialism" embodied by the rayon plants.[41]

Workers' roots in the countryside encouraged resistance and helped them to mobilize support once the strike began. "These workers have come so recently from the farms and mountains . . . and are of such independent spirit," Alfred Hoffmann observed, "that they 'Don't care if they lose their jobs' and cannot be scared." Asked by reporters what would happen if strike activity cost them their jobs, one woman remarked, "I haven't forgotten to use a hoe," while another said, "We'll go back to the farm."[42] Such threats were not just bravado. High levels of farm ownership sustained cultural independence. Within the internal economy of families, individual fortunes were cushioned by reciprocity; an

orientation toward subsistence survived side by side with the desire for cash and store-bought goods.

Stony Creek farmers were solidly behind the sons and daughters they sent to the factories. In county politics Stony Creekers
had historically marshaled a block vote against the town. In 1929
Stony Creek's own J. M. Moreland was county sheriff, and he
openly took the strikers' side. "I will protect your plant, but not
scabs," he warned the company. "I am with you and I want you to
win," he cheered the Tabernacle crowd.[43]

Solidarity flowed not only from the farm families of striking
workers but also from small merchants who relied on those families for their trade. A grocer named J. D. White turned his store
into a union commissary and became a mainstay on the picket
line. A strike leader in the twisting room ran a country store and
drove his working neighbors into town. "That's why he was pretty
well accepted as their leader," said a fellow worker. "Some of them
were cousins and other relations. Some of them traded at his
store. Some of them rode in his taxi. All intertwined."[44]

The National Guard had divided loyalties. Parading past the
plants, the strikers "waved to and called the first names of the
guardsmen, for most of the young men in uniforms [were friends
of] the men and girls on strike." Even when the local unit was
fortified by outside recruits, fraternizing continued. Nettie Reece,
like a number of her girlfriends, met her future husband that way;
she saw him on the street and "knew that was mine right there."
Some guardsmen went further and simply refused to serve. "The
use of the National Guard here was the dirtiest deal ever pulled,"
one protested. "I turned in my equipment when I was ordered to
go out and patrol the road. I was dropped from the payroll two
weeks later."[45]

In this context of family- and community-based resistance,
women had important roles to play. Farm mothers nurtured the
strikers' independence simply by cleaving to the land, passing on
to their children a heritage at odds with the values of the new
order and maintaining family production as a hedge against the
uncertainties of a market economy. But the situation of farm
mothers had other effects as well, and it would be a mistake
to push the argument for continuity too far. As their husbands
ranged widely in search of wage labor, women's work intensified

while their status—now tied to earning power—declined. The female strikers of Elizabethton saw their mothers as resourceful and strong but also as increasingly isolated and hard pressed. Most important, they no longer looked to their mothers' lives as patterns for their own.[46]

The summer after the strike, Bessie Edens attended the Southern Summer School, where she set the group on its ear with an impassioned defense of women's rights:

It is nothing new for married women to work. They have always worked. . . . Women have always worked harder than men and always had to look up to the man and feel that they were weaker and inferior. . . . If we women would not be so submissive and take every thing for granted, if we would awake and stand up for our rights, this world would be a better place to live in, at least it would be better for the women.

Some girls think that as long as mother takes in washings, keeps ten or twelve boarders or perhaps takes in sewing, she isn't working. But I say that either one of the three is as hard work as women could do. So if they do that at home and don't get any wages for it, why would it not be all right for them to go to a factory and receive pay for what they do?[47]

Bessie Edens was remarkable in her talent for translating Southern Summer School teachings into the idiom of her own experiences and observations. But scattered through the life histories written by other students are echoes of her general themes.[48] Read in the context of farm daughters' lives—their first-hand exposure to rural poverty, their yearnings for a more expansive world—these stories reflect the "structure of feeling" women brought to the rayon plants and then to the picket line and union hall. Women such as Edens, it seems, sensed the devaluation of women's handicraft labor in the face of cheap consumer goods. They feared the long arm of their mother's fate, resented their father's distant authority, and envied their brother's exploits away from home. By opting for work in the rayon plants, they struck out for their own place in a changing world. When low wages, high costs, and autocratic managers affronted their dignity and dashed their hopes, they were the first to revolt.

The Elizabethton story thus presents another pattern in the

female protest tradition. In coal-mining communities a rigid division of labor and women's hardships in company towns have resulted, paradoxically, in the notable militancy of miners' wives. By contrast, tobacco factories have tended to employ married women, whose job commitments and associational lives enable them to assume leadership roles in sustained organizing drives. In yet other circumstances, such as the early New England textile mills or the union insurgency of the 1920s and 1930s, single women initiated independent strikes or provided strong support for male-led, mixed-sex campaigns. Where, as in Elizabethton, people were mobilized as family and community members rather than as individual workers, non-wage-earning women could provide essential support. Once in motion, their daughters might outdo men in militancy, perhaps because they had fewer dependents than their male co-workers and could fall back more easily on parental resources, perhaps because the peer culture and increased independence encouraged by factory labor stirred boldness and inspired experimentation.[49]

The fact of women's initiative and participation in collective action is instructive. Even more intriguing is the gender-based symbolism of their protest style. Through dress, language, and gesture, female strikers expressed a complex cultural identity and turned it to their own rebellious purposes.[50]

Consider, for instance, Trixie Perry and a woman who called herself "Texas Bill." Twenty-eight-year-old Trixie Perry was a reeler in the Glanzstoff plant. She had apparently become pregnant ten years before, had married briefly and then divorced, giving her son her maiden name. Her father was a butcher and a farmer, and she lived near her family on the edge of town. Perry later moved into Elizabethton. She never remarried but went on to have several more children by other men. Texas Bill's background is more elusive. All we know is that she came from out of state, lived in a boardinghouse, and claimed to have been married twice before she arrived in town. These two friends were ringleaders on the picket line. Both were charged with violating the injunction, and both were brought to trial.[51]

Trixie Perry took the stand in a dress sewn from red, white, and blue bunting and a cap made of a small American flag. The prosecuting attorney began his cross-examination:

"You have a United States flag as a cap on your head?"

"Yes."

"Wear it all the time?"

"Whenever I take a notion."

"You are dressed in a United States flag, and the colors?"

"I guess so, I was born under it, guess I have a right to."[52]

The main charge was that Perry and her friend had drawn a line across the road at Gap Creek and dared the soldiers to cross it. Above all they were accused of taunting the National Guard. The defense attorney, a fiery local lawyer playing to a sympathetic crowd, did not deny the charges. Instead, he used the women to mock the government's case. Had Trixie Perry threatened a lieutenant? "He rammed a gun in my face and I told him to take it out or I would knock it out." Had she blocked the road? "A little thing like me block a big road?" What had she said to the threat of a tear gas bomb? "That little old fire cracker of a thing, it won't go off."[53]

Texas Bill was an even bigger hit with the crowd. The defense attorney called her the "Wild Man from Borneo." A guard said she was "the wildest human being I've ever seen." Texas Bill both affirmed and subverted her reputation. Her nickname came from her habit of wearing "cowboy" clothes. But when it was her turn to testify, she "strutted on the stand" in a fashionable black picture hat and a black coat. Besides her other transgressions, she was accused of grabbing a soldier's gun and aiming it at him. What was she doing on the road so early in the morning? "I take a walk every morning before breakfast for my health," Texas Bill replied with what a reporter described as "an assumed ladylike dignity."[54]

Witnesses for the prosecution took pains to contradict Texas Bill's "assumed ladylike dignity." A guardsman complained that she called him a " 'God damned yellow son-of-a-bitch' and then branched out from that." Texas Bill offered no defense: "When that soldier stuck his gun in my face, that did make me mad and I did cuss a little bit and don't deny it." Far from discrediting the strikers, the soldiers' testimony added to their own embarrassment and the audience's delight. In tune with the crowd, the defense attorney "enjoyed making the guards admit they had been 'assaulted' . . . by 16 and 18-year-old girls."[55]

Mock gentility, transgressive laughter, male egos on the line— the mix made for wonderful theater and proved effective in court as well. The judge reserved maximum sentences for three especially aggressive men; all the women and most of the men were found not guilty or were lightly fined. In the end even those convictions were overturned by the state court of appeals.[56]

Trixie Perry and Texas Bill certainly donned the role of "disorderly woman." Since, presumably, only extraordinary circumstances call forth feminine aggression, women's assaults against persons and property constitute a powerful witness against injustice. At the same time, since women are considered less rational and taken less seriously than men, they may meet less resistance and be punished less severely for their crimes.[57]

But Trixie Perry and Texas Bill were not just out of line in their public acts; they also led unconventional private lives. It was that erotic subtext that most horrified officialdom and amused the courtroom crowd. The only extended discussion of the strike that appears in the city council minutes resulted in a resolution that read in part:

WHEREAS, it has come to [our] attention . . . that the moral tone of this community has been lowered by reason of men and women congregating in various houses and meeting-places in Elizabethton and there practicing lewdness all hours of the night, in defiance of morality, law and order. . . .

NOW, THEREFORE, BE IT RESOLVED, that the police force of the City arrest and place in the City Jail those who are violating the laws by practicing lewdness within the City of Elizabethton. . . .[58]

Union representatives apparently shared, indeed anticipated, the councilmen's concern. Worried by rumors that unemployed women were resorting to prostitution, they had already announced to the press that 25 percent of the strikers had been sent back to their hillside homes, "chiefly young single girls whom we want to keep off the streets." The townsmen and the trade unionists were thus united in drawing a line between good women and bad, with respectability being measured not only by chastity but by nuances of style and language as well.[59] In the heat of the trial, the question of whether or not women—as workers—had violated the injunction took second place to questions about their status *as women*, as members of their sex. Had they cursed? Had they been on the road at odd hours of the day or night? Was Texas Bill a lady or a "wild man from Borneo"? Fearing that "lewd women" might discredit the organizing drive, the organizers tried to send them home. To protect the community's "moral tone," the city council threatened to lock them up.

There is nothing extraordinary about this association between sexual misbehavior and women's labor militancy. Since strikers are often young single women who violate gender conventions by invading public space customarily reserved for men (and sometimes frequented by prostitutes)—and since female aggressiveness stirs up fears of women's sexual power—opponents have often undercut union organizing drives by insinuations of prostitution or promiscuity. Fearing guilt by association, "respectable" women stay away.[60]

What is impressive here is how Trixie Perry and Texas Bill handled the dichotomy between ladyhood and lewdness, good girls and bad. Using words that, for women in particular, were ordinarily taboo, they refused deference and signaled disrespect. Making no secret of their sexual experience, they combined flirtation with fierceness on the picket line and adopted a provocative courtroom style. And yet, with the language of dress—a cap made of an American flag, an elegant wide-brimmed hat—they claimed their rights as citizens and their place in the female community.

Moreover, that community upheld their claims. The defense attorney chose "disorderly women" as his star witnesses, and the courtroom spectators enthusiastically cheered them on. The prosecuting attorney recommended dismissal of the charges against all the women on trial except Trixie Perry, Texas Bill, and a "hoodlum" named Lucille Ratliffe, on the grounds that the rest came from "good families." Yet in the court transcripts, few differences can be discerned in the behavior of good girls and bad. The other female defendants may have been less flamboyant, but they were no less sharp-tongued. Was Vivian King a member of the UTW? "Yes, and proud of it." Had she been picketing? "Yes, proud of that." What was a young married woman named Dorothy Oxindine doing on Gap Creek at five o'clock in the morning? "Out airing." Did Lena May Jones "holler out 'scab'"? "No, I think the statement made was 'I wouldn't be a scab' and 'Why don't you come and join our organization.'" Did she laugh at a soldier and tell him his gun wouldn't shoot? "I didn't tell him it wouldn't shoot, but I laughed at him . . . and told him he was too much of a man to shoot a lady."[61]

Interviewed over fifty years later, strike participants still refused to make invidious distinctions between themselves and women like Trixie Perry and Texas Bill. Bessie Edens was a settled, self-educated, married woman. But she was also a self-described "daredevil on the picket line," secure in the knowledge that she had a knife hidden in her drawstring underwear. To Edens, who came from a mountain hamlet called Hampton, the chief distinction did not lie between herself and rougher women. It lay between herself and merchants' wives who blamed the trouble on "those hussies from Hampton." When asked what she thought of Trixie Perry and Texas Bill, she answered simply, "There were some girls like that involved. But I didn't care. They did their part."[62]

Nettie Reece, who lived at home with parents who were "pretty particular with [their] daughters," shared Bessie Eden's attitude. After passing along the town gossip about Trixie Perry, she was anxious to make sure her meaning was not misconstrued. "Trixie was not a woman who sold her body," she emphasized. "She just had a big desire for sex. . . . And when she had a cause to fight for, she'd fight." Reece then went on to establish Perry's claim to a certain kind of respectability. After the strike Perry became a hard-working restaurant cook. She was a good neighbor: "If anybody got sick, she was there to wait on them." The six children she bore out of wedlock did well in life, and they "never throwed [their mother] aside."[63]

Family and community solidarity were obvious in the courtroom, implicit in press reports, and confirmed by interviews. By inference, they can also be seen in the living situations of female strikers. Of the 122 activists whose residences could be determined, only six lived or boarded alone. Residing at home, they could hardly have joined in the fray without family toleration or support.[64]

Industrialization, as we know, changed the nature of work, the meaning of time. In Carter County it entailed a shift of economic and political power from the countryside to the town. At issue too were more intimate matters of fantasy, culture, and style.

Implicit in the conflict were two different sexual systems. One, subscribed to by union officials and the local middle class, mandated chastity before marriage, men as breadwinners, and women as housewives in the home. The other, rooted in a rural past and adapted to working-class life, assumed women's productive labor, circumscribed women's roles without investing in abstract standards of femininity, and looked upon sexuality with a more pragmatic eye.

It must be noted at once that this is uncharted territory. There are no studies of gender in preindustrial Appalachia, let alone of sexuality, and discussions of the subject have been limited for the most part to a defense against pernicious stereotypes. The mountain women who people nineteenth-century travel accounts, novels, and social surveys tend to be drudges who married young and aged early, burdened by frequent pregnancies and good-for-nothing men. Alongside that predominant image is another: the promiscuous mountain girl, responsible for the supposed high rate of illegitimacy in the region.[65] We need not dwell on the shortcomings of such stylized accounts, filtered as they are through the lenses of class and cultural "otherness." But it would also be a mistake to discount them altogether, or to oppose them only with examples of mountain folk who conformed quite nicely to outlanders' middle-class norms. The view of married women as drudges is analogous to white observations of Indian life: women may in fact have taken on agricultural responsibilities seen by observers as inappropriate to their sex, while men engaged in hunting, fishing, and moonshining—and later in logging or coal mining—that seemed unproductive or illegitimate or that took them away from home. Similarly, stripped of moralism, there may be a grain of truth in observations about sexual mores in the backcountry South. The women of Elizabethton came from a society that seems to have recognized liaisons established without the benefit of clergy or license fees and allowed legitimacy to be broadly construed—in short, a society that might produce a Trixie Perry or defend "hussies from Hampton" against the snubs of merchants' wives.[66]

This is not to say that the women of Elizabethton were simply acting on tradition. On the contrary, the strikers dressed the persona of the disorderly woman in unmistakably modern garb.

Women's behavior on the witness stand presupposed a certain sophistication: a passing familiarity allowed them to parody lady-hood and to thumb a nose at the genteel standards of the town. Combining garments from the local past with fragments of an expansive consumer culture, the women of Elizabethton assem-bled their own version of a brash, irreverent Jazz Age style.

By the early 1920s radios and "Ford touring cars" had joined railroads and mail-order catalogs as conduits to the larger world. Record companies had discovered hill-country music, and East Tennessee's first country-music stars were recording hits that transformed ballad singing, fiddle playing, and banjo picking into one of America's great popular-music sounds. The banjo itself was an Afro-American instrument that had come to the moun-tains with the railroad gangs. Such cultural interchanges multi-plied during the 1920s as rural traditions met the upheavals of industrial life. The result was an explosion of musical creativity—in the hills of Tennessee no less than in New York City and other cosmopolitan centers.[67] Arriving for work in the rayon plants, young people brought with them the useable past of the coun-tryside, but they quickly assimilated the speeded-up rhythms, the fashions, the popular culture of their generation's changing times.

Work-related peer groups formed a bridge between traditional loyalties and a novel youth culture. Whether married or single, living with parents or on their own, women participated in the strike in same-sex groups. Sisters boarded, worked, and demon-strated together. Girlfriends teamed up in groups or pairs. Trixie Perry and Texas Bill were a case in point. But there were others as well. Nettie Reece joined the union with her parents' approval but also with her whole "dirty dozen" gang in tow. Ethel and M. C. Ashworth, ages eighteen and seventeen, respectively, came from Virginia to work in the plants. "Hollering and singing [in a] Ford touring car," they were arrested together in a demonstration at Watauga Point. Ida and Evelyn Heaton boarded together on Donna Avenue. Evelyn was hit by a car on the picket line, swore out a warrant, and had the commander of the National Guard placed under arrest. After the strike Evelyn was blacklisted, and Ida attended the Southern Summer School.[68]

The sudden gathering of young people in the town nourished new patterns of heterosociability, and the strike's erotic undercurrent surfaced not only in Trixie Perry's "big desire for sex" but also in the behavior of her more conventional peers. The loyalties of the guardsmen were divided, but their sympathy was obvious, as was their interest in the female strikers. Most of the Elizabethton women were in their teens or early twenties, the usual age of marriage in the region, and the strike provided unaccustomed opportunities for courtship. Rather than choosing a neighbor they had known all their lives, under watchful parental eyes, women flirted on the picket lines or the shop floor. Romance and politics commingled in the excitement of the moment, flowering in a spectrum of behavior—from the outrageousness of Trixie Perry to a spate of marriages among other girls.

What needs emphasis here is the dynamic quality of working-class women's culture—a quality that is sometimes lost in static oppositions between modernism and traditionalism, individualism and family values, consumer and producer mentalities. This is especially important where regional history has been so thoroughly mythologized. Appalachian culture, like all living cultures, embraced continuity and discontinuity, indigenous and borrowed elements.[69] As surely as Anna Weinstock—or Alabama's Zelda Fitzgerald—or any city flapper, the Elizabethton strikers were "new women," making their way in a world their mothers could not have known but carrying with them values handed down through the female line. Three vignettes may serve to illustrate that process of grounded change.

Flossie Cole's mother, known by everyone on Stony Creek as "Aunt Tine," was Sheriff Moreland's sister, but that didn't keep her from harboring cardplayers, buck-dancers, and whiskey drinkers in her home. Aunt Tine was also a seamstress who "could look at a picture in a catalog and cut a pattern and make a dress just like it." But like most of her friends, Cole jumped at the chance for store-bought clothes. "That first paycheck, that was it . . . I think I bought me some new clothes with the first check I got. I bought me a new pair of shoes and a dress and a hat. Can you imagine someone going to a plant with a hat on? I had a blue dress and black shoes—patent leather, honey, with real high heels—and a blue hat." Nevertheless, before Cole left home in the morning for her job in the rayon plant, Aunt Tine made sure that around her neck—beneath the new blue dress—she wore a bag of asafetida, a strong-smelling resin, a folk remedy to protect her from diseases that might be circulating in the town.[70]

Then there was Myrtle Simmerly, whose father was killed in a logging accident and whose brothers went "out West" to work, faithfully sending money home so that she could finish school. Myrtle was the first secretary hired at the rayon plant, and she used her earnings to buy a Ford roadster with a rumble seat and a wardrobe of up-to-date clothes. For all her modern trappings, Myrtle defended her "hillbilly" heritage and took the workers' side against what she called the "city fathers, the courthouse crew." Asked why she thought women played such active roles in the strike, she spoke from experience: "They grew up on these farms, and they had to be aggressive to live."[71]

Finally, there is visual evidence: a set of sixteen-millimeter films made by the company in order to identify—and to black-list—workers who participated in the union. In those films groups of smiling women traipse along the picket line dressed in up-to-date clothes.[72] Yet federal conciliator Anna Weinstock, speaking to an interviewer forty years later, pictured them in sunbonnets, and barefooted. "They were," she explained, "what we would normally call hillbillies": women who "never get away from their shacks."[73] This could be seen as the treachery of memory, a problem of retrospection. But it is also an illustration of the power of stereotypes, of how cultural difference is registered as backwardness, of how images of poverty and backwardness hide the realities of working-class women's lives.

The strike, as we know, was defeated, but not without cost to the company and some benefit to the workers. Elizabethton set off a chain reaction across the textile South. "It was supposed to be the leading strike in the South of the textile workers," Bessie Edens explained. "It was the main key to start the labor movement in the South, is what I understood." In Elizabethton itself an autocratic plant manager was recalled to Germany, a personnel officer installed a plant council and an extensive welfare program, wages went up, and hours went down. The new company officials chose symbols of hierarchy and privilege that blended more easily with the American scene. Uniforms were eliminated. At the dedication of a company athletic field in 1930, the "Bemberg-Glanzstoff band" marched around the grandstand, followed first by plant officials, then by workingmen carrying banners, and finally by "beautiful women, dressed in rayon suits and costumes of brilliant hues."[74]

To be sure, blacklisted workers suffered for their choices. The depression, followed by the great drought of 1930–1931, devastated the rural economy and put a powerful bludgeon in company hands.[75] Union support inevitably fell away. Rosa Long, for one, was a pragmatist: "I quit the Union because I didn't see anything to them. Wasn't making me a living talking." Yet a committed remnant, supported by the "Citizens Committee," kept the local alive. When the National Labor Relations Act passed in 1935, the Elizabethton plants were among the first to join the Textile Workers Union of America–Congress of Industrial Organizations. Transferring their allegiance to the UTW-AFL in the late 1930s, Elizabethton's workers formed the largest rayon workers' local in the country.[76]

In the community at large, a muted debate over development went on. The local newspaper kept publishing paeans to progress. But the Citizens Committee saw things differently: "Our sons and daughters have been assaulted, arrested and imprisoned because they refuse to bow to the management of the plants. [Concessions to the companies have] defrauded Carter County out of thousands of dollars of taxes rather than bettering the conditions of the county." In some ways at least, the Citizens Committee seems to have taken the more realistic view. The metropolis dreamed of by Elizabethton boosters never materialized. Having bargained away its tax base, the town was forced to default on its bonded debt. Unfinished streets and sidewalks meandered to an end in open fields; houses in subdivisions sat half-finished; chemical wastes from the rayon plants poured into the Watauga River, polluting the clear spring water that had been one of the site's attractions to industry.[77]

The fate of the Elizabethton women is difficult to discern. Interviews traced the road from farm to factory, then focused on the strike itself; they offered only hints of how the experience of the 1920s fit into whole-life trajectories. Still, circumstantial evidence allows at least a few observations. The first is that from the time the rayon plants reopened in the fall of 1929 until World War II, the number of women they employed steadily declined. Perhaps female strikers were more ruthlessly blacklisted, or men preferentially rehired. Perhaps, disillusioned, women simply stayed away. In any case, shrinking opportunities in the rayon mills did not mean that women abandoned wage labor. Although most of the activists whose subsequent histories are known married and had children, they did not permanently leave the work force. Some returned to the old roles of laundress, cook, and housekeeper; others became telephone operators, saleswomen, and secretaries.[78] Still others eventually slipped back into the rayon plants. "They called back who they wanted," said Flossie Cole. "I was out eighteen years. . . . I probably wouldn't ever have gotten back 'cause they blacklisted so many of 'em. But I married and changed my name and World War II came on and I went back to work." Overall, the percentage of Carter County women who were gainfully employed held steady through the 1930s, then leaped upward with the outbreak of war.[79]

But if the habit of female "public work" persisted, its meaning probably did not. Young women had poured eagerly into the rayon mills, drawn at least in part by the promise of independence, romance, and adventure. As the depression deepened, such motives paled beside stark necessity. One statistic makes the point: the only female occupation that significantly increased during the decade from 1930 to 1940 was domestic service, which rose from 13.4 percent of gainfully employed women to 17.1 percent. When Flossie Cole went "back to the drudge house," she had plenty of company.[80]

Still, despite subsequent hardships, the spirit of the 1920s flickered on. Setting out to explore the strike through oral-history interviews, we expected to find disclaimers or silences. Instead, we heard unfaded memories and no regrets. "I knew I wasn't going to get to go back, and I didn't care," said Bessie Edens. "I wrote them a letter and told them I didn't care whether they took me back or not. I didn't! If I'd starved I wouldn't of cared, because I knew what I was a'doing when I helped to pull it. And I've never regretted it in any way. . . . And it did help the people, and it's helped the town and the country."[81] For those, like Edens, who went on to the Southern Summer School or who remained active in the union, the strike was a pivot around which the political convictions and personal aspirations of a lifetime turned. For them, there were intangible rewards: a subtle deepening of individual power, a belief that they had made history and that later generations benefited from what they had done.

The strike, of course, made a fainter impression on other lives. Women's rebelliousness neither redefined gender roles nor overcame economic dependency. Their desire for the trappings of modernity could blur into a self-limiting consumerism. An ideology of romance could end in sexual danger or a married woman's burdensome double day. None of that, however, ought to obscure a generation's legacy. A norm of female public work, a new style of sexual expressiveness, the entry of women into public space and political struggles previously monopolized by men—all these pushed against traditional constraints even as they created new vulnerabilities.[82] The young women who left home for the rayon plants pioneered a new pattern of female experience, and they created for their post–World War II daughters an environment far different from the one they, in their youth, had known. It would be up to later generations to wrestle with the costs of commercialization and to elaborate a vision that embraced economic justice and community solidarity as well as women's liberation.

Notes

This essay is part of a larger study of southern textile workers cowritten by Christopher Daly, Jacquelyn Dowd Hall, Lu Ann Jones, Robert Korstad, James Leloudis, and Mary Murphy. It began as a collaborative endeavor with Sara Evans of the University of Minnesota, who joined me in gathering many of the interviews on which I have relied. Support for this project came from a University Research Council Grant, an Appalachian Studies Fellowship, and a Woodrow Wilson International Center for Scholars Fellowship.

1. Dan Crowe, *Old Town and the Covered Bridge* (Johnson City, Tenn., 1977), 32, 71; Florence (Cole) Grindstaff interview by Jacquelyn Dowd Hall, July 10, 1981 (in Jacquelyn Dowd Hall's possession). The oral-history component of this essay consists of approximately thirty interviews, the most detailed of which were with pro-union activists, a National Guardsman, one of the original German managers of the Bem-

berg plant, a leader of a company-sponsored organization of "loyal" workers, and members of the sheriff's family. Briefer interviews with workers who remembered the strike but who had not been actively involved are also included.

2. *Elizabethton Star,* March 13, 1929; *Knoxville News Sentinel,* March 13, 1929; Margaret Bowen, "The Story of the Elizabethton Strike," *American Federationist* 36 (June 1929):664–68; U.S. Congress, Senate, Committee on Manufactures, *Working Conditions of the Textile Industry in North Carolina, South Carolina, and Tennessee,* 71st Cong., 1st sess., May 8, 9, and 20, 1929; *American Bemberg Corp. v. George Miller et al.,* minute books "Q" and "R," Chancery Court minutes, Carter County, Tenn., July 22, 1929 (Carter County Courthouse, Elizabethton, Tenn.).

3. For the 1929 strike wave, see Tom Tippett, *When Southern Labor Stirs* (New York, 1931); Liston Pope, *Millhands and Preachers: A Study of Gastonia* (New York, 1942), 207–330; James A. Hodges, "Challenge to the New South: The Great Textile Strike in Elizabethton, Tennessee, 1929," *Tennessee Historical Quarterly* 23 (Dec. 1964):343–57; Irving Bernstein, *The Lean Years: A History of the American Worker, 1920–1933* (Boston, 1960), 1–43; David S. Painter, "The Southern Labor Revolt of 1929" (seminar paper, University of North Carolina, Chapel Hill, 1974, in David S. Painter's possession); and Jesse Creed Jones, "Revolt in Appalachia: The Elizabethton Rayon Strike, 1929" (honors thesis, University of Tennessee, Knoxville, 1974, in Paul H. Bergerton's possession).

4. On Ella May Wiggins, see Lynn Haessly, "'Mill Mother's Lament': Ella May, Working Women's Militancy, and the 1929 Gaston County Textile Strikes" (seminar paper, University of North Carolina, Chapel Hill, 1984, in Lynn Haessly's possession); and Lynn Haessly, "'Mill Mother's Lament': The Intellectual Left's Reshaping of the 1929 Gaston County Textile Strikes and Songs," *ibid.* Proletarian novels, in contrast to historical accounts, took the perspectives and experiences of women as their central concern. See esp. Fielding Burke [Olive Tilford Dargan], *Call Home the Heart* (New York, 1932). See also Sylvia Jenkins Cook, *From Tobacco Road to Route 66: The Southern Poor White in Fiction* (Chapel Hill, 1976), 98–142. For contemporary observations on Elizabethton women, see Matilda Lindsay, "Women Hold Key to Unionization of Dixie," *Machinists' Monthly Journal* 41 (Sept. 1929):638–39, 684; Sherwood Anderson, "Elizabethton, Tennessee," *Nation,* May 1, 1929, 526–27; *Knoxville News Sentinel,* May 17, 1929; and Florence Kelley,

"Our Newest South," *Survey*, June 15, 1929, 342–44. Sara Evans was the first historian to raise questions about women's roles. See Sara Evans, "Women of the New South: Elizabethton, Tennessee, 1929" (seminar paper, University of North Carolina, Chapel Hill, 1970, in Sara Evans's possession).

5. Anne Firor Scott, "On Seeing and Not Seeing: A Case of Historical Invisibility," *Journal of American History* 71 (June 1984):7–8. The new scholarship in Appalachian studies has had little to say about gender. For this point and for a plea for "concrete, empirical, historical research" on class and gender in the region, see Sally Ward Maggard, "Class and Gender: New Theoretical Priorities in Appalachian Studies," paper presented at the Eighth Annual Appalachian Studies Conference, Berea, Ky., 1985, esp. 7 (in Sally Ward Maggard's possession).

6. This scholarship has suggested that the working-class family may serve as a base for resisting exploitation. It has begun to outline the structural factors that include or exclude women from labor movements and to explore the consciousness that informs or inhibits women's collective action. See, for example, Alice Kessler-Harris, "'Where Are the Organized Women Workers?'" *Feminist Studies* 3 (Fall 1975):92–110; June Nash, "Resistance as Protest: Women in the Struggle of Bolivian Tin-Mining Communities," in *Women Cross-Culturally: Change and Challenge*, ed. Ruby Rohrlich-Leavitt (The Hague, 1975), 261–71; Dorothy Thompson, "Women and Nineteenth-Century Radical Politics: A Lost Dimension," in Juliet Mitchell and Ann Oakley, eds., *The Rights and Wrongs of Women* (New York, 1976), 112–38; Jane Humphries, "The Working Class Family, Women's Liberation, and Class Struggle: The Case of Nineteenth Century British History," *Review of Radical Political Economics* 9 (Fall 1977):25–41; Carole Turbin, "Reconceptualizing Family, Work and Labor Organizing: Working Women in Troy, 1860–1890," *ibid.*, 16 (Spring 1984):1–16; Elizabeth Jameson, "Imperfect Unions: Class and Gender in Cripple Creek, 1894–1904," in Milton Cantor and Bruce Laurie, eds., *Class, Sex, and the Woman Worker*, (Westport, 1977), 166–202; Thomas Dublin, *Women at Work: The Transformation of Work and Community in Lowell, Massachusetts, 1826–1860* (New York, 1979), esp. 86–131; Ruth Milkman, "Organizing the Sexual Division of Labor: Historical Perspectives on 'Women's Work' and the American Labor Movement," *Socialist Review* 10 (Jan.–Feb. 1980):95–150; Meredith Tax, *The Rising of the Women: Feminist Solidarity and Class Conflict, 1880–1917* (New York, 1980); Temma Kaplan, "Female Consciousness and

Collective Action: The Case of Barcelona, 1910–1918," *Signs* 7 (Spring 1982):545–66; Susan Levine, "Labor's True Woman: Domesticity and Equal Rights in the Knights of Labor," *Journal of American History* 70 (Sept. 1983):323–39; Linda Frankel, "Southern Textile Women: Generations of Survival and Struggle," in Karen Brodkin Sacks and Dorothy Remy, eds., *My Troubles Are Going to Have Trouble with Me: Everyday Trials and Triumphs of Women Workers* (New Brunswick, 1984), 39–60; Louise A. Tilly, "Paths of Proletarianization: Organization of Production, Sexual Division of Labor, and Women's Collective Action," *Signs* 7 (Winter 1981):400–417; Sharon Hartman Strom, "Challenging 'Woman's Place': Feminism, the Left, and Industrial Unionism in the 1930s," *Feminist Studies* 9 (Summer 1983):359–86; Dolores E. Janiewski, *Sisterhood Denied: Race, Gender, and Class in a New South Community* (Philadelphia, 1985), esp. 152–78; and Ruth Milkman, ed., *Women, Work, and Protest: A Century of US Women's Labor History* (Boston, 1985). In contrast, Leslie Woodcock Tentler has emphasized how family values and the structure of work have encouraged female acquiescence. Leslie Woodcock Tentler, *Wage-Earning Women: Industrial Work and Family Life in the United States, 1900–1930* (New York, 1979), esp. 9–10, 72–80, 180–85.

7. Natalie Zemon Davis, *Society and Culture in Early Modern France* (Stanford, 1975), 124–51. For this phenomenon in the New World, see Laurel Thatcher Ulrich, *Good Wives: Image and Reality in the Lives of Women in Northern New England, 1650–1750* (New York, 1982), 191–97.

8. Michel Foucault, *Power/Knowledge: Selected Interviews and Other Writings, 1972–1977*, trans. and ed. Colin Gordon (New York, 1980), 81.

9. Jesse W. Markham, *Competition in the Rayon Industry* (Cambridge, Mass., 1952), 1–38, 97, 186, 193, 209; Joseph Leeming, *Rayon: The First Man-Made Fiber* (Brooklyn, 1950), 1–82; John F. Holly, "Elizabethton, Tennessee: A Case Study of Southern Industrialization" (Ph.D. diss., Clark University, 1949), 123, 127–28, 133.

10. Bruce Roberts and Nancy Roberts, *Where Time Stood Still: A Portrait of Appalachia* (New York, 1970); William Goodell Frost, "Our Contemporary Ancestors in the Southern Mountains," *Atlantic Monthly*, (March 1899), 311; Arnold J. Toynbee, *A Study of History* (2 vols., New York, 1947), 2:312. For images of Appalachia, see also Henry D. Shapiro, *Appalachia on Our Mind: The Southern Mountains and Mountaineers in the American Consciousness, 1870–1920* (Chapel Hill, 1978). In the 1970s regional scholars posited a neocolonial, or world-systems, model for

understanding the "development of underdevelopment" in the southern mountains. More recently, they have begun to emphasize the role of indigenous elites, class formation, and the similarities between the Appalachian experience and that of other societies in transition from a semisubsistence to a corporate capitalist economy. See, for example, John Gaventa, *Power and Powerlessness: Quiescence and Rebellion in an Appalachian Valley* (Urbana, 1980); David Alan Corbin, *Life, Work, and Rebellion in the Coal Fields: The Southern West Virginia Miners, 1880–1922* (Urbana, 1981); and Ronald D. Eller, *Miners, Millhands, and Mountaineers: Industrialization of the Appalachian South, 1880–1930* (Knoxville, 1982). For an approach to cultural change, see David E. Whisnant, *All That Is Native & Fine: The Politics of Culture in an American Region* (Chapel Hill, 1983).

11. Eller, *Miners, Millhands, and Mountaineers,* 3–38; Steven Hahn, *The Roots of Southern Populism: Yeoman Farmers and the Transformation of the Georgia Upcountry, 1850–1890* (New York, 1983), 1–169; Holly, "Elizabethton, Tennessee," 1–121; Alfred Hoffmann: "The Mountaineer in Industry," *Mountain Life and Work* 5 (Jan. 1930):2–7.

12. J. Fred Holly, "The Co-operative Town Company of Tennessee: A Case Study of Planned Economic Development," *East Tennessee Historical Society's Publications* 36 (1964):56–69; Holly, "Elizabethton, Tennessee," 117–20; Eller, *Miners, Millhands, and Mountaineers,* 86–127; Rebecca Cushman, "Seed of Fire: The Human Side of History in Our Nation's Southern Highland Region and Its Changing Years," typescript, n.d., 142–44, North Carolina Collection (Wilson Library, University of North Carolina, Chapel Hill); *Mountaineer,* Dec. 28, Dec. 31, 1887; Nan Elizabeth Woodruff, *As Rare as Rain: Federal Relief in the Great Southern Drought of 1930–31* (Urbana, 1985), 140–57; Ronald D. Eller, "Class, Conflict, and Modernization in the Appalachian South," *Appalachian Journal* 10 (Winter 1983):183–86; George F. Dugger, Sr., interview by Hall and Sara Evans, Aug. 8, 1979, transcript, 8–14, Southern Oral History Program Collection, Southern Historical Collection (Wilson Library, University of North Carolina, Chapel Hill). See also David L. Carlton, *Mill and Town in South Carolina, 1880–1920* (Baton Rouge, 1982), 1–39. The problems associated with economic change in Carter County were exacerbated by a high birth rate and by the enclosure of half the county's land area for a national forest reserve. See Si Kahn, "The Government's Private Forests," *Southern Exposure* 2 (Fall 1974), 132–44; Margaret J. Hagood, "Mothers of the South: A Population

Study of Native White Women of Childbearing Age of the Southeast" (Ph.D. diss., University of North Carolina, Chapel Hill, 1938), 260–86; and Woodruff, *As Rare as Rain*, 140–41.

13. U.S. Department of the Interior, Census Office, *Report on the Productions of Agriculture as Returned at the Tenth Census (June 1, 1880)* (Washington, 1883), 84–85, 132, 169; U.S. Department of Commerce, Bureau of the Census, *Fourteenth Census of the United States Taken in the Year 1920: Agriculture,* (Washington, 1922), 6, pt. 2:446–47.

14. The negotiations that brought the rayon company to Elizabethton can be traced in the John Nolen Papers (Department of Manuscripts and University Archives, Cornell University Libraries, Ithaca, N.Y.). See esp. John Nolen, "Report on Reconnaissance Survey," typescript, box 27, *ibid.;* and John Nolen, "Progress Report and Preliminary Recommendation," typescript, *ibid.* See also Holly, "Elizabethton, Tennessee," 123, 133–38; Hodges, "Challenge to the New South," 343–44; and Dugger interview, 12–14.

15. Hoffmann, "Mountaineer in Industry," 3; *Elizabethton Star,* March 22, 1929; *Knoxville News Sentinel,* March 14, March 22, 1929; Holly, "Elizabethton, Tennessee," 156, 198. For some indirect evidence of discontent with the course of events, however, see *Elizabethton Star,* Jan. 1, Jan. 17, 1929.

16. Accounts of the size and composition of the work force differ widely. I am relying here on Committee on Manufactures, *Working Conditions of the Textile Industry in North Carolina, South Carolina, and Tennessee,* 95; interview with Arthur Mothwurf, *Knoxville News Sentinel,* May 20, 1929; Noel Sargent, "East Tennessee's Rayon Strikes of 1929," *American Industries* 29 (June 1929):10–11; and Henry Schuettler interview by Hall, n.d. [1981] (in Hall's possession). The city directory for 1930 showed only 21 married women out of 232 town-dwelling female rayon workers, whereas the figures for men were 375 out of 651. It is likely, however, that the directory underestimated married women's employment by listing only the occupation of the male head-of-household. *Miller's Elizabethton, Tenn., City Directory* (Asheville, N.C., 1930), vol. 2. (City directories are extant only for 1926, 1929, and 1930. They were published more regularly after 1936.) Blacks comprised less than 2 percent of the county's population in 1930, and few were employed in the rayon plants. This is not to say that the county's black population was unaffected by industrialization. The pull of urban growth combined with worsening conditions in the countryside drew blacks to town where they

found jobs on the railroads, in construction, and as day laborers. From 1920 to 1930, the black population dropped from 569 to 528 in the county while increasing by 650 percent in Elizabethton. U.S. Department of Commerce, Bureau of the Census, *Fifteenth Census of the United States: 1930, Population* (Washington, 1932), 3, pt. 2:909.

17. Holly, "Elizabethton, Tennessee," 108–10; Thirteenth Census of the United States, 1910, Manuscript Population Schedule, Carter County, Tenn., district 7; *ibid.*, district 15.

18. Thirteenth Census of the United States, 1910, Manuscript Population Schedule, Carter County, Tenn., district 10; *ibid.*, district 12. For the prevalence of women's work in preindustrial societies and for the traditional values that permitted families to send their daughters to take advantage of the new opportunities offered by industrialization, see Joan W. Scott and Louise A. Tilly, "Women's Work and the Family in Nineteenth-Century Europe," *Comparative Studies in Society and History* 17 (Jan. 1975):36–64. For a somewhat different view, see Dublin, *Women at Work*, 23–57.

19. Grindstaff interview.

20. Bessie Edens interview by Mary Frederickson, Aug. 14, 1975, transcript, p. 21, Southern Oral History Program Collection; Bessie Edens interview by Hall, Aug. 5, 1979 (in Hall's possession); *Elizabethton Star,* March 8, 1985.

21. Nettie Reece [pseud.] interview by Hall, May 18 and 19, 1983 (in Hall's possession).

22. Grindstaff interview; *Knoxville News Sentinel,* April 10, April 27, May 20, 1929.

23. For men's working conditions, see Hoffmann, "Mountaineer in Industry," 3; Schuettler interview; *Elizabethton Star,* Aug. 15, 1929; *Knoxville News Sentinel,* May 10, 1929; Duane McCracken, *Strike Injunctions in the New South* (Chapel Hill, 1931), 247; Lawrence Range interview by Hall, Aug. 9, 1979 (in Hall's possession); Thomas S. Mancuso, *Help for the Working Wounded* (Washington, 1976), 75–77; Bessie Edens, "My Work in an Artificial Silk Mill," in *Scraps of Work and Play,* Southern Summer School for Women Workers in Industry, Burnsville, N.C., July 11–Aug. 23, 1929, typescript, pp. 21–22, box 111, American Labor Education Service Records, 1927–1962 (Martin P. Catherwood Library, New York State School of Industrial and Labor Relations, Cornell University, Ithaca, N.Y.); Committee on Manufactures, *Working Conditions of the Textile Industry in North Carolina, South Carolina, and Tennessee,*

85. For women's working conditions, see Christine (Hinkle) Galliher, "Where I Work," in *Scraps of Work and Play*, 23; Ida Heaton, "Glanzstoff Silk Mill," in *ibid.*, 24; Edens interview, Aug. 14, 1975, 1–2, 31–32; Edens interview, Aug. 5, 1979; Grindstaff interview; and Dorothy Conkin interview by Hall, June 16, 1982 (in Hall's possession).

24. Committee on Manufactures, *Working Conditions of the Textile Industry in North Carolina, South Carolina, and Tennessee*, 83; Wilma Crowe interview by Hall, July 15, 1981 (in Hall's possession); Hoffmann, "Mountaineer in Industry," 3; Edens interview, Aug. 14, 1975, p. 32; Grindstaff interview. See also Edens, "My Work in an Artificial Silk Mill."

25. Reece interview. See also Bowen, "Story of the Elizabethton Strike," 666.

26. *Knoxville News Sentinel*, May 13, 1929; *American Bemberg Corp. v. George Miller et al.*, East Tennessee District Supreme Court, Jan. 29, 1930, record of evidence, typescript, box 660, Tennessee Supreme Court Records (Tennessee State Library and Archives, Nashville). See also *Knoxville News Sentinel*, May 14, 1929; *Elizabethton Star*, Feb. 9, 1929; Holly, "Elizabethton, Tennessee," 217; and "Synopsis of Appeal of Major George L. Berry, President of the International Printing Pressmen and Assistants' Union of North America of Pressmen's Home, Tennessee, with Relation to the Elizabethton Situation," n.d., Records of the Conciliation Service, RG 280 (National Archives). For such uses of Americanism, see Corbin, *Life, Work, and Rebellion in the Coal Fields*, 236–52.

27. Ina Nell (Hinkle) Harrison interview by Hall, Aug. 8, 1979, transcript, p. 6, Southern Oral History Program Collection; Albert ("Red") Harrison interview by Evans, Aug. 9, 1979 (in Hall's possession); Evelyn Hardin, written comments in *Scraps of Work and Play*, 25. Most helpful to my thinking about modes of management control were Jeremy Brecher, "Uncovering the Hidden History of the American Workplace," *Review of Radical Political Economics* 10 (Winter 1978):1–23; an Richard Edwards, *Contested Terrain: The Transformation of the Workplace in the Twentieth Century* (New York, 1979), esp. 3–34.

28. Scraps of evidence indicate that a number of short-term walkouts occurred before the March strike, but those walkouts were not reported by the newspapers, and accounts of them differ in detail. See Hoffmann, "Mountaineer in Industry," 3–4; E. T. Wilson to Secretary of Labor, May 25, June 26, 1929, Records of the Conciliation Service; McCracken, *Strike Injunctions in the New South*, 246; *Knoxville News Sen-*

tinel, March 13, March 15, 1929; Holly, "Elizabethton, Tennessee," 307;
and Clarence Raulston interview by Evans and Hall, Aug. 3, 1979 (in
Hall's possession).

29. *Knoxville News Sentinel,* March 14, 1929; Christine (Hinkle) Galliher and Dave Galliher interview by Hall, Aug. 8, 1979, transcript, p. 5,
Southern Oral History Program Collection; Committee on Manufactures, *Working Conditions of the Textile Industry in North Carolina, South
Carolina, and Tennessee,* 79. Although interviews provided important
information about the motives, actions, and reactions of individuals, they
were not a reliable source for constructing a factual, chronological overview of the strike. Nor did they yield a detailed account of the inner
workings of the local union. The most reliable written sources are the
court records; the stories of John Moutoux, a reporter for the *Knoxville
News Sentinel;* and a report commissioned by the Bemberg Corporation,
Industrial Relations Counsellors, Inc., and Konsul Kummer, comps.,
"Bericht über die Striks in Johnson City (Tenn.) ausgebrochen am 12.
Marz und 5. April 1929" (in Hall's possession). Gertraude Wittig supplied me with this document. For the point of view of the local manage-
ment and other industrialists, see Sargent, "East Tennessee's Rayon
Strikes of 1929," 7–32.

30. *Knoxville News Sentinel,* March 14, 1929. For other comments on
the religious atmosphere of union meetings, see Galliher interview, 8–9;
Tom Tippett, "Southern Situation," speech typescript, Meeting held at
the National Board, May 15, 1929, p. 3, box 25, Young Women's Christian
Association Papers, Sophia Smith Collection (Smith College, North-
ampton, Mass.); and Tom Tippett, "Impressions of Situation at Elizabethton, Tenn. May 10, 11, 1929," typescript, p. 1, *ibid.*

31. *Knoxville News Sentinel,* March 20, March 29, 1929; "Instructions
for Adjustment of Wage Scale for Girl Help," March 15, 1929, Records of
the Conciliation Service; "Bemberg-Glanzstoff Strike (Counter Proposition from Workers), March 22, 1929, *ibid.;* "Preliminary Report of
Commissioner of Conciliation," March 22, 1929, *ibid.*

32. Grindstaff interview; Committee of Striking Workers[,] Members of United Textile Workers of America to the Honorable Herbert
Hoover, April 16, 1929, Records of the Conciliation Service. See also
"Preliminary Report of Commissioner of Conciliation," April 16, 1929,
ibid.; William Kelly to James J. Davis, Secretary, U.S. Department of
Labor, April 15, 1929, *ibid.;* "Excerpts," April 16, 1929, *ibid.;* and *Elizabethton Star,* April 15, 1929.

33. Dr. J. A. Hardin to Hon. H. H. Horton, May 16, 1929, box 12, Governor Henry H. Horton Papers (Tennessee State Library and Archives); *Knoxville News Sentinel*, May 6, May 10, May 12, May 14, May 19, May 24, 1929; Bernstein, *Lean Years*, 18.

34. Edens interview, Aug. 14, 1975, pp. 40, 49; Galliher interview, 33; *Knoxville News Sentinel*, March 15, May 14, May 16, May 17, 1929.

35. Mary Frederickson, "Citizens for Democracy: The Industrial Programs of the YWCA," in Joyce L. Kornbluh and Mary Frederickson, eds., *Sisterhood and Solidarity: Workers' Education for Women, 1914–1984* (Philadelphia, 1984), 75–106; Mary Evans Frederickson, "A Place to Speak Our Minds: The Southern School for Women Workers" (Ph.D. diss., University of North Carolina, Chapel Hill, 1981), 92–101; Katharine DuPre Lumpkin interview by Hall, Aug. 4, 1974, transcript, pp. 23–65, Southern Oral History Program Collection; "Marching On," *Life and Labor Bulletin* 7 (June 1929):2. See also Marion W. Roydhouse, "The 'Universal Sisterhood of Women': Women and Labor Reform in North Carolina, 1900–1932" (Ph.D. diss., Duke University, 1980).

36. Alice Henry, "Southern Impressions," Aug. 23, 1927, box 16, National Women's Trade Union League Papers (Schlesinger Library, Radcliffe College, Cambridge, Mass.); Executive Board Meeting, Oct. 30, 1927, box 2, *ibid.; Knoxville News Sentinel*, May 7, March 19, 1929; "Marching On," 1, 3. See also Elizabeth Christman to Mrs. Howorth, June 11, 1929, box 12, Somerville-Howorth Papers (Schlesinger Library).

37. Reece interview; Galliher interview, 26; *Knoxville News Sentinel*, March 14, April 30, May 23, May 25, 1929; Robert (Bob) Cole interview by Hall, July 10, 1981, transcript, p. 12, Southern Oral History Program Collection; Ina Nell (Hinkle) Harrison interview, 4; Tennessee Federation of Labor, *Proceedings of the Thirty-Third Annual Convention* (Pressmen's Home, Tenn., 1929), 38.

38. *Knoxville News Sentinel*, March 19, April 14, April 27, May 5, May 27, 1929; Cole interview, 6–7; Vesta Finley and Sam Finley interview by Frederickson and Marion Roydhouse, July 22, 1975, transcript, 18–19, Southern Oral History Program Collection; *American Bemberg Corp. v. George Miller et al.*, East Tennessee Supreme District Court, Jan. 29, 1930, record of evidence, typescript, box 660, Tennessee Supreme Court Records (Tennessee State Library and Archives); "Hoffman[n] Convicted on Riot Charge: To Appeal Verdict," *Hosiery Worker*, Nov. 30, 1929, 1–2; [company spy] to Horton, April 14, April 15, 1929, box 13, Horton Papers; Mary Heaton Vorse, "Rayon Strikers Reluctantly

Accept Settlement," press release, May 27, 1929, box 156, Mary Heaton Vorse Papers, Archives of Labor and Urban Affairs (Walter P. Reuther Library, Wayne State University, Detroit, Mich.); "Norman Thomas Hits at Strike Efficiency," press release, May 27, 1929, *ibid.;* Ina Nell (Hinkle) Harrison interview, 2; *Chattanooga Times,* May 26, 1929.

39. "Rays of Sunshine in the Rayon War," *Literary Digest,* June 8, 1929, 12; *Charlotte Observer,* June 2, 1929; *Raleigh News and Observer,* May 24, 1929.

40. *Raleigh News and Observer,* May 24, 1929. See also *New York Times,* May 26, 1929, sec. 3, p. 5.

41. Edens interview, Aug. 14, 1975, 43–44; Schuettler interview; Myrtle Simmerly interview by Hall, May 18, 1983 (in Hall's possession); Dugger interview, 22; Ollie Hardin interview by Hall and Evans, Aug. 9, 1979 (in Hall's possession); Effie (Hardin) Carson interview by Hall and Evans, Aug. 6, 1979, transcript, 41, Southern Oral History Program Collection. John Fred Holly, who grew up in Elizabethton and worked at the plant during the 1930s, reported that banker E. Crawford (E. C.) Alexander showed him a copy of an agreement between the company and the Elizabethton Chamber of Commerce assuring the rayon concerns that they would never have to pay weekly wages in excess of ten dollars and that no labor unions would be allowed to operate in the town. Holly, "Elizabethton, Tennessee," 306–307. For earlier manifestations of town-county tensions, see *Mountaineer,* Dec. 28, Dec. 31, 1887, May 2, March 7, 1902. A model for this community-oriented approach to labor conflict is Herbert G. Gutman, *Work, Culture, and Society in Industrializing America: Essays in American Working-Class and Social History* (New York, 1976), 234–60.

42. James Myers, "Field Notes: Textile Strikes in the South," box 374, Archive Union Files (Martin P. Catherwood Library); *Raleigh News and Observer,* March 15, 1929. See also Hoffmann, "Mountaineer in Industry," 2–5; and *Knoxville News Sentinel,* March 14, May 20, 1929.

43. Hoffmann, "Mountaineer in Industry," 2–5; Robert (Bob) Moreland and Barbara Moreland interview by Hall, July 11, 1981 (in Hall's possession); Bertha Moreland interview by Hall, July 11, 1981, *ibid.; Chattanooga Times,* May 26, 1929; "Resolution Adopted at Citizens Meeting," March 11, 1930, Records of the Conciliation Service; *New York Times,* April 22, 1929, p. 17; *St. Louis Post Dispatch,* May 26, 1929; *Knoxville News Sentinel,* March 15, March 20, 1929; *Elizabethton Star,* March 15, 1929; Hardin interview; *American Bemberg Corp. v. George Miller et al.,* East Tennessee Supreme District Court, Jan. 29, 1930,

record of evidence, typescript, box 660, Tennessee Supreme Court Records (Tennessee State Library and Archives). For other support from the countryside, see *Knoxville News Sentinel*, March 21, May 10, May 12, May 20, 1929.

44. *Knoxville News Sentinel*, March 19, May 24, 1929; Tippett, "Impressions of Situation at Elizabethton, Tenn.," 1; "Armed Mob in South Kidnaps Organizer Hoffmann," *Hosiery Worker*, March 30, 1929, 2; *American Bemberg Corp. v. George Miller et al.*, Tennessee Court of Appeals, Sept. 5, 1930, records of evidence, typescript, box 660, Tennessee Supreme Court Records (Tennessee State Library and Archives); Honard Ward interview by Hall, 1981 (in Hall's possession).

45. *Knoxville News Sentinel*, May 15, 1929; Reece interview; McCracken, *Strike Injunctions in the New South*, 246. See also Hardin interview and Raulston interview.

46. Christine Stansell drew my attention to the importance of generational discontinuity. For the argument that precisely because they are "left behind" by the economic developments that pull men into wage labor, woman-centered families may become repositories of alternative or oppositional values, see Mina Davis Caulfield, "Imperialism, the Family, and Cultures of Resistance," *Socialist Revolution* 4 (Oct. 1974):67–85; and Helen Matthews Lewis, Sue Easterling Kobak, and Linda Johnson, "Family, Religion and Colonialism in Central Appalachia or Bury My Rifle at Big Stone Gap," in Helen Matthews Lewis, Linda Johnson, and Don Askins, eds., *Colonialism in Modern America: The Appalachian Case*, (Boone, N.C., 1978), 113–39. For a review of the literature on women and development, see Ellen Carol DuBois, Gail Paradise Kelly, Elizabeth Lapovsky Kennedy, Carolyn W. Korsmeyer, and Lillian S. Robinson, *Feminist Scholarship: Kindling in the Groves of Academe* (Urbana, 1985), 135–44. For a modern example relevant to the Elizabethton case, see Elizabeth Moen, Elise Boulding, Jane Lillydahl, and Risa Palm, *Women and the Social Costs of Economic Development: Two Colorado Case Studies* (Boulder, 1981), 1–16, 22–23, 171–78.

47. Bessie Edens, "Why a Married Woman Should Work," in *Scraps of Work and Play*, 30–31; Edens interview, Aug. 14, 1975, 14, 21, 34–35; Edens interview, Aug. 5, 1975; Millie Sample, "Impressions," Aug. 1931, box 9, American Labor Education Service Records.

48. Marion Bonner, "Behind the Southern Textile Strikes," *Nation*, Oct. 2, 1929, 351–52; "Scraps From Our Lives," in *Scraps of Work and Play*, 5–11; Raymond Williams, *The Long Revolution* (London, 1961), 48–71.

49. Corbin, *Life, Work, and Rebellion in the Coal Fields*, 92–93; Jame-

son, "Imperfect Unions"; Nash, "Resistance as Protest"; Tilly, "Paths of Proletarianization"; Bob Korstad, "Those Who Were Not Afraid: Winston-Salem, 1943," in Marc S. Miller, ed., *Working Lives: The Southern Exposure History of Labor in the South* (New York, 1980), 184–99; Dublin, *Women at Work;* Strom, "Challenging 'Woman's Place.'" For the suggestion that female strikers could fall back on parental resources, see Alice Kessler-Harris, *Out to Work: A History of Wage-Earning Women in the United States* (New York, 1982), 160.

50. For the symbolism of female militancy in other cultures, see Shirley Ardener, "Sexual Insult and Female Militancy," in Shirley Ardener, ed., *Perceiving Women* (New York, 1975), 29–53; Caroline Ifeka-Moller, "Female Militancy and Colonial Revolt: The Women's War of 1929, Eastern Nigeria," in *ibid.,* 127–57; and Judith Van Allen, "'Sitting on a Man': Colonialism and the Lost Political Institutions of Igbo Women," *Canadian Journal of African Studies* 6, no. 2 (1972):165–81.

51. Thirteenth Census of the United States, 1910, Manuscript Population Schedule, Carter County, Tenn., district 7; *Miller's Elizabethton, Tenn., City Directory* (Asheville, N.C., April 1928) vol. 1; *Miller's Elizabethton, Tenn., City Directory* (1930); *Elizabethton Star,* Nov. 14, 1953, Jan. 31, 1986; Reece interview; Carson interview, 25; Nellie Bowers interview by Hall, May 15, 1983 (in Hall's possession); *Knoxville News Sentinel,* May 17, May 18, 1929.

52. *American Bemberg Corp. v. George Miller et al.,* East Tennessee District Supreme Court, Jan. 29, 1930, record of evidence, typescript, box 660, Tennessee Supreme Court Records (Tennessee State Library and Archives).

53. *Ibid.*

54. *Knoxville News Sentinel,* May 17, 1929.

55. *Ibid.; American Bemberg Corp. v. George Miller et al.,* East Tennessee District Supreme Court, Jan. 29, 1930, record of evidence, typescript, box 660, Tennessee Supreme Court Records (Tennessee State Library and Archives).

56. *American Bemberg Corp. v. George Miller et al.,* minute books "Q" and "R," Chancery Court minutes, Carter County, Tenn., July 22, 1929; *American Glanzstoff Corp. v. George Miller et al.,* Court of Appeals, #1, Sept. 5, 1930 (Tennessee Supreme Court and Court of Appeals, Knoxville). On southern women's bawdy humor, see Rayna Green, "Magnolias Grow in Dirt: The Bawdy Lore of Southern Women," *Southern Exposure* 4, no. 4 (1977):29–33.

57. Davis, *Society and Culture in Early Modern France*, 124–51; Ulrich, *Good Wives*, 191–97. For the association of men, rather than women, with individual and collective aggressiveness, see Richard A. Cloward and Frances Fox Pivan, "Hidden Protest: The Channeling of Female Innovation and Resistance," *Signs* 4 (Summer 1979):651–59.

58. Elizabethton City Council, minutes, May 23, 1929, Minute Book, vol. 5, pp. 356–57 (City Hall, Elizabethton, Tenn.).

59. *Knoxville News Sentinel*, May 5, 1929; Myers, "Field Notes." For working-class standards of respectability and sexual morality, see Barbara Taylor, *Eve and the New Jerusalem: Socialism and Feminism in the Nineteenth Century* (New York, 1983), 192–205; Ellen Ross, "Not the Sort That Would Sit on the Doorstep': Respectability in Pre–World War I London Neighborhoods," *International Labor and Working Class History* 27 (Spring 1985):39–59; and Kathy Peiss, *Cheap Amusement: Working Women and Leisure in Turn-of-the-Century New York* (Philadelphia, 1986), esp. 88–114.

60. See, for example, Alice Kessler-Harris, "The Autobiography of Ann Washington Craton," *Signs* 1 (Summer 1976):1019–1037.

61. *Knoxville News Sentinel*, May 18, 1929; *American Bemberg Corp. v. George Miller et al.*, East Tennessee District Supreme Court, Jan. 29, 1930, record of evidence, typescript, box 660, Tennessee Supreme Court Records (Tennessee State Library and Archives).

62. Edens interview, Aug. 5, 1929.

63. Reece interview.

64. I am classifying as "activists" female strikers who appeared as such in newspaper stories, court records, and interviews—and for whom background information could be found.

65. Danny Miller, "The Mountain Woman in Fact and Fiction of the Early Twentieth Century, Part I," *Appalachian Heritage* 6 (Summer 1978):48–56; Danny Miller, "The Mountain Woman in Fact and Fiction of the Early Twentieth Century, Part II," *ibid.*, 6 (Fall 1978):66–72; Danny Miller, "The Mountain Woman in Fact and Fiction of the Early Twentieth Century, Part III," *ibid.*, 7 (Winter 1979):16–21; Edward Alsworth Ross, "Pocketed Americans," *New Republic*, Jan. 9, 1924, 170–72.

66. For colonists' views of Indian women, see Mary E. Young, "Women, Civilization, and the Indian Question," in *Clio Was a Woman: Studies in the History of American Women*, ed. Mabel E. Deutrich and Virginia C. Purdy (Washington, 1980), 98–110. For a particularly interesting account of sexual mores, see Olive Dame Campbell Journal, vol.

4, Jan. 1900–March 1900, esp. 26–27, 30, 33–34, 42–44, 61, 63–65, 67, 72, 78–80, 82, 92, 97, 102, 107–108, 115, 119–20, box 7, John C. and Olive Dame Campbell Papers, Southern Historical Collection; and Whisnant, *All That Is Native & Fine*, 103–79.

67. Charles K. Wolfe, *Tennessee Strings: The Story of Country Music in Tennessee* (Knoxville, 1977), 22–90; Barry O'Connell, "Dick Boggs, Musician and Coal Miner," *Appalachian Journal* 11 (Autumn–Winter 1983–84):48.

68. *Miller's Elizabethton, Tenn., City Directory* (1930); Reece interview; *American Bemberg Corp. v. George Miller et al.*, East Tennessee District Supreme Court, Jan. 29, 1930, record of evidence, typescript, box 660, Tennessee Supreme Court Records (Tennessee State Library and Archives); *Knoxville News Sentinel*, May 16, May 17, 1929; Kelley, "Our Newest South," 343; "Analysis of Union List," Oct. 21, 1929, Records of the Conciliation Service.

69. Whisnant, *All That Is Native & Fine*, 48.

70. Grindstaff interview; Robert and Barbara Moreland interview.

71. Simmerly interview.

72. *Knoxville Journal*, April 22, 1929; sixteen-millimeter film (1 reel), ca. 1929, Helen Raulston Collection (Archives of Appalachia, East Tennessee State University, Johnson City); sixteen-millimeter film (20 reels), ca. 1927–1928, Bemberg Industry Records (Tennessee State Library and Archives). Mimi Conway drew my attention to these films and, more important, helped prevent their loss or destruction when the Bemberg plant closed.

73. Anna Weinstock Schneider interview by Julia Blodgett Curtis, 1969, transcript, 161, 166, 172–73, 177, box 1, Anna Weinstock Schneider Papers (Martin P. Catherwood Library).

74. Edens interview, Aug. 14, 1975, 4; *Watauga Spinnerette* 1 (July 1930).

75. Bessie Edens, "All Quiet on the Elizabethton Front," *News of Southern Summer School for Women Workers in Industry* 1 (Oct. 1930):2, American Labor Education Service Records; Dugger interview, 18–19; Grindstaff interview; Charles Wolff, Plant Manager, to Employees, Feb. 25, 1930. Records of the Conciliation Service; Willson to Secretary of Labor, June 26, 1929; "Analysis of Union List."

76. Spencer Miller, Jr., to Davis, March 21, 1930, Records of the Conciliation Service; *American Bemberg Corp. v. George Miller et al.*, East Tennessee District Supreme Court, Jan. 29, 1930, record of evidence,

typescript, box 660, Tennessee Supreme Court Records (Tennessee State Library and Archives); Holly, "Elizabethton, Tennessee," 336–68; [U.S. National Labor Relations Board], *Decisions and Orders of the National Labor Relations Board*, vol. 23: *April 22–May 28, 1940* (Washington, 1941), 623–29; *ibid.*, vol. 24: *May 29–June 30, 1940* (Washington, 1940), 727–78.

77. *Elizabethton News*, Aug. 13, 1931; "Resolution Adopted at Citizens Meeting"; Tennessee Taxpayers Association, *A Report with Recommendations Covering a Survey of the Finances and Administrative Methods of the City of Elizabethton, Tennessee*, Research Report no. 46 (Nashville, 1940); Holly, "Elizabethton, Tennessee," 179, 212–16, 279.

78. By the fall of 1929, with the rayon plants in full operation, women made up a smaller percentage of the work force than they had before the strike. Whereas they constituted 44 percent of Glanzstoff workers before the conflict, afterward they made up only 35 percent. Although most of that change can be accounted for by an expansion in the number of male workers, the absolute number of women employed also fell from 850 to 797, while the number of men employed rose from 1099 to 1507. *Knoxville News Sentinel*, May 20, 1929; RR to Willson, Oct. 9, 1929, Records of the Conciliation Service. For Elizabethton activists returning to the work force, see *Miller's Elizabethton, Tenn., City Directory* (1930); Carson interview, 2, 35–38; Edens interview, Aug. 14, 1975, 5–7; Hazel Perry interview by Hall, May 20, 1983 (in Hall's possession); Grindstaff interview; Reece interview; Mamie Horne interview by Hall and Evans, Aug. 6, 1979 (in Hall's possession); and Ina Nell (Hinkle) Harrison interview, 9–10.

79. Bureau of the Census, *Fifteenth Census of the United States: 1930. Population*, 3, pt. 2:909; U.S. Department of Commerce, Bureau of the Census, *Sixteenth Census of the United States: 1940. Population* (Washington, 1943), 6, pt. 2:616; Grindstaff interview.

80. *Ibid.*

81. Edens interview, Aug. 14, 1975, 50.

82. For similar conclusions about first-generation immigrant workers, see Peiss, *Cheap Amusements*, 185–88; and Elizabeth Ewen, *Immigrant Women in the Land of Dollars: Life and Culture on the Lower East Side, 1890–1925* (New York, 1985), 264–69. For hints of sexual harassment on the job and for women's vulnerability in a marriage market that was no longer controlled by parents, see Reece interview, and Ina Nell (Hinkle) Harrison interview, 18–22.

Black Power

CATALYST FOR FEMINISM

SARA EVANS

Sara Evans is Professor of History at the University of Minnesota at Minneapolis. She is the author of Personal Politics *(1979) and* Born for Liberty: A History of American Women *(1989). Most recently she has coauthored* Wage Justice: Comparable Worth and the Paradox of Technocratic Reform *(1989) and* Free Spaces: Sources of Democratic Change in America *(1993).*

The essay that follows is excerpted from her first book, Personal Politics: The Roots of Women's Liberation in the Civil Rights Movement and the New Left *(Alfred A. Knopf, 1979).*

It needs to be known that just as Negroes were the crucial factor in the economy of the cotton South, so too in SNCC, women are the crucial factor that keeps the movement running on a day-to-day bais. Yet they are not given equal say-so when it comes to day-to-day decisionmaking. What can be done?—"SNCC Position Paper (Women in the Movement)," November 1964

Black women struck the first blow for female equality in the Student Nonviolent Coordinating Committee (SNCC). Their half-serious rebellion in the spring of 1964 signaled their rising power within the organization. On the front lines black women received their share of beatings and incarceration, but back at the headquarters—the "freedom house"—they still, along with the white women, did the housework; in the offices they typed, and when the media sought a public spokesperson they took a back seat. Gradually they began to refuse this relegation to traditional sex roles. Ruby Doris Smith Robinson, no longer a daring teenager, was on the way to becoming one of the strongest figures in SNCC. Donna Richards reclaimed her maiden name after marrying Bob Moses, one of the most highly respected and influential

men in the organization. Few understood her abrasive rejection of
the slightest hint of sex stereotyping, though many remember it.

The patterns set by such women prepared the way for a new
generation of black women who joined SNCC in 1964 and 1965
firmly believing that a woman could do anything a man could do.
Fay Bellamy, Gwen Patton, Cynthia Washington, Jean Wiley,
Muriel Tillinghast, Annie Pearl Avery—according to Gwen Patton they were equal to any man in SNCC. Taking women like
Diane Nash and Ruby Doris Smith Robinson as models, they
asserted themselves in unmistakable terms. Perhaps at some cost.
Gwen Patton felt that they had to be "superwomen" to maintain
their standing. Others pointed out that anyone who was effective
in SNCC in those days—whether male or female—had to work
long hours, take incredible risks, and refuse to be pushed around
by anyone.[1] Such toughness in women exacted a personal toll:
"Probably if you looked at all our personal lives, we've probably
had a very difficult personal life in terms of relations with men.
Many of us made decisions not to go with SNCC men, because in
some kind of way we didn't need to be fucked . . . it was very
confusing." Patton's fumbling effort to explain the dilemma is
revealing. She did not mean that women had no sexual needs,
though they may have had to set them aside temporarily. The
slang usage of "to be fucked" meant to be abused or taken advantage of. Women found it difficult to be tough and vulnerable at
the same time.

White women on the SNCC staff shared many of the tensions
and ambiguities that affected black women. For a moment it
seemed that their perceptions might coincide as the summer of
1964 raised sexual tensions to new heights. During the summer a
group of women led by Ruby Doris Smith Robinson, and including Mary King, Casey Hayden, and Mary Varela, sat down to
write a paper on the movement's failure to achieve sexual equality.
Yet King, Hayden, and Varela lacked the self-assurance of Robinson, and they were "reluctant, and even afraid to sign" their own
document.[2] As white women they were in an increasingly ambiguous position in a black-led movement. Compared to the black
women's growing power, whites were losing ground. Women like
Hayden and King understood that their roles in many ways had to
be supportive, that the movement must be led by blacks. Yet they

also wanted to be taken seriously and to be appreciated for the contributions they made. To fresh recruits they appeared to be in a powerful position. They had an easy familiarity with the top leadership of SNCC, which bespoke considerable influence, and they could virtually run a freedom registration program; but at the same time they remained outside the basic political decisionmaking process. Staughton Lynd observed the contradiction during the summer of 1964. It was, he said, as if "they had power but they didn't have power." Mary King described herself and Hayden as being in "positions of relative powerlessness." To the extent that they were powerful, it was because they worked very hard. According to King, "if you were a hard worker and you were good, at least before 1965 . . . you could definitely have an influence on policy."

Thus white women, sensing their own precariousness within the movement, held back from a direct engagement on the issue of sex roles and instead raised it anonymously, thereby inadvertently drawing on the growing strength of black women. Racial tension and controversy swirled ominously about the November 1964 SNCC staff retreat at Waveland, Mississippi, where thirty-seven papers were presented on staff relations, SNCC's goals and ideology, organizing, decisionmaking, and race relations among the SNCC staff. On the mimeographed list of paper titles, Number 24 read: "SNCC Position Paper (Women in the Movement)"; the authors' names "withheld by request." Casey Hayden and Mary King had written it in discussion with Mary Varela. They debated whether to sign it, but concluded that they "wouldn't want it to be known at that point that [they were] writing such a thing." Thus they invited a fight but stayed out of the ring.

The paper indicted SNCC in strong, "scrappy" language. "The woman in SNCC," Hayden and King charged, "is often in the same position as that token Negro hired in a corporation. The management thinks that it has done its bit. Yet, every day the Negro bears an atmosphere, attitudes and actions which are tinged with condescension and paternalism . . ." They used their own anonymity as an example: "Think about the kinds of things the authors, if made known, would have to suffer because of raising this kind of discussion. Nothing so final as . . . outright exclusion, but the kinds of things which are killing to the insides—insinuations, ridicule, over-exaggerated compensations."

Evidence of sexual discrimination in SNCC filled the first of three pages: eleven specific examples of the automatic relegation of women to clerical work, exclusion of women from decision-making groups and leading positions, the tendency to refer to men as people and to women as "girls." "Undoubtedly," the argument continued, "this list will seem strange to some, petty to others, laughable to most. The list could continue as far as there are women in the movement." The source of the problem, according to Hayden and King, lay in the "assumption of male superiority . . . as widespread and deep rooted and every much as crippling to the woman as the assumptions of white supremacy are to the Negro." Though such a message would not be well received, they presented it

because it needs to be made know[n] that many women in the movement are not "happy and contented" with their status . . . women are the crucial factor that keeps the movement running on a day-to-day basis. Yet they are not given equal say-so when it comes to day-to-day decision-making.

Unhappy and discontented women, however, had already discovered that men in the movement would find such issues too threatening to discuss. Furthermore, they had found that women also remained "unaware and insensitive." The analogy with black oppression worked once again. Women's lack of consciousness paralleled that of blacks, who failed to "understand they are not free or who want to be part of white America. They don't understand that they have to give up their souls and stay in their place to be accepted." The purpose behind the position paper, therefore, was precisely to provoke discussion and recognition among women of the discrimination they suffered. "And maybe sometime in the future," Hayden and King concluded prophetically,

the whole of the women [sic] in this movement will become so alert as to force the rest of the movement to stop the discrimination and start the slow process of changing values and ideas so that all of us gradually come to understand that this is no more a man's world than it is a white world.

Tucked in among dozens of papers at the Waveland conference, the one on women in the movement provided a certain relief as the butt of ridicule and speculation about its authorship, but otherwise went unnoticed. Many in attendance at the conference have no memory of it at all. Others recall sitting out on the dock after a day of acrimony and rocking with laughter at Stokely Carmichael's rebuttal: "The only position for women in SNCC is prone."

But this was the same conference at which Donna Richards reclaimed her maiden name and her husband, Bob Moses, joined her, publicly adopting his mother's maiden name, Parris. The issues asserted themselves in many forms. Speculation about the authorship of the paper on women centered on black women, particularly Ruby Doris Smith Robinson. Soon it was common knowledge among the white women who cared to remember that Robinson had presented the paper herself. This myth has become a staple in accounts of feminism in the civil rights movement. Its pervasiveness recognized an important truth: that black women occupied positions of growing strength and power which challenged sexual discrimination. Their example inspired white women outside SNCC's inner circles, who believed that if anyone could be expected to write such a paper, it would be black women. In particular the myth honored the memory of Robinson, and it took on reality as tales of the memo and of Carmichael's response generated feminist echoes throughout the country.[3]

Carmichael's barb was for most who heard it a movement in-joke. It recalled the sexual activity of the summer before—all those young white women who supposedly had spent the summer "on their backs." The impact of the freedom summer, then, had both raised the issue of sex roles and infused the issue with racial tensions. For a moment black and white women had shared a feminist response to the position of women in SNCC, but objectively black and white women lacked the trust and solidarity to call each other "sister."

Soon after the summer, some black women in SNCC confronted black men with the charge that "they could not develop relationships with the black men because the men didn't have to be responsible to them because they could always hook up with some white woman who had come down." Deeply resentful of the attraction of white women to black men, they began to search for definitions of femininity that included blackness. Robinson herself hated white women for a period of years when she realized that they represented a cultural ideal of beauty and "femininity" which by inference defined black women as ugly and unwomanly.[4]

The black women's angry demand for greater trust and solidarity with black men constituted one part of an intricate maze of tensions and struggles that were in the process of transforming SNCC and the civil rights movement as a whole. By the winter of 1965 SNCC had grown from a small band of sixteen to a swollen staff of 180, of whom 50 percent were white. The earlier dream of a beloved community was dead. The vision of freedom lay crushed under the weight of intransigent racism; of disillusionment with electoral politics, the system, and nonviolence; and of the differences of race, class, and culture within the movement itself. The anger of black women toward white women was only one element in the rising spirit of black nationalism.

As early as 1963 Ella Baker had sought to counteract growing separatist sentiments:

I can understand that as we grow in our own strength and as we flex our muscles of leadership . . . we can begin to feel that the other fellow should come through *us*. But this is not the way to create a new world. . . . We need to penetrate the mystery of life and perfect the mastery of life, and the latter requires understanding that human beings are human beings.

But such rhetoric of community and brotherhood was a fragile weapon against the realities of racial and class tensions within the movement. Prior to the 1964 summer project, many blacks on the SNCC staff had expressed strong reservations about the impact of large numbers of whites on the movement. They feared that the white college students would try to "take over." Their verbal skills would "put down" local people and impede the development of indigenous leadership.[5]

In specific instances many of these fears were realized. Southern blacks especially distrusted students whom they perceived to be "out for a thrill." Moreover, in many cases the students—sharp, articulate, trained in the verbal skills of the upper middle class— did take over. One volunteer's comments reflected conflicts that were widespread:

. . . Several times I've had to completely re-do press statements of letters written by one of them. . . . It's one thing to tell people who have come willingly to Freedom School that they needn't feel ashamed of weakness in these areas, but it's quite another to even acknowledge such weaknesses in one's fellow workers. Furthermore, I'm a northerner; I'm white; I'm a woman; I'm a college graduate; I've not "proven" myself yet in jail or in physical danger. Every one of these things is a strike against me as far as they are concerned. I've refused to be ashamed of what I cannot change; I either overlook or purposely and pointedly misinterpret their occasional thrusts of antagonism. . . .

Another white volunteer noted that blacks in SNCC, faced with "this onslaught of insensitive Northern energy," would sullenly fade "into the background." The white volunteers were often in the limelight, their bravery constantly extolled in the press. Yet "implicit in all the songs, tears, speeches, work, laughter was the knowledge secure in both them and us that ultimately we could return to a white refuge."[6]

In addition, the summer that motivated young whites to explore their own potentials for courageous action and to build a new vision of social equality also exposed the weakness of a movement whose impulse was fundamentally moral. As they watched their idealism dashed upon the realities of power in American society, SNCC and the Congress of Racial Equality (CORE) workers became bitter and disillusioned. The summer project had been built on the assumption that massive registration of black people in Mississippi, accomplished through publicity and the protection of the federal government against blatant repression, would create real power for black people. It was a naive if noble attempt to force the political process to live up to the democratic ideals it professed.

Those hopes were crushed repeatedly. The federal government continued its policy of protecting people's rights by writing down whatever happened to them. Again and again the FBI and the Justice Department officials would stand by and take notes while demonstrators were beaten and illegally jailed. Finally, at the Atlantic City Democratic Convention the Mississippi Freedom Democratic Party (MFDP) brought the summer to a climax by offering a delegation to challenge the all-white representatives of the state Democratic machine. Fannie Lou Hamer testified to the Credentials Committee that she had been denied the right to vote, jailed, and beaten. At a rally the next day she repeated her story and pleaded: "We are askin' the American people, 'Is *this* the land of the free and the home of the brave?'"

The "compromise" that Democratic officials offered—to seat

the white delegation if they would take a loyalty oath and to give delegate-at-large status to two from the MFDP—seemed to those who had spent the summer in Mississippi unthinkable. That they should be asked to give up so much to white racists after all they had suffered showed them, finally, that those in power could not be compelled by moral considerations. "Atlantic City was a powerful lesson," according to James Forman, "not only for the black people from Mississippi but for all of SNCC. . . . No longer was there any hope . . . that the federal government would change the situation in the Deep South." Others saw the result in racial terms. Stokely Carmichael and Charles Hamilton argued two years afterward:

The lesson, in fact, was clear at Atlantic City. The major moral of that experience was not merely that the national conscience was generally unreliable but that, very specifically, black people in Mississippi and throughout this country could not rely on their so-called allies.[7]

Many movement workers went to Atlantic City with their hope already eroded. Anne Moody, a young black woman from Mississippi, had worked her way through Tougaloo College and in the process become deeply involved in the civil rights movement. By the time she entered a bus to travel to Atlantic City, she had lived through too much to share the movement's optimism:

I sat there listening to "We Shall Overcome," looking out of the window at the passing Mississippi landscape. Images of all that had happened kept crossing my mind: the Taplin burning, the Birmingham church bombing, Medgar Evers' murder, the blood gushing out of McKinley's head, and all the other murders. I saw the face of Mrs. Chinn as she said, "We ain't big enough to do it by ourselves." C.O.'s face when he gave me that pitiful wave from the chain gang. I could feel the tears welling up in my eyes. . . .
We shall overcome some day.
I WONDER. I really WONDER.

The growing bitterness of young blacks in the movement sprang from the depths of their idealism. The commitment they had made—once almost lightly—grew and made new demands daily, even hourly. Danger, fear, monotony, isolation, and loneliness took a heavy toll. A work ethic approaching martyrdom had developed, which made self-denial a condition of participation.

Robert Coles described a "syndrome" of weariness, depression, and guilt as a result of "constant exposure to frustrating social struggle. . . ." The symptoms he found occurred almost universally among young people spending significant amounts of time in seriously dangerous situations. The real danger can hardly be overstated. There were murders. Men, women, and children were beaten severely and publicly humiliated. The effect over time was evident in clinical signs of depression:

Briefly the symptoms reveal fear, anxiety, and anger no longer "controlled" or "managed." Depressions occur, characterized by loss of hope for victory, loss of a sense of purpose, and acceptance of the power of the enemy where before such power was challenged with apparent fearlessness. The youth affected may take to heavy drinking or become silent, sulky and uncooperative. Frequently one sees real gloom, loss of appetite, withdrawal from social contacts as well as from useful daily work in the movement . . . sometimes a precursor of the abandonment of a commitment to nonviolence.[8]

The toll may have been highest on black men in the field. According to Jean Wiley, a woman knew that "the first shot fired wasn't going to be fired at me, it was going to be aimed at a guy. . . ." In addition, men expected more of themselves in terms of courage and audacity and were at the same time less able to express their fears. It was "more legitimate for a woman to say, 'I won't go, I am afraid.'" Women could discuss their feelings with each other and with men, "but whenever men approached the subject they always reduced it to a comic situation."

Yet women too suffered from the constant demands, from reaching beyond themselves day after day. Some just disappeared. "Suddenly they weren't there anymore." Jean Wiley found herself doing the same thing:

I said I was going one place and I knew I wasn't. And I went to the place where one can get lost quickest, and of course that's New York City. I really haven't put that in perspective. But I know that something was lacking . . . not that I wasn't free . . . almost that I'd been too free; that I'd been so emancipated that I couldn't move personally, couldn't sustain having to relate to everything and practically everybody in terms of a larger political situation. There was another side of me that is a very personal side, perhaps a "softer" side that just had to come out, and it couldn't come out there because I just had to be too many things to too many people. So I got lost in the big city.

In the fall of 1964 tensions within the movement were massive and still growing, and SNCC's anarchic lack of structure served only to magnify them. When the staff met in October, eighty-five new members were voted in, most of them summer volunteers who had decided to stay on and work in Mississippi. The meeting was chaotic and alienating. Many recognized that the power base that had been built in Mississippi over the summer would soon be lost, because no one could agree on an internal structure for SNCC, much less build a unifying mass organization for Mississippi. Swollen in size, increasingly diverse, SNCC had split into mutually suspicious factions.

The dominant group in the fall meetings came to be known as the "freedom high" faction. Based largely in Mississippi, it represented a strange amalgam of the oldest and the newest elements in the southern movement. The position they represented was an exaggerated version of "Let the people lead themselves," focusing on individual freedom, reacting against the least suggestion of authority, and romanticizing the local people. James Forman charges that this faction represented the northern middle-class students, black and white, who had come south in 1964. The middle-class idealism and moralism of these youth, added to their own cultural rebellion against the world their parents represented, led them to take ideas like "participatory democracy" to logical extremes. They were frequently the people who challenged any decision not made by the whole group or reached by consensus, who were continually suspicious of anyone they perceived as powerful. They prefigured the anarchist factions of the Students for a Democratic Society (SDS) and the counterculture's "do your own thing" focus on lifestyle and drug culture. Jack Newfield described them more sympathetically as emerging from the summer of 1964 "in the image of Camus' existential rebel," with a "mystical and transcendental faith in the inherent goodness of the poor, even in their infinite wisdom." This was not simply a set of ideas imported from the north. Rather, it was the final distillation of the "beloved community" in the face of too frequent defeat. The informal leadership of the "freedom high" faction was made up not of northern students but of black and white southerners who had been in the movement from 1960. For them the issues were fundamentally moral, and the validation of the individual's sense of personal worth within the movement was the prerequisite for effective action outside it. Racial hostility and a formal, hierarchical structure within the movement thus represented a betrayal of the beloved community, the vision which now formed a core of their identity. And it came at the moment when the physical and psychological damage they had sustained in three or four years of constant work left them desperately in need of a warm, loving, sustaining community.

The "freedom highs" were opposed by the "structure faction," generally longtime field staff whose growing militance and nationalism was born of a disillusion with whites, the impatience of frustrated anger, and a wish to bring coherence and order to the movement, to shift from moral issues to questions of power. James Forman and Ruby Doris Smith Robinson led the fight against hiring the eighty-five new staff members, arguing that SNCC should be black-dominated and black-led and that SNCC staff should undergo both careful training and security checks before being hired.[9]

The southern black field workers carried with them wounds that refused to heal and that intensified the atmosphere of suspicion and recrimination: bitterness that the press was outraged when whites were murdered and hardly noticed when blacks died in the struggle; awareness that the country reveled in stories of blue-eyed blondes living with poor blacks and ignored blacks who had been working in Mississippi for years:

Didn't anyone care about Willie Peacock, born and raised on a Mississippi plantation, who couldn't go back to his home town because he was an organizer for SNCC and the white people would kill him if he went to see his mother? Apparently not.

Hostility toward whites in the movement also reflected a rising militance and impatience with nonviolence, magnified by events outside the south. In 1964 there was the Harlem riot; in 1965 Watts erupted. African nations were demanding and winning their independence with slogans about colonialism, pan-Africanism, and African socialism. Malcolm X began to voice

anti-white attitudes that American blacks had previously expressed only to each other or had been afraid to acknowledge at
all. Many were attracted to his angry words; many more were
jolted by his violent death in the spring of 1965. Alienation from
the concept of nonviolence and "black and white together" was
completed with the Selma campaign that same spring, when the
breach between SNCC militants and the more traditional approach of the Southern Christian Leadership Conference (SCLC)
moderates became unbridgeable. As Julius Lester put it:

Each organizer had his own little techniques for staying alive. Nonviolence might do something to the moral conscience of a nation, but a
bullet didn't have morals, and it was beginning to occur to more and
more organizers that white folks had plenty more bullets than they had
conscience.

By February 1965, the "structure faction" gathered its forces and
prevailed in a "stormy," "traumatic," and "confusing" SNCC staff
meeting. The road to "black power" was clear.[10]

When Mary King asserted that "if you were a hard worker and
you were good, at least before 1965 . . . you could definitely have
an influence on policy," the key phrase in the quote was "at least
before 1965." By 1965 the position of whites in SNCC, especially
southern whites whose goals had been shaped by the vision of the
"beloved community," was in painful decline. Whites were less
and less welcome in any part of the civil rights movement. An
activist in CORE and the Council of Federated Organizations
(COFO) described the situation:

Hostility against white faces was such that even those few white organizers who had earned the respect of their black co-workers found it
impossible, and unnecessarily disagreeable, to operate any longer within
existing movement organizations. . . . Many had been questioning their
own roles for a long time, and . . . their approach had always been that
of consciously working toward their own elimination from leadership
positions.[11]

Most northerners simply returned home, changed but confused,
fearful that in their attempt to do right they had done wrong. The
two northern white women in the inner circles of the SNCC staff,
Betty Garman and Dottie Miller Zellner, sided with the "structure faction" and finally agreed that they too must go. But for

southern white women who had devoted several years of their lives to the vision of a beloved community, the rejection of non-violence and the shift toward a more ideological, centralized, and black nationalist movement was disillusioning and made them bitter. One southern woman felt that she "could understand [the movement] in Southern Baptist terms like 'beloved community,' but not in Marxist terms—that was someone else's fight and someone else's world." And Mary King recalled:

It was very sad to see something that was so creative and so dynamic and so strong [disintegrating]. . . . I was terribly disappointed for a long time. . . . I was most affected by the way that the black women turned against me. That hurt more than the guys. But it had been there, you know. You could see it coming . . .

Many women had simply "burned out" and left the deep south. Jane Stembridge had withdrawn quietly to write. The Southern Student Organizing Committee (ssoc) provided an institutional context within which other whites like Sue Thrasher, Cathy Cade, and Cathy Barrett could continue to function. But for Casey Hayden and Mary King, there was no alternative. Their lives had centered in sncc for years and they could neither imagine leaving nor give up the moral idealism of the "beloved community"—the south was home. What would they do here without the movement?

In the fall of 1965 King and Hayden spent several days of long discussion in the mountains of Virginia. Both of them were on their way out of the movement, although they were not fully conscious of that fact. Finally they decided to write a "kind of memo" addressed to "a number of other women in the peace and freedom movements." In it they argued that women, like blacks,

. . . seem to be caught up in a common-law caste system that operates, sometimes subtly, forcing them to work around or outside hierarchical structures of power which may exclude them. Women seem to be placed in the same position of assumed subordination in personal situations too. It is a caste system which, at its worst, uses and exploits women.

King and Hayden set the precedent of contrasting the movement's egalitarian ideas with the replication of sex roles within it. They noted the ways in which women's positions in society determined such roles in the movement as cleaning house, doing secretarial work, and refraining from active or public leadership. At the same time, they observed,

having learned from the movement to think radically about the personal worth and abilities of people whose role in society had gone unchallenged before, a lot of women in the movement have begun trying to apply those lessons to their own relations with men. Each of us probably has her own story of the various results. . . .

They spoke of the pain of trying to put aside "deeply learned fears, needs, and self-perceptions . . . and . . . to replace them with concepts of people and freedom learned from the movement and organizing." In this process many people in the movement had questioned basic institutions such as marriage and child rearing. Indeed, such issues had been discussed over and over again, but seriously only among women. The usual male response was laughter, and women were left feeling silly. Hayden and King lamented the "lack of community for discussion: Nobody is writing, or organizing or talking publicly about women, in any way that reflects the problems that various women in the movement come across. . . ." Yet despite their feelings of invisibility, their words also demonstrated the ability to take the considerable risks involved in sharp criticisms. Through the movement they had developed too much self-confidence and self-respect to accept subordinate roles passively.

The memo was addressed principally to black women—long-time friends and comrades-in-nonviolent-arms—in the hope that "perhaps we can start to talk with each other more openly than in the past and create a community of support for each other so we can deal with ourselves and others with integrity and can therefore keep working."[12] In some ways it was a parting attempt to halt the metamorphosis in the civil rights movement from nonviolence to nationalism, from beloved community to black power. It expressed Casey Hayden and Mary King's pain and isolation, as white women in the movement. The black women who received it were on a different historic trajectory. They would fight some of the same battles as women, but in a different context and in their own way.

This "kind of memo" represented a flowering of women's consciousness that articulated contradictions felt most acutely by middle-class white women. While black women had been gaining strength and power within the movement, the white women's position—at the nexus of sexual and radical conflicts—had become increasingly precarious. Their feminist response, then, was precipitated by loss in the immediate situation; but it was a sense of loss heightened against the background of the new strength and self-worth the movement had allowed them to develop. Like their foremothers in the nineteenth century they confronted this dilemma with the tools the movement itself had given them: a language to name and describe oppression; a deep belief in freedom, equality, and community—soon to be translated into "sisterhood"; a willingness to question and challenge any social institution that failed to meet human needs; and the ability to organize.

It is not surprising that the issues were defined and confronted first by southern women, whose consciousness developed in a context that inextricably and paradoxically linked the fate of women and black people. These spiritual daughters of Sarah and Angelina Grimke kept their expectations low in November 1965. "Objectively," they said, "the chances seem nil that we could start a movement based on anything as distant to general American thought as a sex-caste system." But change was in the air and youth was on the march. In the north there were hundreds of women who had shared in the southern experience for a week, a month, a year, and thousands more who participated vicariously or worked to extend the struggle for freedom and equality into northern communities. Thus the fullest expressions of conscious feminism within the civil rights movement ricocheted off the fury of black power and landed with explosive force in the northern, white new left. One month later, women who had read the memo staged an angry walkout from a national SDS conference in Champaign-Urbana, Illinois. The only man to defend their action was a black man from SNCC.

Notes

1. Interviews with Howard Zinn, Betty Garman, Jean Wiley, Gwen Patton, and Fay Bellamy.

2. Mary King to Sara Evans, personal letter, January 26, 1975.

3. "SNCC Position Paper (Women in the Movement)," Waveland,

Mississippi, November 1964. I am grateful to Clayborne Carson, Jr., for sending this document to me. For an account of the Waveland meeting, see Carson, "Toward Freedom and Community: The Evolution of Ideas in the Student Nonviolent Coordinating Committee, 1960–66" (unpublished Ph.D. dissertation, University of California at Los Angeles, 1975), 260–86. Interviews with Sandra Carson, Kathie Sarachild, Mary King, and Jimmy Garrett; [Myrna Wood], "Ruby Dorris," *New Left Committee Bulletin,* 1:1 (November 1967). See Maren Lockwood Carden, *The New Feminist Movement* (New York, 1970), xxi.

4. Interview with Jimmy Garrett; Josephine Carson, *Silent Voices: The Southern Negro Woman Today* (New York, 1969), 254–55.

5. Howard Zinn, SNCC: *The New Abolitionists* (Boston, 1964), 186–88. See also Mary Aicken Rothschild, "Northern Volunteers and Southern 'Freedom Summers' 1964–65: A Social History" (unpublished Ph.D. dissertation, University of Washington, 1974), 26–27.

6. Elizabeth Sutherland, ed., *Letters from Mississippi* (New York, 1965), 185; Sally Belfrage, *Freedom Summer* (New York, 1965), 79–80.

7. Hamer quoted in *ibid.,* 239; Jane Forman, *The Making of Black Revolutionaries: A Personal Account* (New York, 1972), 395–96; Stokley Carmichael and Charles V. Hamilton, *Black Power: The Politics of Liberation in America* (New York, 1967), 96. See also Carson, "Toward Freedom and Community," 242–59.

8. Ann Moody, *Coming of Age in Mississippi* (New York, 1968), 384; interview with Jean Wiley and Betty Garman; Robert Coles and Joseph Brenner, "American Youth in a Social Struggle: The Mississippi Summer Project," unpublished paper, 308.

9. Forman, *Making of Black Revolutionaries,* 413–22; Pat Watters, *Down to Now: Reflections on the Southern Civil Rights Movement* (New York, 1971), 332; Jack Newfield, *A Prophetic Minority* (New York, 1966), 3.

10. Julius Lester, "The Angry Children of Malcom X," in *Black Protest Thought in the Twentieth Century,* ed. by August Meier, Elliot Rudwick, and Francis L. Broderick (2d ed., Indianapolis, 1971), 473, 477–79; Forman, *Making of Black Revolutionaries* 437–38, 441; Debbie Louis, *And We Are Not Saved* (Garden City, N.Y., 1970), 208, 220–47; Carson, "Toward Freedom and Community," 284–99; interview with Betty Garman.

11. Louis, *Not Saved,* 239, 243.

12. Casey Hayden and Mary King, "Sex and Caste: A Kind of Memo," *Liberation,* 10 (April 1966): 35–36.

Library of Congress Cataloging-in-Publication Data

Half sisters of history :
southern women and the American past /
Catherine Clinton, editor.
p.   cm.
ISBN 0-8223-1483-5 (acid-free paper).
ISBN 0-8223-1496-7 (pbk. acid-free paper)
1. Women—Southern States—History.
I. Clinton, Catherine, 1952–   .
HQ1438.S63H35 1994   305.4'0975—dc20
94-7822   CIP